THE AMERICAN NATION
A HISTORY

FROM ORIGINAL SOURCES BY ASSOCIATED SCHOLARS

EDITED BY
ALBERT BUSHNELL HART, LL.D.
PROFESSOR OF HISTORY IN HARVARD UNIVERSITY

ADVISED BY
VARIOUS HISTORICAL SOCIETIES

IN 28 VOLUMES
VOL. 23

*HENRY WHITTEMORE
LIBRARY*

*STATE COLLEGE
FRAMINGHAM, MASS.*

THE AMERICAN NATION
A HISTORY

LIST OF AUTHORS AND TITLES

Group I

Foundations of the Nation

Vol. 1 European Background of American History, by Edward Potts Cheyney, A.M., Prof. European Hist., Univ. of Pa.

" 2 Basis of American History, by Livingston Farrand, LL.D., President Univ. of Colo.

" 3 Spain in America, by the late Edward Gaylord Bourne, Ph.D., formerly Prof. Hist., Yale Univ.

" 4 England in America, by Lyon Gardiner Tyler, LL.D., President William and Mary College.

" 5 Colonial Self-Government, by Charles McLean Andrews, Ph.D., Prof. Am. History, Yale University.

Group II

Transformation into a Nation

Vol. 6 Provincial America, by Evarts Boutell Greene, Ph.D., Prof. Hist. and Dean of College, Univ. of Ill.

" 7 France in America, by the late Reuben Gold Thwaites, LL.D., formerly Sec. Wisconsin State Hist. Soc.

Vol. 8 Preliminaries of the Revolution, by George Elliott Howard, Ph.D., Prof. Polit. Science. Univ. of Neb.
" 9 The American Revolution, by Claude Halstead Van Tyne, Ph.D., Head Prof. Hist. Univ. of Michigan.
" 10 The Confederation and the Constitution, by Andrew Cunningham McLaughlin, A.M., Head Prof. Hist., Univ. of Chicago.

GROUP III

DEVELOPMENT OF THE NATION

Vol. 11 The Federalist System, by John Spencer Bassett, Ph.D., Prof. Am. Hist., Smith College.
" 12 The Jeffersonian System, by Edward Channing, Ph.D., Prof. Ancient and Modern Hist., Harvard Univ.
" 13 Rise of American Nationality, by Kendric Charles Babcock, Ph.D., Dean Col. Arts and Sciences, Univ. of Illinois.
" 14 Rise of the New West, by Frederick Jackson Turner, Ph.D., Prof. Hist., Harvard University.
" 15 Jacksonian Democracy, by William MacDonald, LL.D., Prof. Government, Univ. of California.

GROUP IV

TRIAL OF NATIONALITY

Vol. 16 Slavery and Abolition, by Albert Bushnell Hart, LL.D., Prof. Government, Harvard Univ.

Vol. 17 Westward Extension, by the late George Pierce Garrison, Ph.D., formerly Prof. Hist., Univ. of Texas.
" 18 Parties and Slavery, by Theodore Clarke Smith, Ph.D., Prof. Am. Hist., Williams College.
" 19 Causes of the Civil War, by Rear-Admiral French Ensor Chadwick, U.S.N., retired, former Pres. of Naval War College.
" 20 The Appeal to Arms, by James Kendall Hosmer, LL.D., formerly Librarian Minneapolis Pub. Lib.
" 21 Outcome of the Civil War, by James Kendall Hosmer, LL.D.

Group V

National Expansion

Vol. 22 Reconstruction, Political and Economic, by William Archibald Dunning, Ph.D., Prof. Hist. and Political Philosophy, Columbia Univ.
" 23 National Development, by Edwin Erle Sparks, Ph.D., Pres. Pa. State College.
" 24 National Problems, by Davis R. Dewey, Ph.D., Professor of Economics, Mass. Inst. of Technology.
" 25 America as a World Power, by John H. Latané, Ph.D., Prof. Am. Hist., Johns Hopkins University.
" 26 National Ideals Historically Traced, by Albert Bushnell Hart, LL.D., Prof. Government, Harvard University.
" 27 National Progress—1907-1917, by Frederic Austin Ogg, Ph.D., Prof. Political Science, Univ. of Wisconsin.
" 28 Index to the Series, by David Maydole Matteson, A.M., Harvard College Library.

COMMITTEES ORIGINALLY APPOINTED TO ADVISE AND CONSULT WITH THE EDITOR

THE MASSACHUSETTS HISTORICAL SOCIETY

Charles Francis Adams, LL.D., President
Samuel A. Green, M.D., Vice-President
James Ford Rhodes, LL.D., 2d Vice-President
Edward Channing, Ph.D., Prof. History Harvard University.
Worthington C. Ford, Chief of Division of MSS., Library of Congress.

THE WISCONSIN HISTORICAL SOCIETY

Reuben G. Thwaites, LL.D., Secretary and Superintendent.
Frederick J. Turner, Ph.D., Prof. of American History, Wisconsin University.
James D. Butler, LL.D., formerly Prof. Wisconsin University.
William W. Wight, President
Henry E. Legler, Curator

THE VIRGINIA HISTORICAL SOCIETY

William Gordon McCabe, Litt. D., President
Lyon G. Tyler, LL.D., Pres. of William and Mary College
Judge David C. Richardson
J. A. C. Chandler, Professor Richmond College
Edward Wilson James

THE TEXAS HISTORICAL SOCIETY

Judge John Henninger Reagan, President
George P. Garrison, Ph.D., Prof. of History, University of Texas
Judge C. W. Raines
Judge Zachary T. Fullmore

THE AMERICAN NATION: A HISTORY
VOLUME 23

NATIONAL DEVELOPMENT

1877–1885

BY

EDWIN ERLE SPARKS, PH.D.

PROFESSOR OF AMERICAN HISTORY, UNIVERSITY OF CHICAGO

NEW YORK AND LONDON
HARPER & BROTHERS PUBLISHERS

Republished, 1970
Scholarly Press, 22929 Industrial Drive East
St. Clair Shores, Michigan 48080

Library of Congress Catalog Card Number: 70-145311
Standard Book Number 403-01223-6

This edition is printed on a high-quality,
acid-free paper that meets specification
requirements for fine book paper referred
to as "300-year" paper

Copyright, 1907, by HARPER & BROTHERS.

PRINTED IN THE UNITED STATES OF AMERICA

D-S

CONTENTS

CHAP.		PAGE
	Editor's Introduction	xi
	Author's Preface	xiii
I.	The New Spirit of '76 (1876–1877) . . .	3
II.	The People and Their Distribution (1877–1880)	20
III.	Invention and Discovery (1877–1885) . .	37
IV.	Problems of Transportation (1875–1885) .	53
V.	Industrial Problems (1875–1885)	68
VI.	President Hayes and the South (1876–1877)	84
VII.	Republican Dissensions (1877–1878) . . .	103
VIII.	The Federal Election Laws (1876–1881) .	119
IX.	Currency and Fisheries (1877–1881) . . .	137
X.	Civil Service Evils (1877–1880)	154
XI.	Presidential Election of 1880 (1880–1881)	165
XII.	Civil Service Reform (1881–1884) . . .	182
XIII.	The Isthmian Canal (1877–1885)	202
XIV.	The Chinese Question (1879–1885) . . .	229
XV.	The Far West (1876–1888)	251
XVI.	The Indian Question (1877–1885)	265
XVII.	The Tariff of 1883 (1873–1883)	282
XVIII.	Inland Commerce (1875–1885)	305
XIX.	The Election of 1884 (1882–1884) . . .	327
XX.	Critical Essay on Authorities	352

CONTENTS

EDITOR'S INTRODUCTION

THE previous volume in this series, Dunning's *Reconstruction*, deals with the later phases of a Civil War, the consequences of which, and the adjustments resulting from which, occupied men's thoughts for a dozen years after hostilities in the field had ceased. Then came a distinct break between those old issues and the immediate, vital question of the adaptation of American government to the industrial and social needs of the country. It is at this turning-point, the year 1877, that Professor Sparks begins this volume.

The first five chapters are devoted to a summary of the social and economic conditions of the time, including invention, transportation, and labor. This prepares the way for chapters vi.–viii., on the party struggles due to President Hayes' withdrawal of the federal troops from the South. In chapters ix.–xii., the author develops two other questions — silver coinage and the national civil service—which aroused lively discussion. Then he turns (chapters xiii., xiv.) to the two principal questions of foreign policy, the Isthmian Canal and the exclusion of the Chinese. Two chapters (xv., xvi.) bring out the effect on the nation of the rapid settling up of the West, and the consequent pressure on the Indians. In chapters xvii. to xix. are described the struggles over the tariff, the new conditions of transportation, and the election of 1884, by which Cleveland came to the White House, the first Democrat since Buchanan.

To deal with a period so near the present time, to handle judiciously controversies which are still warm, is not an easy task. Professor Sparks has succeeded in bringing out the contrast between the issues and prepossessions of his period as against those of the Civil War. He has put into relief the filling up of the West, and the creation of arteries of communication, as factors in national politics and policies. He has shown how new organization of capitalists, laborers, and agencies of transportation compelled the nation to consider a new theory of the relation of government to private and corporate business. He has thus prepared the ground for the further discussion of the problem of control of industry, as it is described in the next volume of the series, Dewey's *National Problems*.

AUTHOR'S PREFACE

THE work of reconstructing the political standing of certain southern states, impaired by attempted secession, was wellnigh completed by 1877. In the decade following, the foundations were unconsciously laid for the national edifice which is the glory of the present age. Old precedents were gone, new industrial conditions were confronted, new routes of commerce were discovered, and new political policies were worked out. Modern accumulation of wealth and modern combinations of labor here found a beginning. The national credit, impaired by depreciated paper issues, was restored by the resumption of specie payments.

Increased Asiatic immigration to California caused the first barriers to be erected against the admission of a foreign people; and conditions in Utah demanded federal regulation of a social question, thus establishing a new precedent. Many of the limitations through constitutional interpretation, which had been a hinderance to congressional action, disappeared after the final arbitration of war; thenceforth expediency and the general good were to be the criteria of action.

AUTHOR'S PREFACE

The result of the Civil War produced among other nations a renewed confidence in the perpetuity of the United States and inaugurated at home the active foreign policy characteristic of the present day. The "peace policy" of Grant towards the American Indians was fully developed and a beginning made of the final task of converting tribal nomads into self-supporting individuals.

Above all, the political conception which saw in a party a vast machine warranted in using its control of both national and state governments in order to perpetuate itself and to benefit its members, was weakened by the final collapse of the reconstruction contrivances and by the activity of the civil service reformers. In this decade, therefore, may be sought not only the beginnings of modern industrial and economic triumphs, but also a quickening of the higher sentiment which regards public service as a public trust and civic duty as akin to religious obligation. In 1884 the awakening brought about the election of a "reform president" for the first time in half a century, and appropriately rounded out the decade.

EDWIN ERLE SPARKS.

NATIONAL DEVELOPMENT

NATIONAL DEVELOPMENT

CHAPTER I

THE NEW SPIRIT OF '76
(1876-1877)

THE one hundredth anniversary of the birth of American independence came opportunely to mark an epoch in American history. The material damage wrought by the Civil War was wellnigh repaired by time and industry. The discord in the hearts of the people was disappearing, as the policy of restoring the Union by force was gradually abandoned. How the specific problems of reconstruction were met has been described in a preceding volume of this series.[1] How the beneficent policy of President Hayes eradicated the last evils of reconstruction and hastened a true reunion is to be told in later chapters of this volume.

But there was a reconstruction going on in a larger sense; a reconstruction of industries, an adjustment of new sources of supply to new processes of manufacture, a co-ordination of means of transportation

[1] Dunning, *Reconstruction* (*Am. Nation*, XXII.).

with the demands of population, an adaptation of national vision to the new order of things, and a realization that neither secession, civil war, nor reconstruction had circumscribed the future of the republic. Millions of acres of unoccupied lands stretched invitingly towards the west; vast mineral resources lay undeveloped in the earth; forests covered the mountain slopes and spread over large areas in the northwestern and southern states; and unimproved opportunities for new ways of transportation presented themselves all over the continent and across the adjacent waters. Burdened no longer by slavery and sectionalism, the republic seemed to enter upon a new era of life as it neared the first centennial of its birth.

To celebrate fittingly and in this spirit the year 1876, public thought turned towards a national fair which should illustrate by proper exhibits the century's progress in the United States, and in which other nations might be invited to join. Doubtless the success of the Paris Exposition in 1867 and the Vienna Exhibition of 1873 suggested this form of celebrating the American centennial year. As early as March 3, 1871,[1] Congress provided for an exhibition of American and foreign arts, products, and manufactures to be held in 1876 in the city of Philadelphia, the first capital of the federal republic and the scene of the drama of the Declaration of Independence. The president of the United States was

[1] *U. S. Statutes at Large*, XVI., 470.

authorized to appoint a board of commissioners to have charge of the enterprise, and also to invite other nations to participate. The national government was expressly held free from expense or financial liability; and by another act, June 1, 1872, a board of finance was incorporated to raise the required capital.[1] By joint resolution, June 5, 1874, the president was authorized to invite other nations to take part in the celebration.[2] The federal government further patronized the undertaking by erecting a building in which to illustrate the functions and workings of its different departments. A tract of more than two hundred acres, a part of Fairmount Park in Philadelphia, was placed by the city at the disposal of the exposition authorities.

From its inception the enterprise encountered difficulties; previous experience with world's fairs little guided the uncertain steps of its promotors; and the financial panic of 1873 caused many subscriptions to be cancelled, and threatened, if it continued, to reduce materially the number of visitors. Thirty-nine nations accepted the invitation to join in the exhibition. Some erected buildings and others asked for housing at the expense of the finance board. Being now threatened with a lack of space in the six buildings contemplated, the managers hastily constructed additional buildings and annexes, the expense of which, added to the four and one-half millions spent on the main buildings, exhausted

[1] *U. S. Statutes at Large*, XVII., 203.   [2] *Ibid,*, XVIII., 53.

their resources. They appealed to Congress to save the project and caused a debate in both House and Senate on the power of Congress to make an appropriation for this purpose, in which the survivors of strict construction made a last stand. The debate marked the passing of constitutional quibbling and showed the helplessness of old doctrines before the new demands of national pride.

Advocates of the proposition to advance one and a half million dollars to the Centennial Commission could find no precedent except the acts whereby appropriations were given for American representation in the London Exhibition of 1851, and the later Paris Exposition and Vienna Exhibition. The total of seven hundred thousand dollars spent for this purpose seemed to have excited little opposition or alarm at the time; but the Democratic opponents of the proposed relief measure for the Centennial board were now insistent that Congress had no power under the constitution to warrant the proposed appropriation. Its defenders waived the letter of the constitution, claiming that the enterprise was entitled to national support because it was national in its inception and organization. One speaker asked: "Where did Congress derive the power to embellish and decorate the grounds and buildings of the Government? Where did it derive the power to purchase works of art which adorn these Halls and add to their attractiveness? Where did it derive the power to purchase the magnificent library of which we boast? Where did it derive the power to fit out expeditions to explore the polar seas and to travel to foreign countries to observe the transit of Venus? Where did it derive the power to appropriate money on three different occasions to promote international exhibitions held in other countries? Where did it derive the power to encourage art, to promote science, to advance practical and useful industry, to maintain an Agricultural Department, or a horticultural garden, a National Observatory, or a Signal corps?"[1]

Many of the acts thus appealed to had been passed by Democratic Congresses, thus placing that party upon the defensive. One member illustrated in his argument the microscopic care with which the strict constructionists had been compelled to search each line of the constitution to justify the action which national growth and necessity demanded from time to time. He refused to accept the easy doctrine of "implied powers" and sought an explicit clause for each statute. The right to fire a salute in the army and navy he justified by the provision of the constitution authorizing Congress to raise armies and support a navy; the erection of the ornamental dome to the Capitol was warranted by the phrase "and other needful buildings"; the purchase of works of art for adorning the building was extenuated by court decisions that pictures were included as part of a building; the appropriations for the

[1] *Cong. Record*, 44 Cong., 1 Sess., 479.

entertainment of foreign ambassadors was vindicated under the power "to receive public ministers and ambassadors"; the polar expedition and that sent to observe the transit of Venus were grounded on the power to maintain a navy; and grants of public lands for educational purposes were warranted by the power given to Congress to "dispose of" the territory and other property of the United States.[1] Henry Clay was jokingly quoted as declaring in the bank bill debate in 1811,[2] that when any one was in search of ground for a doubtful action he went to the clause in the constitution giving Congress the right to regulate commerce. Yet some of the justifications named above were almost as far-fetched.

Advocates of the proposed measure wished to rise superior to constitutional quibbles such as supposedly went out of fashion in the Civil War, and to ground the appropriation on the right to save the national honor and to promote the national pride. Instances were cited of the appropriation for constructing a tomb for Washington and the money spent in entertaining Lafayette in 1824—each of which could be justified only by the patriotic impulse of the people. "Many things have been done," confessed one speaker, "perhaps not within the strict letter of the Constitution; but we have high authority for the saying, 'The letter killeth, the spirit giveth life.' The power which saved a nation's

[1] *Cong. Record*, 44 Cong., 1 Sess., 511, 512.   [2] *Ibid.*, 510.

life can save a nation's honor." [1] The appeal to the nation's honor was successful in overcoming whatever of narrow-constructionism, once voiced by Jefferson, by Madison, and by John Taylor of Caroline,[2] survived the fire of the Civil War. "Expediency" had replaced "constitutionality" as the criterion. The bill was passed and became a law February 16, 1876,[3] and the financial success of the project was no longer in doubt. In addition to this loan, the government expended on the exposition, by erecting a building, by making exhibits, and by admitting foreign exhibits free of duty, about six hundred thousand dollars more.[4]

Thus relieved of financial difficulties, the Centennial Exhibition was opened in May, 1876, with elaborate ceremonies and maintained until November of the same year. Twenty-six states of the Union and many foreign nations erected characteristic buildings for the housing of their exhibits, in several of which structures native building material was employed exclusively. Some of the principal trades and manufactures also erected buildings in which they showed their products or processes.[5]

The Exhibition had a marked and unexpected effect in stimulating travel. Preparations to carry

[1] *Cong. Record*, 44 Cong., 1 Sess., 479.
[2] See Channing, *Jeffersonian System* (*Am. Nation*, XII.), chap. vi.   [3] *U. S. Statutes at Large*, XIX., 3.
[4] *Exec. Docs.*, 44 Cong., 3 Sess., No. 74, p. 13.
[5] Centennial Exhibiton of 1876, *Report*, IV.; *Harper's Weekly*, XX., 422; cf. Dunning, *Reconstruction* (*Am. Nation*, XXII.), 292.

the visitors included the completion of the Bound Brook route from New York to Philadelphia, and an extension of the Lehigh Valley Railway to Buffalo. At least three million individuals must have visited Philadelphia, of whom more than two millions came from a distance of one hundred miles or more. Up to this time Americans had, as a whole, travelled little: the modern exodus to Europe had not begun, and the few returned travellers were always sure of an audience to hear of their novel experiences abroad. Even their own land was to most Americans a *terra incognita*. The man who had visited California was a second Marco Polo or Sir John Mandeville. In Philadelphia the world was brought together in a small compass: most of the visitors for the first time saw the carvings of India, fabrics, bronzes, and jewelry from France, lacquered work from the Netherlands, lace from Brussels, German textiles and dyestuffs, Bohemian glassware, Swiss watches, wrought-iron and earthenware from Sweden, silver filigree-work from Norway, Russian enamels and furs, Italian ornaments, Egyptian embroideries, Mexican onyx, Orange Free State ivory and skins, Hawaiian corals and shells, Brazilian woods and fruits, Chilian leather, and Oriental marvels of delicate workmanship. For the first time, thousands saw Chinese carpenters at work in truly antipodal manner, drank Paraguayan maté or tea, marvelled at the many uses of gutta-percha, examined the wooden clocks from the Black Forest, were amused by the figures clad in peasant costumes from Sweden and from China, discussed a new floor covering known as "linoleum," and wondered at the cunning workmanship and artistic invention of the almost unknown Japanese.

Even more potent in their beneficent results were the educational and art exhibits.[1] The American educational system had been wrought out largely from subjective experience and suffered from self-sufficiency and complacency. The school exhibits sent from other nations, especially Belgium, were a revelation in the matter of sanitary school surroundings and hygienic conditions. America was deficient, it was also found, in the cultivation of artistic sense and agreeable environment of the school-buildings. Germany and Switzerland excelled all in methods of teaching manual training, beginning with childhood.[2] Two buildings on the Centennial grounds were devoted solely to the kindergarten methods of training children, and this valuable factor in education was widely introduced into America. In 1873 there were only forty-two kindergarten "institutes" in the United States; in 1878 the number had increased to one hundred and fifty-nine, with nearly five thousand pupils.[3]

A permanent building of granite, glass, and iron, known as Memorial Hall, housed the art collection.

[1] *Senate Exec. Docs.*, 45 Cong., 3 Sess., No. 74, pp. 14-17.
[2] *North Am. Rev.*, CXXXII., 64.
[3] U. S. Comr. of Education, *Report*, 1878, p. lxxvi.

American art was confessedly crude and undeveloped and the exhibit was for the most part made up of foreign productions; but good judgment was shown in making the American collection largely an assemblage of historical paintings and portraits especially appropriate for a centennial display. Great Britain and Austria led in paintings loaned for the occasion, and Italy in marbles.

Notwithstanding the presence of these paintings and marbles, some disappointment was felt by lovers of art that the contribution from European centres was so meagre. America was not yet known as a patron of art. Few works of value had been imported, and American productions of permanence were almost as rare. Only thirteen recognized "art collections" existed in the entire United States in 1876, that of the Corcoran Gallery in Washington and of the Metropolitan Art Museum in New York being most praiseworthy. The buildings of the Centennial did not compare favorably with later expositions, after a refined taste and skilled creators had been evolved.

America made slow progress in architecture as well as in art. Planting colonies and clearing the backwoods required immediate and usable dwellings and other buildings, with little regard for appearance' sake. Time was required for an awakening to the possibilities of the higher art of construction. Yet the Philadelphia display opened the eyes of the American people to the value of art in its more material aspects of manufacture. Industrial drawing in the schools speedily replaced or gave life to the inane "free-hand"; better designs in fabrics and furniture were brought out; and manual training received a place among legitimate studies of the school curriculum.[1] Men of wealth sought to acquire real works of art for private or public collections, and the artistic factor was introduced into modern American life, without which the present industrial age would be one of hopeless materialism. The bare walls and windows of many school-rooms were soon adorned with works of art and with potted plants. In the home, artistic and rare furnishings began to replace crude and glaring specimens of amateurish handiwork.

At the Centennial, in the popular estimation a painting representing a violin hanging on a panelled door was rivalled only by the Corliss engine. No visit to Philadelphia was complete without a view of these two crowning glories. The "monster" engine of fourteen hundred horse-power was sufficient to move all the machinery in the Exposition.[2] The people were able to see produced before their eyes newspapers, pins, boots and shoes, bricks, envelopes, candies, tacks, nails, corks, carpets, dress-goods, and shingles. At one place could be seen a method for driving piling by the force of exploding gunpowder;

---

[1] U. S. Comr. of Education, *Report*, 1876, pp. cci.–ccxii.; 1877, pp. ccii.; 1878, pp. cxcvi.; 1893–1894, pp. 877–950.
[2] *Harper's Weekly*, XX., 421 (May 27, 1876).

at another a contrivance for unloading vessels by an automatic railway. Pneumatic tubes for transporting small parcels with great speed by exhausting the air in front was a strange device at the time. The Westinghouse air-brake and other contrivances for the safety of railway passengers were objects of special interest. A variety of typewriters was shown, the first of which was put on the market in 1872, although a patent was granted for this object as early as 1829; but the machines were considered novelties rather than necessities. The patent office displayed sixty thousand drawings and five thousand models to show what had been accomplished in America by inventors.[1]

The effect of the inspiration of the Centennial Exhibition in its manufacturing aspect was manifest in the increase of engineering courses offered in the colleges and in the founding of new schools devoted to technical education. Under the patronage of grants of public land authorized by the federal government in 1862, the old "farm-schools" had been replaced in the various states by agricultural colleges, intrusted also with teaching the "mechanic arts." Lacking the traditional classical and cultural courses, these led a precarious existence, until touched by the magic of engineering in the dawn of the industrial age. Here were laid the broad foundations for many of the modern state universities and the technical and agricultural colleges which

[1] U. S. Tenth Census (1880), IV.

are credited with achieving for technical education what the sectarian colleges have done for general education. In these schools manual labor has been ennobled and farming has been raised from drudgery to a skilled profession through the application of science to its art.

To this end, indeed, the agricultural exhibit at Philadelphia conduced largely. It was the most novel feature of the exhibition, compared with previous European expositions. The display of farm implements and machinery showed that America was far in advance of other nations in these particulars; and it was argued that the immense space of tillable lands and paucity of adequate labor had combined to quicken the mechanical skill and invention of cultivators of the soil. The food-producing possibilities of the various states were a revelation to the inhabitants themselves. Even far-away Washington territory sent a creditable display of agricultural products and fruits. Among the novelties of the day was the use of Spanish moss from the southern states for upholstering purposes, and "an apparatus for hatching chickens." Bake-shops were established on the grounds to demonstrate the making and to further the use of the crusted bread and rolls known to the Old World. Soon a "Vienna bakery" could be found in every city.[1]

The total number of admissions to the Exposition

---

[1] See the numerous *Guides* and *Hand-Books* of the Centennial Exhibition.

was about ten millions and the admission receipts were nearly four million dollars. To this source of income were added subscriptions from individuals, from the United States government, the state of Pennsylvania, and the city of Philadelphia, swelling the total assets to more than eleven million dollars. After all expenses were met and the loan repaid to the United States treasury, there remained a sufficient balance to return to each subscriber nearly a fifth of his subscription.[1]

An interesting sequence of the Philadelphia fair may be found in the increased export trade in the years immediately following. The attention of foreign visitors was called to the superior advantages of certain American manufactures useful in their business, and to the low price of certain raw materials required in their factories. Cheap American food products found a ready market abroad. For instance, "butterine," or oleomargarine, a food scorned by American working-men, was exported in 1878 to the value of almost half a million dollars. Indian-maize, or "corn," it was hoped, would also find a sale in Europe and Asia, being one of the cheapest foods known;[2] but it was soon demonstrated that popular prejudice would militate against its use except in years when a shortage of wheat or other accustomed grains made a resort to maize necessary.

[1] *Senate Exec. Docs.*, 45 Cong., 3 Sess., No. 74, pp. 18, 152.
[2] U. S. Tenth Census (1880), III., 485.

From this date is reckoned the growing importance of the United States as the food producer for a large part of the Old World. In 1876 40,000,000 bushels of corn and 70,000,000 bushels of wheat went from the United States ports to various foreign lands; in 1880 the wheat export reached 150,000,000 bushels, and that of corn 91,000,000 bushels,[1] being nearly one-third the entire crop of each. In the Centennial year the cotton crop reached permanently the 4,000,000 bales mark, a figure reached before the war only in 1859 and in 1860. In 1881 the crop aggregated 6,000,000 bales, nearly two-thirds of which went to Europe, forming about one-half the cotton consumed there.[2] The wool crop of the United States was about a sixth of the total for the world; but almost the whole of it was retained for home consumption.[3] Only a thousand tons of pig-iron and an equal amount of iron and steel rails were exported in 1880.[4] Manifestly the United States was destined to become the source of supply for food before her manufactures would be demanded.

The amount of dried fruit sent abroad increased in 1877 twenty times over the amount exported during any preceding year. Ripe fruit also was shipped on steamships in iced chambers, with some degree of success. Still more novel was the experiment of sending dressed beef to Europe in large refrigerating

---

[1] *U. S. Statistical Abstract*, 1900, pp. 328, 329; *Railway Gazette*, August 1, 1881.   [2] *U. S. Statistical Abstract*, 1900, p. 331.
[3] *Ibid.*, 334.   [4] *Ibid.*, 362.

chambers constructed in steamships. In 1876 nearly twelve thousand carcasses of beeves were shipped in this way and the experiment proved that such a method was feasible.[1] Live cattle had frequently been shipped to England and a steady market for American beef had been built up; but the dressed beef could not command so high a price as the livestock, and the expense of the refrigerators was too heavy to make the practice profitable except in times when cattle were unusually cheap. However, improved methods were introduced in due time, and by 1881 the trade in dressed meat had grown to the value of $6,000,000. In 1884 the export trade in live cattle amounted to nearly $18,000,000, and that of fresh beef to $12,000,000. In the same year, $34,000,000 worth of bacon and nearly $25,000,000 worth of lard went from the United States to feed the people of other countries.[2]

In return, stock raisers imported live-stock for breeding purposes to the value of $415,000 in 1873; but steadily increased their importations until they reached $1,245,000 by 1881.[3] Percheron horses, Jersey cows, Poland China hogs and other established breeds began to replace the mongrel stock on the farms, and placed cattle, sheep, and hog raising in a class distinct from farming.[4]

[1] *Frank Leslie's Weekly*, XLIV., 84.
[2] U. S. Bureau of Statistics, *Report*, 1884, p. xx.
[3] *Appleton's Annual Cyclop.*, 1882, p. 487.
[4] *Harper's Weekly*, XXV., 266.

It is a coincidence, and probably merely a coincidence, that the Centennial year marked the permanent shifting of the balance of trade in the United States from the import to the export column. In only three years before that date—viz., 1857, 1862, and 1874, did the United States sell more goods than it bought; but after 1876 there were only three years, 1888, 1889, and 1898, when the purchases exceeded the sales.[1]

[1] *U. S. Statistical Abstract*, 1900, p. 92.

CHAPTER II

THE PEOPLE AND THEIR DISTRIBUTION
(1877–1880)

NEAR the principal entrance in the Centennial Exhibition grounds was placed upright a forearm and hand of cyclopean size, grasping a torch of like dimensions. They were parts of a gigantic female figure symbolizing "Liberty enlightening the world," which was erected in 1886 in New York Harbor, the gift of the French to the American people. Past it came the swarms of immigrants from the European hives to aid in filling the land which lay beyond its welcoming torch.

The population of the United States showed, when proper corrections were applied to the census of 1870, an increase between 1860 and 1870 of 26.6 per cent.; between 1870 and 1880, of 26 per cent.; in the next decade of 24.9 per cent.[1] The Civil War caused no decrease in the steady growth of population; yet during no decade following that convulsion did the growth equal the 33 per cent. which many prior decades showed. Changed conditions and the natural check of a partly supplied demand acted as a drag.

[1] U. S. Twelfth Census (1900), I., xx.

The region of greatest growth between 1870 and 1880 was, as usual, in the West, because of the westward movement of the people. The story of the marvellous increase of population in Ohio, in Illinois, and in Iowa during preceding decades[1] was to be repeated in Kansas, Nebraska, Colorado, the Dakotas, and Texas. In 1860 the census map showing the distribution of population located the technical "frontier"—*i. e.*, more than two people and less than six people to the square mile—not far from the ninety-fifth meridian.[2] The thin edge of settlement lay in central Minnesota, central Iowa, the eastern counties of Kansas and Nebraska, western Arkansas, and half across Texas. In 1880 it had advanced beyond the ninety-seventh meridian, extending down the Dakota-Minnesota boundary-line to Nebraska, and throwing out slender projections along the Platte, the Kansas, and the Arkansas rivers quite to Wyoming and Colorado. In 1860 a fringe of people extended up the Missouri River as far as Fort Randall in the Dakota territory. Twenty years later the people had spread out over the southern part of the territory and were creeping up the Red River of the North; there they multiplied in numbers over one hundred times between 1860 and 1890, owing to the development of agriculture in the Red River valley and the discovery of gold in the Black Hills.[3]

[1] Garrison, *Westward Extension* (*Am. Nation*, XVII.), chap. i.
[2] U. S. Tenth Census (1880), I., xviii.
[3] U. S. Twelfth Census (1900), I., 2.

In 1860 there was a long, narrow "island" of people in the Rocky Mountains, stretching irregularly from Cheyenne to El Paso. About three thousand of them were engaged in agriculture and mining in Colorado; ten years later, although their number had grown to thirty-nine thousand, statehood still seemed remote; but several "rushes" of people followed the discovery of new mining-fields, and in 1876 Colorado had sufficient population to warrant its admission to the Union as the "Centennial state."

Fortune continued to smile on Colorado after statehood was gained. Placer-mining had long been carried on, for example, in the lake district in the heart of the mountains; but declined until, in 1877, there were only some twenty cabins to show where the Stray Horse Gulch and kindred claims had once attracted thousands of miners. In that year the rejected carbonates were found to be rich in silver, and vast cerusite deposits were opened containing lead; new processes were invented for extracting the metals, and Leadville arose, a city of fifteen thousand people, in a sage-brush valley at an altitude of ten thousand feet above sea-level. In 1880 it was shipping gold, silver, and lead to the value of more than a million dollars a month. Miners and prospectors were swarming over the slopes of every mountain-range in the state, rushing madly into some promising locality, living under frightful unsanitary conditions, and then stampeding to another place where fickle fortune seemed to disclose herself. In Leadville, during the first seven and a half months of 1879, there were one hundred and fifteen deaths, one-fourth of the number due to violence.[1]

Enticed by these demands for transportation, railroad companies accomplished wonders in railway engineering, came to actual combat in their rivalry for some possible route of construction in the mountain-passes, enlisted miners' mobs in their quarrels, and finally appealed to the courts when passions had become sufficiently cool. In May, 1879, the first train passed through the Royal Gorge in the Grand Cañon of the Arkansas, following an old rock-bound river-path known to the Spaniards over a hundred years before.[2] In 1870 there were 157 miles of railroad within the state; ten years later there were 1750 miles.[3]

This development of Colorado brought an increase of more than four hundred per cent. in her population between 1870 and 1880, and widened out her settled area into a broad triangle, the base of which rested on the northern boundary of New Mexico. The latter territory seemed about to recover from the loss in population suffered in the preceding decade, and to feel the effects of the approach of the railroad. Arizona territory, freed from hostile Ind-

[1] Colorado Board of Health, *Report*, quoted in *Appleton's Annual Cyclop.*, 1879, p. 157.   [2] *Ibid.*, 161.
[3] *U. S. Statistical Abstract*, 1900, p. 381.

ian wars and made accessible by the construction of the Southern Pacific Railroad, almost trebled its population between 1870 and 1880.[1] Nebraska made the next largest gain, followed by Washington territory, Kansas, Wyoming territory, and Idaho territory in order.[2]

Four hundred miles to the west of Denver, in the midst of the wilderness, the Mormons planted civilization in 1847 and extended their settlements in a long north and south group through Utah parallel to the Colorado group. By their systematic solicitation of converts in all countries, the Mormons peopled the territory with a regularity in strong contrast to the hegiras which marked the settlement of other western states and territories. This steady growth was due also to the persistence of the Mormons in encouraging agriculture and developing the art of irrigation, while discouraging mining with its attendant speculation and frenzies. In 1880 the territory contained nearly fifty thousand people, and might expect early statehood, unless prevented by antagonism to its peculiar institution, Mormonism.[3]

The Colorado and Utah groups were islands of people far in advance of the mainland of population and separated from it by the arid tracts on the eastern side of the Rockies, which were responsible

---

[1] *Frank Leslie's Newspaper*, XLIV., 44.
[2] U. S. Eleventh Census (1890), I., xiii.
[3] U. S. Tenth Census (1880), I., 531; *Appleton's Annual Cyclop.*, 1881, p. 859; Linn, *Story of the Mormons*, chap. vi.

for the misnomer, "The Great American Desert," applied originally to the Great Plains. To the east of the arid regions, the main advance of people was slowly rounding into form on the prairies under more favorable conditions than the first immigrants experienced. Railroads transported them and their belongings to their new homes and returned their products to market. In 1880 more than six million acres of public lands were patented under the homestead law, three-fourths being located in states and territories to the west of a line drawn through the western boundary-lines of Iowa and Missouri. The Dakotas received most of these immigrants, with Nebraska a close second. Minnesota also attracted large numbers to the public lands lying along the Red River quite up to the Canadian line. These fertile prairies of the West were becoming the food-producing region for the older states. In 1860 Minnesota raised only ten million bushels of wheat, but in 1880 produced thirty-four million. The Dakota crop during the same period increased from a thousand bushels to nearly three million.[1] Kansas grew six million bushels of corn in 1860 and over a hundred million in 1880.[2]

Cattle-grazing in Wyoming in 1870 was scarcely inaugurated, only eleven thousand head being listed in the entire territory. A decade later the number had increased to five hundred and twenty-one thousand, the herds roving freely and identified only

[1] U. S. Tenth Census (1880), III., 440, 564.   [2] *Ibid.*, 470.

by branding-marks in the great "round up." The space of country covered in this industry could be realized only by examining the posted notices for the annual in-gathering of the cattle and noting that frequently the drag-net would be drawn over four hundred miles of grazing lands and would involve weeks of hard riding.[1] In 1880 sixty thousand head were shipped from Wyoming to the Chicago stockyards, and an equal number to Kansas City. Even at this time the sheep industry was beginning to drive the cattle from Wyoming, and wars between rival owners and herdsmen were only too frequent. Between 1870 and 1880 the number of sheep in the territory increased from six thousand to four hundred and fifty thousand, although the grazing lands were far from fully occupied.[2]

Texas rivalled its northerly neighbors in the extension of the frontier. In 1870 the front line of people had scarcely passed Fort Worth; but in the next ten years it advanced to the one-hundredth meridian, and developed some of the future industries of the state. About 1880 the small and inferior Spanish sheep were improved by crossing the breed with the Merinos, with the result that the Texas woolclip advanced from four and one-half million pounds to twenty-two million pounds between 1870 and 1880.[3] Of even more importance was the utilization

[1] Hough, *Story of the Cowboy*, chap. ix; *Reed Anthony, Cowman.*
[2] U. S. Tenth Census (1880), III., 1018.
[3] U. S. Twelfth Census (1900), III., 978.

of the vast herds of wild cattle which roamed the plains of Texas, degenerates of the domesticated animals brought to America by the Spaniards. As early as 1856 a herd of these long-horned Texan cattle was driven on foot to Chicago and sold profitably. During the Civil War the high price of meat caused fixed shipments of these cattle to be made to eastern markets, and in 1871 no less than four hundred thousand head were collected and shipped, chiefly from Abilene, Kansas, for many years a railway terminus.[1] To this point the wild cattle and also those improved by cross-breeding were driven on foot from Texas.

Instead of being injured, it was found that the cattle were improved by being taken north before shipment; hence arose the annual "drive" from Texas into Kansas, Colorado, and Wyoming. The "cattle boom" of 1881 doubled the price of the Texan product and made fortunes for its participants. Stock companies were formed, attracting capital and drawing young men from England and Scotland. Northern farmers complained that the "drive" disseminated "Texas fever" and other cattle diseases among their domesticated stock; the small farmers along the route attempted to fend the droves from their farms; and a long warfare ensued between cattlemen and individual holders in which barbed-wire fence and "blue-devil" nippers were weapons, before the great cattle ranges were cut up into

[1] U. S. Twelfth Census (1900), III., 965.

small farms or made into ranches from which the cattle were shipped by the newly opened railways of Texas. State enactments barring Texas cattle were declared an unconstitutional exercise of interstate commerce power by the federal courts,[1] thus paving the way for and demonstrating the demand for federal regulation of trade between the states.

The frontier, advancing from the east, seemed hastening to meet a counter-wave of people penetrating the Sierra Nevada and the Cascade ranges from the Pacific coast side.[2] The development of agriculture and fruit-growing in California, which began to compete with the mining industry between 1860 and 1880, caused a more even distribution of population in that state, filling up the vacant spaces until, in the latter year, only the extreme northeastern and southeastern corners were unoccupied. Nevada passed the highest point of growth soon after being admitted as a state in 1864, although the loss of population, due to the decrease of mining and the impossibility of developing agriculture under the conditions of the times, was not manifest until 1890. Oregon, after the "rush" of 1850 to 1860, settled down to a steady growth; while Washington territory began the increase of population which caused her, between 1870 and 1890, to surpass the remarkable records made earlier by California and by Oregon.

---

[1] Hannibal, etc., Railroad Co. *vs.* Husen, 95 U. S., 465.
[2] U. S. Eleventh Census (1890), I., **xix**.

The expansion of the people over the unoccupied grazing, farming, and mineral lands of the West was rivalled by the growth of manufacturing cities in the East. A city arose at the head and foot of every navigable river, perhaps on a portage-path which the feet of explorer, trader, or Jesuit missionary had worn deep into the earth by years of usage, but always at a point favorable to the transportation of raw material and manufactured products, and always as near as might be to cheap fuel. To these strategic points in the eternal warfare between man and nature first came the craftsman who made from wood and iron the utensils and furniture demanded by his neighbors. He was followed by the organizing capitalist, who established a factory and exported the surplus factory-made goods. Hither came to dwell the operators and laborers, who provided mind and muscle for the factories and mills; the merchants who disposed of the goods; the wagoners and freight-handlers who placed them on board the cars for shipment; and frequently the trainmen and sailors who carried them away and brought back the raw material in return.

Both skilled and unskilled laborers flocked into these industrial centres, boys from the farms and immigrants from Europe, forming the cities which were a necessary concomitant of the industrial age. In 1800 only one-twentieth of the people of the United States dwelt in cities of more than eight thousand; in 1870 the proportion had grown to one-fifth; and in 1880 it had increased to one-fourth.[1] These centres of population not only interfered with the due-west advance of the people, but counteracted it in some instances by a return movement. They not only produced millionaires but also the proletariat, to form the problems of cities; and they further wrought great changes in the maps. Boston, for example, absorbed the town of Roxbury in 1867, Dorchester in 1870, and Charlestown in 1874, raising the population of Boston from 177,000 to 362,000. In 1873 the towns of Morrisania, West Farms, and Kings Bridge disappeared in New York City.[2]

In 1880 New York City was first in magnitude, as she had been since the first census was taken, with Philadelphia in the second rank. Chicago had just passed St. Louis in the race for fourth place. Within the last ten years Boston passed Baltimore and St. Louis, San Francisco overtook New Orleans, while Washington, Cleveland, and Pittsburg pushed Buffalo from the tenth to the thirteenth place. Spokane was a village of three hundred and fifty people in 1880, and Seattle had only three thousand inhabitants. Certain modern industrial centres, such as South Omaha, Nebraska, and Superior, Wisconsin, had not yet appeared on the map. Kansas City, Kansas, and Birmingham, Alabama, now grown to large manufacturing cities, had a population of little over three thousand each in 1880. Many modern

[1] U. S. Tenth Census (1880), I., 416–425.
[2] U. S. Twelfth Census (1900), I., lxxx.

cities, which owe their existence to mining industries, were as yet embryonic. Butte, Montana, had three thousand population, and "Last Chance Gulch," transformed into Helena, had only the same number; Anaconda had not yet appeared on a Montana map; Bisbee and other mining cities of Arizona had no existence; and the future Oklahoma City lay in an Indian territory in which not even a census had as yet been taken.[1]

An examination of the place of birth of the native-born people living in the newer states in 1880[2] showed that the direction of interstate migration continued to be from east to west. To the peopling of Dakota territory, Wisconsin contributed most largely, with New York second and Minnesota third. Nebraska drew most heavily upon Illinois, then upon Ohio, New York, Pennsylvania, and Indiana in decreasing order. To people Texas, Alabama contributed most freely her sons and daughters, with Tennessee, Mississippi, and Georgia following in order. While more than twelve thousand Vermonters had chosen to move to Wisconsin, only one hundred and thirty-five were found in Louisiana. On the other hand, Georgians to the number of fifteen thousand selected Louisiana as a home, but only one hundred and ninety-seven went up to dwell in Wisconsin.[3] Only the magnetism of cities, drawing

---

[1] U. S. Twelfth Census (1900), I., 430–433.
[2] U. S. Tenth Census (1880), I., 480–483.
[3] U. S. *Summary of Commerce and Finance*, 1903, p. 4336.

equally from all directions, was able to check in later years this unfortunate tendency to perpetuate lines of sectionalism in the intermigration of the people.

Immigration may be regarded as the barometer of American prosperity. During "good times" laborers are attracted and add to the general prosperity; during adverse periods, demand ceases, their coming is checked, and the loss of their potential labor adds to the general shrinkage. The number of aliens arriving in the United States, which reached four hundred thousand in 1854, fell to seventy thousand in the midst of the war, but a little more than recovered its former proportions by 1870. Checked again in the panic of 1873, the number of arrivals slowly waned until 1879, when a reaction set in and the number rapidly increased. In 1880 nearly half a million inhabitants of Europe sought to better their conditions by coming to the United States, and three years later the number grew to 788,992, the high-tide of immigration until 1893.[1] Up to this time the nativity of the new-comers varied little in relative proportion from the beginning of the movement to America. Germany and Ireland continued to supply nearly one-half the total number, with Canada, England, Sweden, Norway, and Scotland following in decreasing order.[1] Of these the Scandinavian countries, which sent a little over one per cent. of the total immigration in 1860, contributed in 1870 nearly

[1] *U. S. Summary of Commerce and Finance*, 1903, p. 4340; cf. Hart, *National Ideals* (*Am. Nation*, XXVI.), chap. iii.

five per cent. and in 1880 more than six per cent. of the entire number of arrivals. They settled almost exclusively in the agricultural regions of the Northwest.[1] The influx of French Canadians, which has manifested itself in recent times particularly in New England and the north border states, reached only a little over one-tenth of all the immigration of 1880. Nor was the modern invasion from Austro-Hungary, including Bohemia, and from Italy and Poland, more in evidence in 1880. United, they made up only four per cent. of the total immigration, and gave no evidence that twenty years later they would constitute nearly one-fourth of the entire number.[2] These peoples, unaccustomed to agricultural pursuits above the peasant class, furnished laborers for manufacturing plants, and consequently contributed to the growth of cities and the complexity of the municipal problem.

The rehabilitation of the southern states progressed steadily during the period under consideration, although under unfavorable conditions. Deprived of slave labor and unable to attract foreign laborers, with public attention fixed on the surface of the soil, ignoring both mineral resources and forests, and with inadequate means of transportation, the southerner, was handicapped in the start of the industrial race.[3]

---

[1] *North Am. Rev.*, CXXXIV., 162.
[2] *U. S. Summary of Commerce and Finance*, 1903, pp., 4346–4350.
[3] Cf. Hart, *Slavery and Abolition* (*Am. Nation*, XVI.), chap. iv.

But reinforced by the industrial "carpet-bagger," he undertook to open mines and mills, to build and operate factories, and to find a home market for both raw material and manufactures. In 1870 Virginia sent several hundred agents to Germany and to England and printed thousands of copies of pamphlets in both German and English to persuade emigrants to settle in that state; but the established lines of movement, and the concentration of the emigrant steamship lines in New York, kept Virginia from realizing large returns in the way of settlers.[1] Consequently the southern cities continued to show almost unmixed American blood, averaging only two foreigners out of each hundred inhabitants. Immigrants followed lines of railways into the interior of the country; and the disproportion of almost three miles of railway north of the Mason and Dixon line to one mile south of it directed them to the northern section.

Nevertheless, local mining and manufacturing industries were developing in the South. In 1880 coal was mined in Alabama, Arkansas, Georgia, Kentucky, Maryland, Missouri, North Carolina, Tennessee, and Virginia, in more than four hundred establishments and to the value of over six million dollars—nearly one-eighth of all produced in the United States. Iron was manufactured in over two hundred establishments, embracing nearly every southern state, with a total value of $25,000,000.

[1] *Am. Annual Cyclop.*, 1870, p. 132.

Cotton mills, of which a considerable number existed before the war, rapidly increased in number and in size. In 1870, in the southern states, 11,000 looms were employing 417,000 spindles and consuming 45,000,000 pounds of their own cotton; ten years later the number of looms had increased to 15,000, the spindles to 714,000, and they were using 102,000,-000 pounds of cotton.[1] New England still remained the cotton-weaving centre, consuming more than 500,000,000 pounds of raw material in 1880; but the mills in operation in the South attested the industrial recovery of that section as well as the possibility of maintaining her people by her own resources.

The freedmen continued to be an important element in southern population. About 1879 an unorganized and irregular movement of these people set in towards the free states, especially Kansas, where they hoped to find a new Canaan, in which their domestic and political status would be more secure than in their former homes. The exodus, which had partly a religious motive, caused relief to the southern people in general but alarm to those engaged in cotton culture, and in some instances they forcibly turned back the refugees. Conventions of white men met in various cities to secure easier contract laws between white and black and to protest against northerners alluring laborers from the cotton-fields. Influenced by the enactment of more rigid suffrage and property laws in many of the

[1] *Appleton's Annual Cyclop.*, 1880, p. 132.

southern states, and under the political excitement of the campaign of 1880, the migration increased until more than forty thousand negroes had gone into Kansas alone. They came for the most part from Mississippi, Texas, Tennessee, and Louisiana. Organized charity contributed more than two hundred thousand dollars for their relief, and colonies of them were planted on the public lands.[1] Gradually the craze subsided, and the movement of the centre of negro population south rather than north, since the Civil War, proves that no important redistribution of population followed.[2]

[1] *Appleton's Annual Cyclop.*, 1879, p. 354; 1880, p. 417; 1881, p. 812. Also see *Senate Reports*, 46 Cong., 2 Sess., No. 693; *Nation*, XXVIII., 242, XXX., 431.
[2] U. S. Twelfth Census (1900), p. clxviii.

CHAPTER III

INVENTION AND DISCOVERY
(1877–1885)

AS has been pointed out above, in 1880 nearly one-fourth of the people were gathered in cities of eight thousand or more inhabitants, causing serious problems of housing, lighting, and transportation.[1] The population naturally spread out into the suburbs, but the usual system of street-cars, drawn by horses, was no longer possible for the long distances to be traversed, at a satisfactory speed. In 1876 work was begun in New York City upon a system of overhead railways supported on iron pillars or arches resting on the curb of the street or in the roadway. Passenger-trains were drawn upon its rails by diminutive locomotives weighing less than fifteen tons. Nearly forty miles of these "elevated roads" were planned to traverse the principal streets of New York City and to extend to its most populous suburbs.[2]

Three years later the engineering world turned its attention to San Francisco, where many and steep hills prohibited the use of horse or steam cars. To

---
[1] U. S. Eleventh Census (1890), I., lxxxiii.
[2] *Appleton's Annual Cyclop.*, 1878, p. 284.

overcome the difficulty a small subway was built between the rails in the street, with a slit on its upper side through which passed a grappling arrangement descending from the car to an endless steel wire rope moving in the subway. This rope was kept in motion by being passed about a huge revolving drum in a power-house adjacent to the car line. By clutching or releasing the slowly moving cable the car could be started or stopped at will.[1] Used at first only to draw the cars over hills on Clay Street, the system was soon installed on other streets of San Francisco, and initiated in other cities as a cheap method of intramural transportation. The "cable" was so great an improvement upon the horse-car that it was regarded as permanent; but within twenty years it was almost wholly superseded by the electric "trolley" car.

Experimental electric cars antedated the cable by nearly fifty years; Dever's model was exhibited at Springfield, Massachusetts, in 1835.[2] Another model electric railway, illustrating the use of a third rail in carrying the current, was shown at Stockbridge, Massachusetts, in 1879, the year that Siemans and Halske made a success of their "trolley" road at the Berlin exhibition. In 1882, Edison operated a car by electricity at Menlo Park, New Jersey,[3] and the following year a miniature road carried passengers

[1] *Appleton's Annual Cyclop.*, 1879, p. 346.
[2] U. S. Bureau of the Census, *Special Report, Street and Electric Railways* (1902), 160.   [3] *Ibid.*, 161.

at the electric exhibit at Chicago. In 1884 a tiny train drawn by electricity was used at the Philadelphia Electrical Exposition on a track four hundred feet long.[1]

During the same year Professor Short operated an experimental electric road at Denver, and Bentley and Knight one at Cleveland. Depoele's electric road carried passengers at the New Orleans Exposition in 1885.[2] Credit for the first electric railway constructed through the streets of a city and operated for profit is shared by the Sprague system installed on two and a half miles of track at Richmond, Virginia, in 1885, and the Daft system placed on a line between Baltimore and Hampden, two miles long, during the same year.[3] In 1886 there were only these two lines in operation in the United States; four years later the number had increased to forty-nine.[4]

Since the time of Davy it had been known that a current of electricity passing through two sticks of charcoal slightly separated produced a brilliant light, and an "arc" light of this kind was used in the siege of Paris in 1871, and in certain light-houses on the British coast. The difficulty was to find carbon

---

[1] Franklin Institute, *Journal*, CXXII., 401.
[2] U. S. Census Bureau, *Special Report, Street and Electric Railways* (1902), 163–165.
[3] *Science*, August 28, 1885; for sketch of electric railway inventions, see decision in Adams Elect. Ry. Co. *vs.* Lindell Ry. Co., 77 Fed. Rep., 433.
[4] U. S. Eleventh Census (1890), *Transportation on Land*, 681.

points which would glow steadily and adjust themselves while burning. European scientists were also experimenting on a current passed through a closed tube in an atmosphere of high rarefaction in order to obtain a light; but no material suitable for such combustion could readily be found. As late as 1872, when Tyndall was delivering his scientific lectures throughout the United States, he was obliged to carry with him a battery of a hundred cells to supply a current for his experiments. No effort had been made as yet to supply a current outside a laboratory; but from several inventors there came almost simultaneously machines which revolved an armature, consisting of coils of wire wrapped about an iron core, between the poles of one or more electro-magnets.[1] These were known as "magneto-electric" machines, or as "dynamo-electric" machines, a name soon shortened to "dynamo." A current generated on such a machine could be carried to a distance on a wire and utilized in any desired manner.

These successful attempts to convey a current along a wire were not reached without long and tedious experimentation. It was one hundred and twenty years after Franklin demonstrated that lightning was a discharge of electricity, and seventy years after Volta announced that electricity could be produced by chemical action,[2] before electrical energy

---

[1] Iles, *Flame, Electricity, and Camera*, 107, 108.
[2] Bigelow, *Franklin's Works*, I., 276-281; Iles, *Flame, Electricity, and Camera*, 100.

was turned to commercial use in the magnetic telegraph. Just before Morse perfected that invention, Faraday and Henry[1] suggested that currents of electricity could be produced by a revolving magnet, yet thirty years elapsed before the armature was invented which made modern applications possible.

After many improvements by various inventors, C. F. Brush, of Cleveland, produced an arc light suitable for streets and parks; and in 1879 the first electric lighting station under this system was installed at San Francisco.[2] Experimenters working on the bulb or vacuum light were using for the filament to be illuminated cotton thread, cartridge-paper, and platinum wire. In 1879, Thomas Edison, an American inventor, after searching the vegetable kingdom of the world, adopted a filament of bamboo supported on platinum wires, and gave out the first practical incandescent light.[3] By arranging the lights in a multiple series and by dividing the current and conveying it along different lines, the power supplied to the several lamps was properly regulated and the lighting of large areas from the same plant made possible. In 1882 the first Edison electric lighting plant for incandescent lighting was opened in New York City, the current being carried

[1] Tyndall, *Faraday as a Discoverer*, passim; Smithsonian Institution, Board of Regents, *Proceedings*, 1887.
[2] U. S. Eleventh Census (1890), *Manufactures*, Part III., 239.
[3] Iles, *Flame, Electricity, and Camera*, 124; *Harper's Weekly*, XXV., 456; Edison, "The Success of the Electric Light," in *North Am. Rev.*, CXXXI., 295.

from a common station by wire instead of having a storage battery in each house, as was contemplated by a rival system.[1] So rapidly had the American methods improved that two of the four lights shown at the Electrical Exhibition in Paris in 1881 came from the United States. In 1880 there were over seventy establishments in the United States engaged in manufacturing electrical supplies to the value of two and a half million dollars. When Garfield was inaugurated, in 1881, the city of Washington was illuminated by electricity. At the Philadelphia Exhibition of 1884, twelve engines, combining 1800 horse-power, furnished the current for hundreds of electric lights, aggregating 1,500,000 candle-power. Of these 5600 were incandescent lamps, some with colored bulbs, arranged in effective manner about the buildings and grounds. A monster arc light, said to be of one hundred thousand candle-power, shone from a tower; and numerous lights of a similar kind made the grounds as light as the interior of a building.[2]

It was not enough that electricity should be made to convey people and illuminate cities; it must perform other tasks. Among the curiosities shown at the Centennial Exposition was a "lover's telegraph," which consisted of a string connecting two boxes or bits of tubing with a flexible diaphragm closing one end of each, the ends of the string being

[1] U. S. Twelfth Census (1900), X., 157.
[2] *Appleton's Annual Cyclop.*, 1884, pp. 304-310.

attached to these diaphragms. The vibrations made
by the voice of a person speaking in one box were
conveyed to the string by the diaphragm, and could
be heard by the person at the other box.[1] Attempts
were next made to send the vibrations through a wire
by the aid of the electric current, and success soon
followed. In 1877 the newspapers told exciting
stories of a concert in New York, the music of which
was carried to a distance by means of a wire and
distinctly heard through the use of the "telephone,"
the invention of Elisha Gray. Another instrument,
serving the same purpose, the invention of Professor
Bell of Boston, conveyed distinctly the sound of
voices over a wire stretched between Boston and
Salem.[2] Conversation was carried on by the participants concerning the weather and the railway
strike. The Salem people were amazed to hear that
it was raining in Boston. At the request of the inventor, who was in Salem, his letters were opened in
his Boston office and their contents heard in Salem,
"with as much clearness," said an astonished reporter,
"as though Mr. Watson had been a private secretary
at his elbow."[3] There seemed no limit to the commercial uses to which this invention could be put when
once the wires were strung between cities. Many predicted that it would soon replace the telegraph.

[1] Iles, *Flame, Electricity, and Camera*, 239.
[2] Prescott, *Bell's Electric Telephone* (1884), passim; *Frank Leslie's Weekly*, XLIV., 124 (March 24, 1875).
[3] *Independent*, March 28, 1877.

The demand for rapid transportation in the cities produced another invention of unlimited potentiality, although injured by too much popularity which made it a temporary "fad." At the Centennial Exposition was displayed an imported "bicycle," an adaptation of the velocipede which had been in limited use for the past fifty years. Two years later an American company was organized to manufacture the modern machine. In 1884 no les than six thousand bicycles were manufactured by half a dozen companies, and it was estimated that at least thirty thousand were in use. Bicycle "meets" were held in various cities,[1] and bicycle clubs made long tours through the country, adding to the comity of the people. The machine consisted practically of one large wheel over which the rider was mounted, balanced by a small wheel at the rear. The danger of this precarious position led to the invention in 1884 of a "safety" machine, with two moderate wheels of equal size. Being adapted to both sexes, it speedily replaced the former style of build. In 1886 the public realized the possibilities of the bicycle and the craze was begun. In 1890 it was necessary to create a special department of the patent office to consider the numerous applications for patents connected with the bicycle. The use of the machine, although eventually superseded by the automobile, led to a renewed interest in sports and in the study of nature, aided in scattering the crowded people of the

[1] *Harper's Weekly*, XXV., 400.

cities into the suburbs,[1] and thus furthered a reaction in favor of country life.

Prominent among the names connected with these startling experiments and inventions, which established the American reputation for applied genius, was that of Thomas A. Edison, a typical American. Among other devices, he arranged in 1877 a revolving wax cylinder upon which vibrations from the human voice or a musical instrument made indentations through the medium of a receiver. When the wax cylinder was revolved in a "transmitter," these impressions were reformed into the original sounds. Records of persons speaking and singing, as well as of musical instruments, were made and reproduced at will by this sound-writer or "phonograph," which it was supposed would greatly influence the agencies employed in business.[2] To Edison was also accredited, in 1879, the invention of the megaphone, a simple paper funnel through which "conversation could be carried on at a distance of from one and a half to two miles," as the reporters described it. More complicated and less appreciated was Edison's electric pen which wrote from the telegraph, his micro-tasimeter which detected minute variations in temperature, and his "carbon" telephone. Several men had experiment-

[1] U. S. Twelfth Census (1900), I., xc.; *Appleton's Annual Cyclop.*, 1884, p. 80.
[2] Edison, "The Phonograph of the Future," in *North Am. Rev.*, CXXVI., 527.

ed by placing tuning-forks on telegraph transmitters and receivers and sending messages tuned to different pitches. In this manner it was possible to send two messages each way over the same wire simply by tuning them to different keys. From this suggestion, Edison eventually evolved his sextuplex telegraph.[1]

In few of the arts was more progress made in this period of preparation for the industrial age than in photography. A sensitized paper was devised upon which the negative could be made direct in the camera, thereby avoiding the weight and frequent breakage of glass plates. At the same time, experiments were being made with a substitute for ivory made chiefly from gun-cotton and camphor and known as "celluloid." Presently some one thought of sensitizing long strips of the celluloid rolled to fit a camera, and thus was the modern era of amateur photography inaugurated. A "composite" photograph was formed by the collection of a number of negatives of different persons made in the same relative position of the eyes or mouth or some other feature. From these negatives, superimposed one on another, a new negative was made in which harmony of features in the persons composing the composite was emphasized by distinct lines and shadows in the picture, and deviations by blurs.[2] The inven-

---

[1] Iles, *Flame, Electricity, and Camera*, 168, 210, 213.
[2] *Ibid.*, 319; *Nature*, May 23, 1878; *McClure's Magazine*, September, 1894.

tion, it was presumed, would be of value to students of ethnology and in tracing effects of the law of heredity in families. About the same time a San Francisco photographer named Muybridge, in order to settle the long-standing dispute among artists about the motions made by a horse in trotting, arranged a row or battery of cameras beside a race-track. Sensitized plates were exposed in turn by electricity as the horse passed in front of the cameras, which operated with a length of exposure of about the thousandth part of a second.[1] The result startled all observers by the seemingly unnatural positions of the animal, settled all disputes of this nature, and paved the way for the later motion-pictures, reproducing travelling regiments and other moving bodies. Photography was henceforth to play an important commercial part in advertising, in selling goods by sample, in science, and in the instruction and entertainment of the people.

Science as applied to the well-being of the people was demonstrated in Washington, Pennsylvania, in 1875, by the construction of a building for the purpose of incinerating dead bodies in accord with the ancient Greek custom.[2] The body of Baron de Palm, who died in New York, was successfully cremated, December, 1876, the entire process requiring less than four hours. Although the desirability

---

[1] Iles, *Flame, Electricity, and Camera*, 312, 360; *Appleton's Annual Cyclop.*, 1878, p. 723.
[2] *Frank Leslie's Newspaper*, XLV., 75.

of the practice from hygienic grounds was admitted, it was opposed by many because of sectarian beliefs, and as contrary to long-standing sentiment.

An engineering triumph upon which the people of the West based large hopes was the Sutro tunnel in Nevada. More than three miles in length, it furnished an outlet to the mines in the rich Comstock lode and drained the entire system of mines in that vicinity of the water which bade fair to ruin them.[1] Unfortunately, before it was finished most of the mines were exhausted. The discovery of gold in the Black Hills caused the introduction of improved mining machinery, and stimulated railroad building in the West. By 1884 the completion of four Pacific railways in the United States and one in Canada[2] testified to the liveliness of the people, the skill of engineers, the generosity of the national government, and the accumulation of American capital.

Inspired by these achievements, visionists even contemplated through trans-continental service for passenger-trains from ocean to ocean. In 1877 an enterprising publisher chartered a special train, which passed unbroken from New York to San Francisco and returned to its initial point.[3] The public interest and rejoicing in this and similar feats seemed a

[1] *Appleton's Annual Cyclop.* 1878, p. 288.
[2] Roberts, *Hist. of Canada*, 373, 383, 402; *Appleton's Annual Cyclop.*, 1882, p. 217.
[3] *Frank Leslie's Newspaper*, XLIV., 140, and succeeding numbers.

revival of old times, when canal and railway were rivals, and the national pulse was quickened by an "American system." A Nicaraguan ship canal and a Tehuantepec ship railway were kept before the people as future triumphs for American engineers.

In 1869, John A. Roebling and his son began to construct a suspension bridge, with a middle span of 1595 feet, between New York and Brooklyn, which was opened to the public in 1883.[1] At the same time a double-track cantilever railroad bridge was thrown across the chasm below the Niagara Falls. The congestion in the streets of New York City was relieved by the construction of the elevated railroads.[2] In many suits for damages instituted against the company by owners of adjacent real estate, the courts decided that the streets were public property and the railway a public necessity; but after years of litigation some damages were finally awarded against the company.[3] In 1885 more than nine acres of partly submerged reef in the East River above New York, commonly known as Hell Gate, were removed by firing a hundred and forty tons of explosives placed in twenty miles of shafts and tunnels which had been honey-combed through it.[4] The federal government made further provision for

[1] *Appleton's Annual Cyclop.*, 1883, p. 580. [2] *Ibid.*, 568, 580.
[3] *Ibid.*, 1882, p. 616; *Harper's Weekly*, XXVI., 675; *Railroad Gazette*, XIV., 648.
[4] *Harper's Weekly*, XXIV., 824; *Appleton's Annual Cyclop.*, 1876, p. 377; 1880, p. 250; 1881, p. 250.

commerce by constructing a dam across the Ohio River six miles below Pittsburg, intended to be the beginning of a scheme for a slack-water navigation between that city and New Orleans. If ever completed, it would relieve the demand for better transportation facilities in the iron regions, and cotton belt, where improved methods of cultivation were producing constantly increasing crops.

The progress of the southern states in the production of cotton was illustrated by an International Cotton Exposition in Atlanta, Georgia, in 1881. Eighteen hundred exhibits were displayed and viewed by nearly three hundred thousand visitors. Many improved machines connected with the cotton culture were shown, especially those designed to clean and rescue the "storm" cotton, which amounted to one-sixth the crop. Cotton seed, which had been thrown away before 1860, was now utilized for a fertilizer, cattle food, and the cheaper kinds of carbon, after the valuable oil had been extracted. In beds adjacent to the exposition buildings, cotton culture was shown in all its stages, and possible improvements demonstrated. There were exhibits of jute and other new products of the South, to give hope that dependence need not always rest on one crop. The displays of the Wesson cotton mills of Mississippi, those of Augusta, Columbus, and West Point, Georgia, Piedmont, South Carolina, and elsewhere, showed a vigorous competition with the old source of cotton goods in New England. The exposition proved an inspiration for the new industrial South.[1]

Government exploring expeditions, beginning with that of Lewis and Clark, had long since outlined most of the topographical features of the United States, and some extended surveys had also been made. In 1879,[2] Congress authorized the organization of a United States Geological Survey, to undertake systematically the task of locating and describing the mineral treasures to be exploited during the coming industrial age; and thus greatly aided the surveys already made by many of the states. The United States also assumed its share in the task of Arctic exploration. In 1878, Lieutenant Schwatka, of the United States navy, sailed on a two years' search for relics of the lost Sir John Franklin expedition of 1847. Schwatka cleared up many points concerning the fate of the unfortunate English expedition, made a remarkable sledge journey of thirty-two hundred and fifty miles, and secured valuable geographical information concerning the north.[3] The following year the ill-fated *Jeannette*, under Commodore De Long, sailed from San Francisco via Bering Strait to find a supposed polar sea. Two anxious years followed before her few survivors found their way to the mouth of the Lena River and thence into

[1] *Appleton's Annual Cyclop.*, 1881, p. 260.
[2] *U. S. Statutes at Large*, XX., 394.
[3] *Senate Exec. Docs.*, 48 Cong., 2 Sess, No. 2; *Appleton's Annual Cyclop.*, 1880, p. 298.

Siberia.[1] According to an international agreement, the United States in 1881 sent Lieutenant Greely to establish a station for scientific observation in northern Greenland. In attempting to carry out his orders, Greely incidentally reached 83° 24', the most northerly point thus far attained. He and a remnant of his party were rescued in 1884 by the third relief expedition sent out to them, under command of Captain Winfield S. Schley.[2] While these intrepid spirits were winning prestige for American enterprise and American valor in the Arctic regions, equally courageous leaders were demanded at home to grapple with problems arising from the new industrial conditions—especially in the matter of transportation.

[1] *Appleton's Annual Cyclop.*, 1879, p. 417; 1880, p. 288; 1881, p. 322; 1882, p. 331. See also the numerous public documents cited in *Tables of U. S. Public Docs.*, 426.

[2] *Appleton's Annual Cyclop.*, 1881, p. 325; 1883, p. 420; *House Misc. Docs.*, 49 Cong., 1 Sess., No. 393; *Harper's Weekly*, XXVIII., 485, 517.

CHAPTER IV

PROBLEMS OF TRANSPORTATION
(1875-1885)

TRANSPORTATION is an essential agency in an industrial age. The rapid extension of railways during the years immediately following the industrial recovery of the United States from the Civil War was both indicative of the approach of an industrial age and a preparation for it. The 9000 miles of railways of 1850 reached 30,000 in 1860, and 52,000 in 1870, showing a steady growth of about 20,000 miles every ten years. In 1880 there were 87,801 miles in operation, 9416 miles under construction, and 35,293 miles projected, a large gain on the preceding decade.[1] During 1872 alone, 7439 miles had been added, the banner year for railroad construction until 1893. Part of this additional mileage represented links to connect short lines having the same general direction and thus to form a "trunk" line between prominent shipping points. Cornelius Vanderbilt, president of the Hudson River Railroad, in 1869 consolidated it with the

---

[1] U. S. Tenth Census (1880), IV., 290; cf. Dunning, *Reconstruction* (*Am. Nation*, XXII.), chap. ix.

New York Central, making possible shipment in bulk on one road from New York to Buffalo. In 1873 he leased the Lake Shore & Michigan Southern, forming a through freight line between New York and Chicago.[1] The Pennsylvania Company, about 1869, under the legal advice of Samuel J. Tilden, leased the Pittsburg, Fort Wayne & Chicago, giving it entrance to Chicago. In 1874 the Baltimore & Ohio Company built an extension from its Ohio Central line to Chicago, and the Grand Trunk opened a lake and rail line from Detroit to Milwaukee, making five trunk lines to compete for the business between Lake Michigan and the seaboard. This number was increased about 1882 by the completion of the West Shore and the "Nickel Plate," and also by the extension of the Erie Railroad to Chicago. As yet no great and prosperous north and south lines had been built; the volume of trade flowed in an east and west direction.

Vanderbilt's aim in forming a through line to Chicago was to secure some of the extensive carrying trade between the lakes and the ocean, over which the lake and canal route had enjoyed a monopoly for nearly fifty years. In the Erie Canal, the artificial waterway seemed to have reached its highest stage of efficiency, though it could not compete with the railroad in passenger traffic and not even in freight, except in goods which permitted slow transportation and in limited bulk. About 1867 the carriers on the Great Lakes and Erie Canal first felt

[1] *Railroad Gazette*, IX., 13.

the force of competing railways, although no trunk line had yet been formed. In that year grain was carried by water from Chicago to the seaboard for 24 cents a bushel. In 1870 the water rate fell to 17 cents a bushel, because the railroads were charging only 33 cents for their more rapid transit. In 1880 the rail rate dropped to 19 cents and the canal had to cut to 12 cents. Four years later the rail carriage was reduced to 13 cents and the canal to 6 cents, a rate which left no profits.[1]

As a result of these and similar conditions, part of the three thousand miles of canals, which had been constructed in the United States before 1875, was already abandoned, and no new artificial waterway was under construction, although a widening of the Erie Canal to give it larger capacity was contemplated.[2] To maintain inland water traffic, Congress continued to appropriate large sums of money for improving the rivers and harbors. In 1879 the aggregate appropriation for this purpose was $6,648,-517, and the amount was increasing annually. In ocean commerce, while the amount of imports and exports to and from America grew steadily, the American shipping and ship-building industry suffered an atrophy, because wooden shipping was being replaced by iron vessels.[3] The total trade

[1] Haines, *Restrictive Railway Legislation*, 158; *U. S. Statistical Abstract*, 1900, p. 391; *Railroad Gazette*, XII., 320.
[2] For the Erie and other canals, see Poor, *Manual of Railroads*, 1881, pp. i.–xix.; U. S. Tenth Census (1880), IV., 731.
[3] *North Am. Rev.*, CXXXII., 466.

through American ports in 1877 was valued at $1,176,580,817, of which American vessels carried only 14 per cent. as against 28 per cent. ten years before.[1] Great Britain led, with Germany second, in the American carrying-trade. Some steps were taken towards developing American lines to compete with these: in connection with the Pennsylvania Railroad, the American Steamship Company was organized in 1873 to operate vessels between Philadelphia and Liverpool; and during the same year the Red Star Line was formed, as a Standard Oil enterprise, to be maintained between Philadelphia and Antwerp as oil carriers; it soon developed into a New York freight and passenger route to Belgium.

No sooner were trunk lines formed between prominent points, as Chicago and the seaboard, Chicago and St. Louis, Chicago and Omaha, than competition began to illustrate the evils of over railroad building, because it reduced the rates of carriage. In 1877 twenty lines were competing for the St. Louis-Atlanta trade, although they differed in length from 526 miles to 1858 miles. The long haul received no more for its service than the short haul.[2] In attempting to secure business between these and other competing points, scouts were maintained by each company to solicit trade; a free hand was given to them in the making of rates; freight carriage was soon reduced to a ruinous figure; and an occasional

[1] *U. S. Statistical Abstract* (1900), 454.
[2] *Railroad Gazette*, IX., 327.

"passenger war" made returns still smaller. Between competing points, freight was sometimes carried a thousand miles for a lower sum than the same bulk was carried one hundred miles where no competition had to be met. This was fortunate for shippers who enjoyed competing lines, but exasperating to those shipping from isolated places.

Railroads must endeavor to meet expenses, and they soon learned to make the shipping points which had no competition pay for the cutting of rates at competitive points. Thus they gained an argument which they have used frequently since in pleading against competition: for a rate war, instead of benefiting the shipper, might ruin him. Cattle were once carried from the Missouri River to Chicago for eighty-one cents a car-load. A large number was thus suddenly thrown upon the market; prices fell; and many western farmers suffered in consequence. Lines of water transportation also felt the effects of competition in lowering rates. In 1867 a ton of ore carried from Escanaba, Michigan, to Cleveland, earned its carrier $4.25. In 1870 it brought only $2.50.

Of the various devices employed by railroads to overcome competitors, rate agreement was the easiest, and is said to have been tried as early as 1858 by the New York Central and the Erie, in competing for the trade between Lake Erie and the city of New York.[1] Having witnessed the disastrous effects of Chicago-New York rate wars in 1869, 1875,

[1] Johnson, *Am. Railway Transportation*, 217.

and 1876, Cornelius Vanderbilt was convinced that unchecked competition meant ruin, and that combination of competing lines was as necessary as combinations of connecting roads had been in the process of forming trunk lines. He realized that the expense of operation, of repair, and of deterioration continued whether the volume of business was large or small; and consequently devoted the latter years of his life to perfecting a plan of agreement among the five lake-to-seaboard routes for "one rate from the lakes to the Atlantic." A central board of arbitration was formed to establish rates for carrying various classes of goods and to maintain the established tariff. The Baltimore & Ohio and the Grand Trunk refused to be bound, and the so-called "iron-clad agreement" went to pieces soon after Vanderbilt's death in 1877. Seven coal-carrying railroads in Pennsylvania and New York formed a similar agreement, which established fixed rates for delivering coal at principal points, regardless of the road which carried it, and also limited the output of the mines. A committee of the New York Assembly in 1878 decided that the arrangement was not in contravention of the state laws.[1]

The device of "pooling" the earnings was tried as early as 1870 by the Northwestern, the Rock Island, and the Burlington railway companies, to regulate competition in the freight service between Chicago and Omaha. Each company retained about half its

[1] *Appleton's Annual Cyclop.*, 1878, p. 619.

earnings, and the remainder was divided equally among all the companies. In 1875 Albert Fink formed the "Southern Railway and Steamship Association," to control competition among the cotton carriers in states south of the Potomac and Ohio and east of the Mississippi River.[1] The success of this pool resulted in Fink being called in 1877 to form the Chicago-New York roads into a pool.[2] A common treasurer was authorized to receive the earnings of each road entering the pool, and to redistribute them among the roads at the end of a given period according to some prearranged percentage. In the apportionment of the west-bound traffic the New York Central and the Erie were each to have 33 per cent., the Pennsylvania 25 per cent., and the Baltimore & Ohio 9 per cent.[3] The greatest difficulty encountered by the combination arose from the fact that there was not sufficient business for each road, and solicitors continued to cut rates, causing complaints on the part of the smaller roads in the pool that they were obliged to do more than their proportion of the labor, or to have their share of the profits withheld. Rates continued to decline throughout the pooling days, although the people imagined the combination gave the roads great advantages in profits. No attempt was made to enforce the rules of the pooling association by law, possibly because the roads did not desire to raise

[1] *Railroad Gazette*, IX., 314.
[2] Johnson, *Am. Railway Transportation*, 232.   [3] *Ibid.*, 236.

the question of the legality of their combining even in this simple manner.

The railroad was regarded as a public benefactor in its early days. Before 1872 the federal government had promised as an aid to railroad building 155,-000,000 acres of public lands, an area almost equal to the New England states, New York, and Pennsylvania combined;[1] nineteen different states had voted sums aggregating two hundred million dollars for the same purpose; and municipalities and individuals had subscribed several hundred million dollars to help railway construction. Attempts to regulate railway charges were confined almost wholly to limitations placed in the railway charters by the state authorities; but these were so liberal that the roads rarely were in danger of violating them. In 1869 Massachusetts formed a state board of railroad commissioners whose duty included hearing complaints of discrimination or unjust treatment of shippers. It had power to prescribe and enforce a uniform system of accounts, but possessed no judicial authority. Commissions were formed in many states, some with advisory, and others with mandatory power, and a few with general powers over corporations.[2] In 1877 appeared the first report on internal commerce from the United States bureau of statistics, a division in the department of the interior founded

[1] Johnson, *Am. Railway Transportation*, 314.
[2] For map showing character of commissions by states, see *ibid.*, 360; Haines, *Restrictive Railway Legislation*, 234.

as a result of the Senate committee on transportation lines to the seaboard.

The railway as a national problem was presented first in the interstate combinations by which "trunk lines" were formed; yet Congress had placed itself on record in the act of 1866,[1] commonly known as "the charter of the American railway system," as favoring such unification. The act was intended to "facilitate commercial, postal, and military communication among the several states," and permitted steam railroads to carry passengers and freight from one state to another and connect with roads of other states to form continuous lines, but without affecting state charters. No serious attempt was made by state or federal powers to interfere with these early consolidations.

About 1870 a change in public feeling towards the railroads, because of discrimination in rates, manifested itself in hostile legislation, especially in the western states. The farmer and rural shipper were indignant because they paid higher rates than the city shippers, and their wrath was intensified by the panic of 1873. The general discontent was largely responsible for the spread among the western farmers of the organization called the Patrons of Husbandry, but commonly known as the "Grangers."[2] Its object was to do away with the "middle-man" and his profit by direct dealing between the pro-

[1] *U. S. Statutes at Large*, XIV., 66.
[2] Dunning, *Reconstruction* (*Am. Nation*, XXII.), 228.

ducer and consumer. The so-called Granger laws, passed by Illinois, Iowa, Wisconsin, and Minnesota—the grain-producing states of that time—were intended to establish a uniform rate for transporting and warehousing grain and other classified products, and to require schedules of rates to be published each day together with the rates in force during the previous year. The agitation was responsible for the insertion of a provision in the constitution of California in 1879 requiring railroad rates to be fixed by the state through a commission.

This legislation ignored the fact that railroad tariffs are most difficult things to form, involving more than forty elements in the computation.[1] The volume of traffic, cost of construction, climate, products, land, water, grades, and competition are a few of the many factors to be considered. Like most legislation of the kind, the Granger laws went too far: the roads insisted that enforcement of the laws would mean confiscation of their property, and they stopped railway extension in every hostile state, thereby injuring its prospects until the objectionable legislation was repealed. They also found it easy to delay prosecutions in the local courts through the practice of giving free transportation.

Many of these Granger cases found their way into the Supreme Court of the United States, and decisions were rendered in 1876 and the years fol-

[1] Noyes, *Am. Railroad Rates*, chap. iii.; Haines, *Restrictive Railway Legislation*, chap. vii.

lowing. A majority of the court held in the case of Munn *vs.* Illinois[1] that a state had power to regulate charges made by a common carrier—in this instance a warehouse—and that such regulation was not in violation of the company's charter as a contract; that the public was, in fact, a partner in such a public corporation; but that state regulation must not establish rates so low that they would be equivalent to confiscation of the property of the carrier. Also, the right to regulate rates within the state might legally effect commerce passing outside the state, until the federal government legislated upon interstate commerce. Dissenting justices held that the state had no right to meddle with railroad corporations because engaged in private and not public business. The principles here established held in the remaining cases with some variations.[2]

Whatever advantage the public might have gained from these decisions was destroyed by the continued critical financial condition of the railways. In 1873 more than two-fifths of the total railway mileage was in the hands of court receivers; and in 1877 the aggregate debts of the railway companies was estimated at more than double the national debt. Be-

[1] Munn *vs.* Illinois, 94 U. S., 113; McPherson, *Hand-Book of Politics*, 1878, p. 97.
[2] The other prominent "Granger cases" were: C. B. & Q. R.R. Co. *vs.* Iowa, 94 U. S., 155; Peik *vs.* C. &. N. W. Ry. Co., 94 U. S., 164; C. M. & St. Paul R.R. Co. *vs.* Ackley, 94 U. S., 179; Winona & St. Peter R.R. Co. *vs.* Blake, 94 U. S., 180; Shields *vs.* Ohio, 95 U. S., 319.

tween 1876 and 1879 nearly four hundred and fifty railroads were sold under foreclosure of mortgage. Real recovery was not felt until about 1881. The Grangers, not confining their reforms to one line and courting various political parties, lost their influence in the state legislatures. The states began to repeal the restrictive laws; new issues arose to attract public attention; and the agitation subsided for the time being, to arise a few years later in a demand for federal regulation of railroads.

In 1872 President Grant suggested to Congress an investigation of "various enterprises for the more certain and cheaper transportation of the constantly increasing surplus of western and southern products to the seaboard.[1] The result was the Windom report, made in the Senate in 1874,[2] which suggested that Congress had the power to construct as well as to regulate railroads and to bring the pooling companies to terms in that manner. At the same time the House heard the McCrary report[3] and passed the McCrary bill, which provided for regulation of railroads along the line of the Granger acts; but the Senate failed to pass it. In 1881 the House considered the Reagan bill, which prohibited pools, required publicity of rates, but left the enforcement of the act to the federal courts.[4] It was considered

[1] Richardson, *Messages and Papers*, VII., 195.
[2] *Senate Reports*, 43 Cong., 1 Sess., No. 307.
[3] *House Reports*, 43 Cong., 1 Sess., No. 28.
[4] McPherson, *Hand-Book of Politics*, 1882, pp. 125-129.

at subsequent sessions but never became a law. In 1885 each branch of Congress passed a bill to regulate interstate commerce, but the two houses failed to agree on a common bill.

The debates on these various bills disclosed some of the inconsistencies of railway rating; for instance, goods could be shipped from Pittsburg to Cincinnati by the Ohio River and thence to Philadelphia by rail cheaper than they could be sent direct from Pittsburg to Philadelphia by rail, for the Pennsylvania had a monopoly between these cities, while Cincinnati was favored with several competing lines to Philadelphia. A car-load of freight could be shipped from Omaha to San Francisco, it was said, and returned to stations in Nevada cheaper than if shipped direct to Nevada points.[1]

The people manifested their interest in the correction of these abuses by presenting hundreds of petitions to Congress in 1881 and 1882, asking federal regulation of railway rates. It will be remembered that the Supreme Court, in the Granger cases, established the right of a state to regulate its local traffic and even to operate indirectly upon outside commerce until Congress legislated on traffic between the states. State legislatures took comparatively no advantage of this suggestion, and the privilege was withdrawn in the Wabash case, in 1886, when the Supreme Court reviewed its former decision. It now held that regulation of goods

[1] *Cong. Record*, 46 Cong., 3 Sess., 365.

transferred under one contract from the interior of the state of Illinois to New York was national in its character and belonged exclusively to Congress. "Notwithstanding what was said in Munn *vs.* Illinois and other cases, this court holds that a statute of a state intended to regulate or to tax or to impose any other restrictions on the transmission of persons, property, or telegraphic messages from one state to another is not within that class of legislation which states may enact in the absence of legislation by Congress." [1]

This limitation of the power of the state hastened action on the report of the Cullom committee, which had investigated railway conditions; and, in 1885, reported to the Senate in favor of establishing a federal railway commission.[2] The final result was the interstate commerce act of 1887, as described in a later volume.[3]

As the country recovered from the financial difficulties of 1873, the railroad situation gradually improved; and by 1881 only five important lines remained in the hands of receivers. The short agricultural crop of 1883 might have brought another period of disaster, but it was averted because powerful combinations of capital had absorbed the smaller lines, and from the earnings on some portions of the system were able to carry the less remunera-

[1] Wabash, St. L. & P. Ry. Co. *vs.* Illinois, 118 U. S., 557.
[2] *Senate Report*, 49 Cong., 1 Sess., No. 46.
[3] Dewey, *National Problems* (*Am. Nation*, XXIV.), chap. vi.

tive. Organization, solidarity, and economy told in the management of the railroads, as better construction, longer trains, and increased earnings told in their operation. In 1882 the railroads of the United States paid total dividends amounting to one hundred million dollars,[1] the new states in the Northwest making the best showing, where population was rapidly extending. To absorb the small lines, the large companies secured their stock, often listed at values far above their cost, and thus caused the securities of twenty of the largest roads to aggregate nearly half a billion dollars. The railways were the first forms of industrialism to combine; and their employés soon imitated their example.

[1] *U. S. Statistical Abstract*, 1900, p. 385.

CHAPTER V

INDUSTRIAL PROBLEMS
(1875–1885)

THE spasmodic labor organizations and accompanying labor troubles, which had been known since the Revolution, assumed importance with the dawn of the industrial age. The agitation for a limited number of hours for a working-day won a victory in 1840 when President Van Buren by executive order established the "ten-hour system" for the labor of federal employés.[1] Following the Civil War, which placed a new value on free labor by ending slave labor, an agitation was begun for an eight-hour laboring-day, for better conditions for the working-man, for fixed hours and cash payment of wages, for sanctity of contract, and for liability of employers. Congress in 1868 constituted eight hours a day's work for all laborers, workmen, and mechanics employed by the government,[2] and President Grant by proclamation ordered no reduction of pay because of the shortened time of labor.[3]

[1] Richardson, *Messages and Papers*, III., 602.
[2] *U. S. Statutes at Large*, XV.
[3] Richardson, *Messages and Papers*, VII., 15, 175.

No demand was made for uniform wages by legislation, but united demands for changes of conditions in individual crafts and workshops were growing more frequent. Injunctions and "conspiracies" were products of a later period.[1] Influenced by requests for these and similar laws, as well as by accompanying complaints and grievances, Massachusetts in 1864 created a labor bureau, an example followed before 1890 by twenty-two other states. The chief officer of the state bureaus was known as a commissioner, a chief, or a secretary, and in many cases he was a member of some labor organization.

The oldest labor union now in existence in the United States is said to be that of the printers, organized in New York City in 1853. It followed very largely the lines of the trades-unions of England, as these in turn followed the principles of the guild of the Middle Ages. The locomotive engineers organized a union in 1863, the cigar-makers in 1864, the bricklayers in 1865, the railway conductors in 1868, the railway firemen in 1869, and the iron and steel workers in 1876.[2] By this time hostility was apparent between organized capital and organized labor.[3] "Capital has assumed to itself the right to own and control labor for its own greedy and selfish end," said the organized bricklayers in

---

[1] Wright, *Industrial Evolution of U. S.*, chap. xix.; Dewey, *National Problems* (*Am. Nation*, XXIV.), chap. iii.
[2] McNeill, *Labor Movement*, 324–329.
[3] Commons, *Trade-Unionism and Labor Problems*, chap. xxi.

1865.[1] Beneath lay the inherited antagonism between class and mass; between privilege and prohibition. An interview, real or imaginary, with a locomotive engineer is significant in these incipient days of America's labor troubles. He instituted a comparison between the hard-working, begrimed man in the locomotive cab on the lookout for danger, and the high-salaried officials sitting over their wine in a private car attached to the train he was drawing. His wage must necessarily be diminished by the large salaries and by the extravagance of the surroundings of these officials. Even their private car must be hauled at a dead loss to the company.[2] Evidently the laborer had not grown accustomed to lavish display on the part of the affluent.

The public demand for regulation of railway rates was met by the statement that it would reduce still more the wages of the railway employés, already feeling the effects of the financial embarrassment of the railroads. Editors declared that a partial remedy would be a schedule of rates on the "live and let live" basis: the roads must charge enough to pay their men decent wages. Reduction of wages was one method of retrenchment which had been adopted by many roads, although in some instances the Brotherhood of Locomotive Engineers and the Order of Railway Conductors blocked the attempt by threats to desert their posts in a body. This hap-

[1] Quoted by Ely, *Labor Movement*, 63.
[2] *Frank Leslie's Newspaper*, XLIV., 382 (August 11, 1877).

pened on the Reading, the Grand Trunk, and the Boston and Maine railroads in the spring of 1877.

The essential principle of the "strike" and the "boycott" were employed in coercing the Tories in Revolutionary times, and those weapons were not unknown to concerted labor movements in later days; but no serious or wide-spread disorder attended a strike in the United States before 1877. In July of that year the Baltimore & Ohio railroad directors, who had reduced the wages of their employés no less than three times in the seven years preceding,[1] announced a still further reduction for all men receiving over one dollar per day. Of all the organized classes of employés the freight brakemen and firemen received the lowest wages, averaging on this road from $1.50 to $1.75 per day. Even this sum could not be depended upon because of the uncertainty of the "runs."[2]

In justification of the reduction, the company showed that the profits of all the railroads to their stockholders had been reduced from $46,000,000 in 1873 to $22,000,000 in 1876, while the freight charges were one-third less on coal transportation; and that the pay of firemen on some other roads was as low as $1.25 a day, and for brakemen $1.56 a day. The company also argued that the reduction in wages of railway employés was not greater than in other occupations. As to irregularity of "trips,"

[1] *Nation*, XXIV., 158, 173.
[2] *Appleton's Annual Cyclop.*, 1877, p. 625.

the company claimed that it acted solely for the good of the men in dividing the limited business it could secure among all of them rather than to discharge some portion of them.

Upon receipt of the notice of the intention of the company, the freight firemen on the Baltimore & Ohio road resolved to resist it, and the brakemen joined them.[1] They saw the futility of adopting the mild tactics threatened by their more skilled fellow-employés, the engineers and conductors; they realized that the company could easily find other men to take their places. Consequently, when they stopped work, as they did in Baltimore and at points along the line in Maryland and West Virginia, they refused to permit the freight-trains to proceed with other operatives. The fever spread rapidly to the employés of other roads, which had made no reduction and contemplated none. Demands were made on superintendents, schedules of wages presented, and various grievances aired. Through fourteen states the disaffection spread, from New York to Kansas and from Michigan to Texas. Resolutions were adopted by the strikers in some localities not to interfere with the United States mails and not to permit violence. The futility of peaceful men adopting these resolutions when lawless characters were to be found in every city was soon demonstrated.[2]

[1] *Frank Leslie's Newspaper*, XLIV., 371 (August 4, 1877); McNeill, *Labor Movement*, 155.
[2] *Frank Leslie's Newspaper*, XLIV., 371; *Harper's Weekly*, XXI., 626.

To furnish opportunity for mischief, it chanced that the land was full of idle men, made so by the four dull years which followed the panic of 1873. Some of the idle laborers turned vagrant, commonly known as "tramps," and went begging from door to door, thus increasing the habitually nomadic class. They wandered along railways, collected in camps near the tracks, and swarmed over moving freight-trains. They were reported to have a system of marks to be placed upon houses to show the disposition of the occupants. Incendiary fires were attributed to their vengeance, and many states passed vagrancy laws to control them.

Rioting and bloodshed marked the strike from the beginning. Pittsburg, a great railroad centre, was for days in the hands of a mob, which burned the Union depot, train-sheds, freight depots, round-houses, and offices, looted gun-stores, and came near burning the entire city, the flames being turned aside only by the force of the prevailing winds. The loss, including 125 locomotives, 1400 loaded cars, and 600 empty cars, was estimated at this place alone at ten million dollars.[1] In other cities, east and west, mobs were formed which blocked the moving of trains and went from workshop to mill, compelling peaceful working-men to abandon their tasks and follow the crowd.

This awakening of the slumbering giant of Amer-

[1] McNeill, *Labor Movement*, 159; *Appleton's Annual Cyclop.*, 1877, p. 429.

ica, the mob, known to exist but presumably amendable to a show of authority, demonstrated in a most disagreeable manner the feeble coercive power naturally resident in an unmilitary republic. Pennsylvania and New York had large forces of militia at command, but for these the mob felt nothing but contempt. Two days were required to convey the Pennsylvania militia from Philadelphia to Pittsburg, and when they reached their destination and were compelled to fire upon the rioters, they were deserted by the Pittsburg militia, driven out by the infuriated citizens, pursued to the woods, and barely escaped with their lives. The people of Baltimore attacked the militiamen of Maryland as they passed through the streets on their way to Cumberland. Several soldiers and citizens were killed in this affray.[1]

However inadequate the state militia was seen to be in coping with the mobs, the executives of West Virginia and Maryland had comparatively no forces of this nature at their disposal. This was due to a lack of military spirit in these states, and also to the antipathy of a large number of their citizens to an armed force in time of peace. Within two days after the strike was inaugurated, the governor of West Virginia, of which the legislature was not in session, invoked the constitutional guarantee of each state against "domestic violence" by requesting aid

[1] Andrews, *Last Quarter Century*, I., 305; McNeill, *Labor Movement*, 157.

of President Hayes; and three days later the governor of Maryland followed his example. The president responded by ordering troops to the scenes of disorder, under command of General Hancock, and by issuing proclamations commanding all good citizens to preserve the peace. Soon after, the governor of Pennsylvania, who was travelling in the West, called for federal aid in addition to the state militia, and it was supplied. One week after the inauguration of the strike it reached Chicago, and the governor of Illinois requested troops. In Indiana and Missouri, whose governors hesitated for political reasons to call upon President Hayes, federal troops were used upon demand of the United States marshals, a practice authorized by the act of 1795 and utilized in reconstruction days. To the request of the governor of Indiana that the commandant of the United States arsenal at Indianapolis render him assistance, and to the appeal of the governor of California that the United States vessels at the navyyard take up a position in front of the city of San Francisco to awe the strikers, the president replied that federal troops could be used only to suppress domestic violence. A similar attitude was assumed towards the governor of Wisconsin, who wished to employ the veterans in the soldiers' home near Milwaukee as a guard.[1]

Awed by the federal forces more than by the state

[1] *Federal Aid in Domestic Disturbances*, 189–205; *Frank Leslie's Newspaper*, XLIV., 382 (August 8, 1877).

troops, the rioters dispersed in the many railroad centres in which they had collected, the strikers opened negotiations with their employers, and within two weeks from its beginning the strike was at an end, each side claiming a victory. An interesting aspect of the strike with significant results was seen in southern Illinois where a federal judge, who had appointed a receiver for a railroad, issued a command to strikers not to interfere with the operation of the road. Upon his call for aid, federal troops were used under the marshal of his court to enforce his mandate. When the strike was ended, further illustration was seen of the superiority of the federal courts over the state courts. Eight men were brought before the United States district court at Peoria, Illinois, in August, 1877, were convicted of having interfered with the operation of a train on the Toledo, Peoria, and Warsaw Railway, a road in the hands of a receiver, and were sentenced to fine and imprisonment.[1] Fifteen other offenders in Indianapolis received similar punishment for similar misdemeanors. The leader of the strikers on the Erie, a railroad in the hands of a federal court, was also prosecuted and imprisoned.[2] The mails were sent around the points of disturbance as much as possible, for the railway mail service had not yet developed sufficiently to make it a factor for national protection. The security of the mails was to be

---

[1] *Railway Gazette*, IX., p. 368.
[2] *Appleton's Annual Cyclop.*, 1877. p. 432.

warranted later, through federal injunctions and interstate commerce action.

Railroad companies not in the hands of federal receivers were less fortunate during the strike. Through the state courts they were able to collect damages from the several counties in which their property had been destroyed; but being under state and not national charter, they enjoyed no such close connection with the national authorities as did their rivals, the steamboat lines. The reason why one class of common carriers should be under state and another under federal control must be sought in the early definition of "commerce" as including water traffic both coast and inland. By resolution of the Congress of the Confederation, May 12, 1786,[1] the navigable waterways of the Northwest were made free to all citizens of the United States; and by a Supreme Court decision in 1824 state monopoly of steam navigation on navigable waters was forbidden.[2] Almost from its beginning, Congress legislated for the protection of immigrants on shipboard,[3] and in 1860 extended this protection to women travelling on any waterway of the United States.[4] Travellers by land had only state protection, which was sometimes virtually no protection.

"The raising of the black flag and the stoppage of

[1] *Journals of Congress*, IV., 637.
[2] Gibbons *vs.* Ogden, 9 Wheaton, 1.
[3] For example, see acts of March 2, 1819, February 22, 1847, May 17, 1848, March 3, 1849, and March 3, 1855.
[4] *U. S. Statutes at Large*, XII., 3.

all vessels on the Great Lakes and on the Mississippi and Ohio rivers," said the president of the Pennsylvania Railroad Company, "would not produce one tithe of the damage to the whole country that has resulted from the recent stoppage of the great trunk lines. The burning of the vessels and their cargoes in these waters would raise a storm of wrath which no mob would dare face, and would be visited by the United States government under existing laws with most exemplary punishment. . . . The authority of the United States, now potent to protect commerce moving upon the waters, should be equally potent when the same commerce is exposed to greater peril upon land. . . . It will hardly be contended that the railway companies must become bankrupt in order to make secure the uninterrupted movement of traffic over their lines, or to entitle them to the efficient protection of the United States government."[1] Manifestly the companies were about to be driven to demand national protection as the public was already seeking national regulation.[2]

The outcome of the railway strike was watched eagerly by the anthracite coal-miners of eastern Pennsylvania, and some of them even took part in it from sympathy. Their wages had been reduced until they claimed that the best miner under the most favorable conditions could not earn more than fifteen dollars a month, and many were forced to be

[1] *North Am. Rev.*, CXXV., 351-362 (September, 1877).
[2] *Frank Leslie's Newspaper*, XLIV., 414 (August 25, 1877).

content with half that sum. For these conditions they blamed the railroad pool, which had restricted the output of the mines; the railway companies, in turn, blamed competition, which compelled them to form the pool. Before the close of July, 1877, all the miners in the anthracite region were on strike, and the contagion spread to the bituminous districts of the state and even to Indiana and Illinois. Rioting accompanied the demonstration, but was suppressed by the state authorities. The companies generally agreed to advance wages ten per cent., and the strikers gradually returned to work during August.[1]

The next labor outbreak occurred among the miners at Leadville, Colorado, May 26, 1880, ostensibly to secure an increase of wages from three dollars a day to four dollars a day, and a reduction of working hours to eight for a shift; but it was understood that the real grievances were the strict rules adopted generally by the mining companies. About five thousand men took part in the strike, the state militia was called out and martial law proclaimed, before the disagreement was ended by concessions on both sides. The total loss was estimated at four million dollars.[2]

During the railroad strike of 1877, suggestions were made that all the railway employés form a "trainmen's union" to cope with their employers.

[1] Powderly, *Thirty Years of Labor*, 209–221.
[2] *Appleton's Annual Cyclop.*, 1880, p. 119; McNeill. *Labor Movement*, 166.

The idea assumed another form in the extension of lodges of the Knights of Labor, a secret protective association of garment-cutters which had been formed in Philadelphia in 1869.[1] By 1878 it extended to other trades and other states, and established a "national resistance fund" to be used by "brothers in need against the aggressions of employers." This parent of allied labor unions declared war against the power of aggregated wealth and unjust accumulation, and proposed to secure for the laborer the fruits of his toil. It advocated the establishment of bureaus of labor, co-operative industries, granting public lands to actual settlers, the removal of technicalities in the administration of justice, abolition of the contract-labor system, weekly payment of wages, and an eight-hour working day. Women were made eligible for membership, and in 1882 the organization had one hundred and forty thousand members, grouped into forty-four district assemblies in twenty-two states and territories.[2]

In March, 1882, the Knights of Labor fathered a strike of the Cumberland, Maryland, coal-miners, which lasted six months, entailed poverty and suffering on the strikers and their families, and resulted in a victory for the companies, many of which refused to re-employ the strikers. Independently of the

[1] McNeill, *Labor Movement*, 397.
[2] Ely, *Labor Movement in America*, 75; Powderly, *Thirty Years of Labor*, 186–196; Wright, *Industrial Evolution*, 245–263; U. S. Tenth Census (1880), XX., last report; *North Am. Rev.*, CXXXV., 118–126.

Knights of Labor, the Amalgamated Association of Steel and Iron Workers, with a membership of seventy-five thousand and a strike fund of five hundred thousand dollars in its treasury, declared a strike in Cleveland, Ohio, May 9, 1882. Their demand for an advance in wages was declared inadmissible by the iron manufacturers, especially at a time when the market was dull and steel rails had experienced a remarkable fall in price. The employers took advantage of the strike to close their mills and so reduce the output, or to make repairs; and after many months the workmen were starved into returning to the mills at the former wage scale.[1]

The year 1882, which followed a short-crop year and witnessed a corresponding advance in the price of provisions, was prolific of labor troubles. The freight-handlers of New York City struck in June, demanding an advance of wages from seventeen to twenty cents an hour, making a total increase of thirty cents a day. For several weeks a freight blockade was maintained in New York and Jersey City; the companies endeavored to secure laborers from the immigrant offices, but found them unskilled and inefficient. Eventually most of the strikers returned to work at the old terms.[2] An interesting phase of this strike was a notice from the chancellor

---

[1] *Appleton's Annual Cyclop.*, 1882, pp. 455, 456; *Harper's Weekly*, XXVI., 378.
[2] *Harper's Weekly*, XXVI., 451; *Appleton's Annual Cyclop.*, 1882, p. 456.

of the state of New Jersey that the Erie Railroad was in the hands of a court receiver and interference with its management would be punished as contempt of court. The shippers of New York City contributed a novel feature by bringing suit against the several railway companies for a writ of mandamus to compel them to perform their duties as common carriers under penalty of having their charters revoked. The companies replied that they must be allowed to select their employés and determine their wages without a judicial mandamus. "Is it discreet or practicable," they asked, "for the court to undertake to regulate the employment of men by carriers whether individuals or corporations?" The court decided that the redress of the shippers lay in a suit for damages against the company and not in a writ of mandamus.[1] This decision of a single justice made in chambers was reversed in January, 1883, by the court in general session, the majority of the justices holding that railroads could be compelled to fulfil their public obligations and that a plea of interference by a strike was no excuse.[2]

Among the lessons learned in these early days of labor outbreaks was the general inefficiency of the state militia, the power of the judiciary, the necessity for employers giving their employés a hearing,

---

[1] People *vs.* N. Y. L. E. & W. and N. Y. C. & H. R. Rw. Cos., N. Y. Rep., 63 Howard, 291.
[2] *Appleton's Annual Cyclop.*, 1882, p. 614; *Railway Gazette*, XV., 51 (January 19, 1883).

the strength of allied trade-unionists, and the need of appeal to the principles of arbitration if labor and capital were to abandon barbaric methods of fighting each other. As an agency for the study of the labor problem, Congress created in 1884 a bureau of labor statistics as a branch of the department of the interior, to "collect information upon the subject of labor, its relations to capital, the hours of labor, and the earnings of laboring men and women, and the means of promoting their material, social, intellectual, and moral welfare." Its investigations would be of service, it was hoped, to legislators in framing laws for the industrial needs of the country.[1]

[1] *House Reports*, 48 Cong., 1 Sess., No. 342. For bureau's investigation of labor disturbances in Pennsylvania in 1887–1888, see *House Reports*, 50 Cong., 2 Sess., IV., No. 4147. See also Bureau of Labor, *Annual Reports* in Secretary of the Interior, *Reports*. For general conditions in 1885, see Senate Com. on Labor and Capital, *Report*, 48 Cong. (1885), 4 vols.

CHAPTER VI

PRESIDENT HAYES AND THE SOUTH
(1876-1877)

MARCH 4, 1877, fell upon Sunday. For the third time in the history of the United States it was necessary to postpone the inauguration of a president until the following day; but never before was it deemed advisable to take precautions against possible interference by force with the legal inauguration on March 5. Nearly forty-eight hours before the term of President Grant expired, the oath of office was given privately to his successor, Rutherford B. Hayes, in the executive mansion, upon the invitation and in the approving presence of President Grant, owing to an unwarranted rumor that Tilden, the Democratic candidate, intended setting up a rival government in New York.[1] On the following Monday, at high noon, the ceremony was repeated publicly at the east front of the Capitol—a fitting end to the many extraordinary circumstances attending the presidential election of 1876.

[1] Badeau, *Grant in Peace*, 251; Bigelow, *Tilden*, II., 112; French, *U. S. Grant*, 421; *Frank Leslie's Newspaper*, XLIV., 22.

The "returning boards" of South Carolina, Florida, and Louisiana pronounced the Democratic majorities in those states fraudulently obtained, and cast out a sufficient number to give the states to the Republican electors. Congress referred the ensuing dispute to an electoral commission,[1] whose work was not completed on March 1, 1877, within four days of the date of inauguration. Tilden, the Democratic candidate, remained quietly in New York, but Hayes, the Republican candidate, felt impelled, from information he had received concerning the probable result, to start for Washington. When he bade farewell to his friends at Columbus, Ohio, where he resided as governor of that state, he said: "I understand very well the uncertainty of affairs at Washington. I understand very well that possibly next week I may be with you again to resume my place in the governor's office as your fellow-citizen." At four o'clock on the following morning, March 2, he was roused from his sleep on the train by the notification that the commission had decided in his favor.[2] "Hayes is elected," was the message which flashed across the continent and brought relief to the tension of four months. At daybreak on that day the citizens of Washington began decorating their buildings, the action representing more than the usual preparations for an inauguration: they were celebrating the passing of the electoral ma-

[1] Dunning, *Reconstruction* (*Am. Nation*, XXII.), chap. xxi.
[2] *Frank Leslie's Newspaper*, XLIV., 21.

chinery through the severest test to which it had yet been subjected.

The only inauguration under comparable conditions was that of Abraham Lincoln, sixteen years before,[1] confronted, as he said, by "great and peculiar conditions"—a threatened sectional division of the people; yet the danger must inevitably rally one section to his support; Hayes had the united support of neither section. Lincoln's title to office was beyond question; that of Hayes was clouded by suspicion of fraud. Each was the victim of conditions beyond his control; yet as time went on the conditions rallied to Lincoln not only his own party but made friends from his enemies, while the conditions of the later days alienated the party from Hayes. Armed resistance followed the inauguration of Lincoln; threats of a similar appeal to force were current when Hayes entered the office.

Yet in addressing the twenty thousand people assembled under cloudy skies at the east front of the Capitol March 5, and shielding themselves from snow flurries, Hayes chose to think of the present as an occasion of rejoicing rather than of alarm and precaution. To the world was given, he said, "the first example in history of a great nation, in the midst of the struggle of opposing parties for power, hushing its party tumults to yield the issue of the contest to adjustment according to forms of law."[2] The con-

[1] Chadwick, *Causes of the Civil War* (*Am. Nation*, XIX.), chap. xvii.   [2] Richardson, *Messages and Papers*, VII., 446.

flicting claims having been amicably adjusted, he
thought the general acquiescence of the nation ought
surely to follow. When informed that Lincoln had
been peaceably inaugurated, the commanding general of the army, stationed in the Capitol grounds
with a battery, exclaimed, "Thank God!"; a similar
expression framed itself on thousands of lips when
the last fragments of fireworks burned out on Pennsylvania Avenue on March 5, 1877, and the Inauguration Day of a doubtful election was ended without
untoward incident. The Democratic press and party
leaders generally accepted the verdict and redeemed
their promise to abide by the decision of the electoral
commission.[1] The good judgment of the people prevailed once more.

Few presidents created a more favorable impression
personally than did Hayes. At the inauguration,
newspaper correspondents described his admirable
bearing, his manifest sincerity, and his avoidance
of ostentation.[2] Old-timers in Washington circles
could find no comparison for the new president except to recall the Apollo-like Franklin Pierce. They
hailed the simplicity shown by the president's family
in a social way, and contrasted it with the ostentation of the preceding residents of the White House.[3]
Evidently the "court," which had been inherited
from the military days of 1861 to 1865, was not to
be continued.

[1] See *Frank Leslie's Newspaper*, XLIII., 418.
[2] *Independent.* March 15, 1877. [3] *Harper's Weekly*, XXI., 206.

As a Republican president, placed in office by the vote of the Republican members of the electoral commission, Hayes might expect the support of his party against the sneers and attacks of the opposition, especially since he entered office unhampered by factional obligations. The eight years which had elapsed since he left Congress to become governor of Ohio enabled him to avoid the factional following which blessed or cursed Blaine, Conkling, Morton, and other party leaders, preventing each from securing the presidential nomination which came to Hayes. Because Hayes was without a body of organized followers was in their minds a warrant that he would be a "safe" man; that he would be careful of party interests; would be mindful of party policies, and amendable to party dictation. He was said to belong to the "illustrious obscure" and to be "negatively honest." Indeed, the fear that he would be a "man of putty" in the hands of the party leaders cost him some Republican votes in the popular election. Few candidates have taken as little part in the canvass and have depended as solely on the party managers as did Hayes. Notwithstanding these auspicious party beginnings Hayes lost the support of his party leaders within six weeks, primarily because of his pacific action towards the South—a policy attributed by his enemies to double-dealing and faint-heartedness, but characterized by his friends as generous and far-sighted statesmanship.

The pacification of the South had been a prominent issue in the late campaign. The Democratic platform denounced the attempts of the Republicans to "light anew the dying embers of sectional hate between kindred peoples once estranged but now reunited." [1] The Republican platform pledged the party to a "permanent pacification of the southern section of the Union and the complete protection of all its citizens in the free enjoyment of their rights." [2] On this platform Hayes in his speech of acceptance asserted that the "moral and national prosperity of the southern states can be most effectually advanced by a hearty and generous recognition of the rights of all by all." If elected, he promised to aid "the efforts of the southern states to obtain for themselves the blessings of honest and capable self-government." [3]

The people of the prostrate states had succeeded, through the Ku-Klux Klan and other devices, in gradually regaining control, until only in two states—Louisiana and South Carolina—did the Republicans maintain even the shadow of a government, and there only by virtue of detachments of federal troops occupying the state buildings. In Louisiana, Packard, a Republican carpet-bagger from Maine, claimed to have been elected governor and was inaugurated, while his Democratic opponent, Nicholls, a native of Louisiana and a crippled veteran of the Confederate service, was also inaugurated and set up a rival gov-

[1] Stanwood, *Hist. of the Presidency*, 377.   [2] *Ibid.*, 370.
[3] McPherson, *Hand-Book of Politics*, 1876, p. 212.

ernment. Chamberlain, the Republican claimant to the governorship of South Carolina, came from Massachusetts during the Civil War, became nominally a cotton planter but primarily an office-holder, and finally reached the governorship. A rival government set up the Democratic candidate, Wade Hampton, Carolinian born, of a distinguished family, and a Confederate veteran.[1] President Grant stationed federal troops in the capitals of each state, but refused to permit them to support either claimant.[2] Such were the conditions when Hayes became president. If he reversed the action of Grant and ordered the troops to sustain the Republican claimants, reconstruction by force would continue in the South; if he withdrew the troops, federal interference was at an end, the government would return to the people of the two states, and the period of reconstruction would be closed.

Shortly before his inauguration, Hayes received a letter from a Unitarian minister which confirmed his opinion on the inefficacy of continuing pacification by force of arms. "I was in New Orleans," wrote the Reverend W. G. Eliot, "in charge of a congregation, part of two winters immediately following the War, and am sorry to say that nothing has been gained

---

[1] On these statesmen, see *Appleton's Cyclop. of Am. Biog.*, I., 564; III., 70; IV., 512.

[2] *Federal Aid in Domestic Disturbances*, 182; *House Exec Docs.*, 44 Cong., 2 Sess., No. 30; Dunning, *Reconstruction* (*Am. Nation*, XXII.), chap. xix.; McPherson, *Hand-Book of Politics,* 1878, pp. 57–68.

since that time. Both the color line and the party line are more marked, political and social animosity is increased."[1]

Unwilling to proceed rashly even with such testimony at hand, and acting in accord with a resolution previously made, Hayes sent a commission to Louisiana, April 2, 1877, to bring about a recognition of one legislature and one governor, and to report upon the feeling of the people of the state. "An attentive consideration of the conditions," said their instructions, "under which the Federal Constitution and the acts of Congress provide or permit military intervention by the president in protection of a state against domestic violence, has satisfied the president that the use of this authority in determining and influencing disputed elections in a state must carefully be avoided."[2] The commission consisted of Wayne MacVeagh, former United States minister to Turkey; General Hawley, ex-president of the board of Centennial Commissioners; Charles B. Lawrence, ex-chief-justice of Illinois; General John M. Harlan, of Kentucky, former attorney-general—all Republicans; and ex-Governor John C. Brown, former Confederate general from Tennessee, a Democrat. They held moderate rather than radical views, and could recall remote rather than present activity in party councils. Considering the members and their in-

---

[1] Eliot, *W. G. Eliot*, 287.
[2] Haworth, *Disputed Presidential Election*, 207–300; *House Exec. Docs.*, 45 Cong., 2 Sess., No. 97, p. 2.

structions, the result of their investigation could easily have been foreseen.

The commission found Packard at the head of a "rump" government, without state senate or courts and with few followers. Recognizing the impossibility of supporting his claims in the face of a hostile people, the commission confined its labors to securing guarantees from Nicholls and his legislature that order would be maintained by them and the rights of all citizens would be regarded, if the other government were withdrawn. The commission also persuaded several members of the Packard legislature to take seats in the Nicholls body.[1] President Hayes, being informed by telegraph of these favorable conditions, ordered the regular forces to be withdrawn from the public buildings of the state. At noon, April 9, 1877, the troops to the number of one hundred and sixty, headed by their band, marched from the Orleans Hotel to the Jackson barracks, while the Louisiana state battery fired one hundred guns on the levee in token of the evacuation. The Packard government now yielded to the inevitable and quietly dissolved. Louisiana, the first state to pass from local to national control in the process of reconstruction, had at last returned to her own.[2]

The unhorsed Republican governor, Packard, issued an address in which he waived none of his

---

[1] McClure, *Our Presidents*, 267; *Appleton's Annual Cyclop.*, 1877, p. 463; McPherson, *Hand-Book of Politics*, 1876, pp. 19-47.
[2] *Frank Leslie's Newspaper*, XLIV., 192.

legal rights but yielded only to a superior force. "It grieves me beyond expression," said he to his faithful followers, "that the heroic efforts you have made and the cruel sufferings you have undergone to maintain Republican principles in Louisiana have had this bitter ending." He advised them to continue their organization against the day when the state would raise itself again to Republican principles. The Nicholls administration began cleaning house by cutting down the extravagant fees established for officials under the Reconstruction government, arranging payment of the enormous state debt, creating new election laws, and investigating affairs in the subordinate state offices. The state debt recognized at this time as legitimate amounted to $11,785,293.21; the city debt of New Orleans, bonded and floating, was $21,894,714.74, though the total assessment of property in city and state was only $180,000,000.[1] Proceedings were instituted against the members of the returning board which had turned the state over to the Hayes electors, charging them with perjury, forgery, and altering returns.

South Carolina had never rivalled Louisiana as the storm centre of reconstruction; consequently Hayes simply invited both claimants to her governorship to a conference with him at Washington. After full and frank conversation with both men, in which Governor Hampton gave assurance of the

[1] *Appleton's Annual Cyclop.*, 1878, p. 499.

maintenance of peace and order and acceptance of the constitutional amendments in his state if his government were recognized, Hayes, with the full consent of his cabinet, ordered the federal troops to be withdrawn from the state-house at Columbia, April 10, 1877; Chamberlain, in an address, agreed no longer to press his claim, and Hampton took possession of the state offices.[1] His administration signalized the resumption of home rule by reducing the pay of members of the general assembly from six hundred dollars per annum with mileage, as it was established under Republican rule, to five dollars a day. The reform was continued by investigating the state debt; levying a tax for the support of free schools; and taking steps towards a university or college for the education of colored people. Three former Republican officials, two of them negroes, were prosecuted for bribery, fraud, and forgery.[2]

Inasmuch as promises made in party platforms had come to be platitudes, and protestations of a desire for pacification were regarded as catch-words, the generous motives announced by Hayes were open to suspicion. Charges of a political "bargain" were made, and have been repeated as persistently as those concerning Adams and Clay in 1825. It was asserted that the electoral votes of South Carolina and Louisiana were delivered to Hayes on his

---

[1] Haworth, *Disputed Presidential Election*, 295; Foulke, *Morton*, II., 486; McPherson, *Hand-Book of Politics*, 1878, pp. 74–81.   [2] *Appleton's Annual Cyclop.*, 1877, p. 697.

promise that the federal troops would be withdrawn from those states. Unfortunately for this story, the eight Republican members of the commission who delivered the presidency to him were by no means a unit in wishing the troops withdrawn. Another rumor said that the possible opposition in the Democratic House of Representatives to receiving the report of the commission was checked by a promise from the managers of Hayes that the troops would be withdrawn.[1] The chief evidence was a letter written February 17, 1877, by Stanley Matthews and Charles Foster, two friends of Hayes, from Ohio, in which they promised Senator Gordon, of Georgia, and John Y. Brown, of Kentucky, that they would use their efforts to have Hayes "adopt such a policy as will give to the people of the states of South Carolina and Louisiana the right to control their own affairs in their own way." They also had the utmost confidence that such would be the policy of his administration.[2] Certain self-impeached political henchmen, like McLin, of Florida, who were disappointed in gaining office as reward for their disreputable work, placed their testimony against the word of men like ex-Governor Noyes and General Lew Wallace to prove that Hayes was privy to some kind of a "bargain." Stress was also laid on a series of conferences in Washington between Hayes Repub-

[1] *Cong. Record*, 45 Cong., 2 Sess., 2047.
[2] *House Misc. Docs.*, 45 Cong., 3 Sess., No. 31, II., 624; Haworth, *Disputed Presidential Election*. 272.

licans and leading Democrats. In one of these, held during the House debates on the report of the electoral commission, in which Watterson, Burke, and Ellis represented the Democrats, while Garfield, Sherman, Matthews, and others spoke for the Republicans, it was claimed that plans were laid and pledges exchanged which bound Hayes in the event of his inauguration to remove the troops.[1]

In later sessions of Congress the charges were ventilated in debate. Ellis, one of the Democratic participants in the Washington conference, said: "These gentlemen pledged nothing for Mr. Hayes; they bound him by no promise. The language they held to us was, 'We know him; we know the language of his letter of acceptance. We have his sentiment with regard to the South; we know he believes in self-government for those states, and without speaking authoritatively for him we yet say to you in our opinion he will give the blessings of free government to those two states.'"[2] Another participant in the conference, Foster, said: "I defy mortal man to bring evidence that I pledged anybody to do anything in consequence of anything that might be done by others."[3]

Careful and candid consideration of the testimony cannot fail to show that many men in both parties

---

[1] *House Misc. Docs.*, 45 Cong., 3 Sess., No. 31, I., 978–990; II., 595–633; Andrews, *Last Quarter-Century,* I., 226; cf. Dunning, *Reconstruction* (*Am. Nation*, XXII.), 339.
[2] *Cong. Record,* 45 Cong., 2 Sess., 1011.   [3] *Ibid.,* 1010.

earnestly desired peace, wished to put an end to reconstruction methods in both sections, and trusted the sincerity of Hayes in his professions of a healing policy. To the radicals in each party, any step taken by these middle-men would seem a "bargain," and if Hayes had wished to drive a bargain, opportunity surely was not wanting. Yet to a New Orleans editor who journeyed to Columbus to get an assurance, he would say nothing more than to reiterate the sentiments in his letter of acceptance which all might read.[1] Sherman visited him, but could gain no intimation of the purpose in his mind beyond the friendly and encouraging words of that letter.[2] In a private communication to Sherman, Hayes expressed the opinion that a fair election at the South would have given him forty electoral votes. "But," he added, "we are not to allow our friends to defeat one outrage and fraud by another. There must be nothing crooked on our part."[3]

To Schurz, Hayes wrote of the use of the military force in the South as already at an end, never to be employed again except in emergencies which he did not think possible to occur.[4] When Foster, who represented Hayes's district in Congress, openly stated in the House that the policy of Hayes, if inaugurated, would be to restore the Union without

---

[1] *House Misc. Docs.*, 45 Cong., 3 Sess., No. 31, pp. 875–89
[2] John Sherman, *Recollections*, 561.
[3] Ohio Arch. and Hist. Soc., *Publications*, IV., 351.
[4] Haworth, *Disputed Presidential Election*, 270, note 1.

sectional lines, and to reinstate all freemen as citizens,[1] Hayes did not hesitate to approve his words. Whatever bargain was made, Hayes was not privy to it, and as a "bargain" it was nothing more than an attempt of men of peace in each party to reach a common ground, a motive which will gain approval as the years pass, as partisanship cools, and as judgment takes the place of passion.

Although Hayes was liberal in adopting a policy of peace, he was a party man and followed the old custom of rewarding his faithful followers. Nearly every Republican who had been connected with the delivery of the Louisiana and Florida electoral vote received a federal office.[2] Perhaps it was nothing more than the accustomed reward for party effort; yet it gave color to the charge that Hayes was redeeming his pledges.[3] In some instances, when the character of the southern manipulators became known to the president, he withdrew the commission; but if he had displayed the courage on making appointments which he later showed on dismissals, the result would have been more fortunate.

During the summer following the inauguration, many incidents trivial in themselves were taken as significant by the friends of Hayes and his healing policy. The ceremony of placing flowers on the graves of deceased soldiers, inaugurated in some

[1] *Cong. Record*, 45 Cong., 3 Sess., 1708.
[2] Rhodes, *United States*, VII., 289; Bigelow, *Tilden*, II., 53.
[3] *House Misc. Docs.*, 45 Cong., 3 Sess., No. 31, 381–394.

southern states and adopted officially by many states in the Union, was not observed jointly by Federal and Confederate veterans; but each maintained its own observance of an appointed day. Yet on May 30, 1877, President Hayes was invited to speak in Tennessee; Reagan, ex-Confederate postmaster-general, was asked to address the people of Ohio; and General Pryor, an ex-Confederate of Virginia, spoke in Brooklyn, New York. Supporters of the new policy also called attention to the fact that the federal military band at Chattanooga assisted in the decoration of both Union and Confederate graves; and that at New Rochelle, New York, no distinction was made in the distribution of the flowers in the cemeteries. Stanzas appeared in newspapers on the unusual spectacle of the "blue and the gray" marching side by side in many cities during the processions of the day. In September, Hayes made a trip through some of the southern states and was well received.[1]

Governor Chamberlain returned to New York, and soon after made a visit to Iowa, where he was received as a martyr, according to newspaper descriptions.[2] "Governor" Packard eventually reached Maine, having spent fifteen years in his unsuccessful mission for the Republican party in the South. Through the medium of newspaper interviews he informed the northern people that the Republican

[1] *Nation*, XXV., 190 (September 27, 1877).
[2] *Ibid.*, XXIV., 302 (May 24, 1877).

party was on the road to its dissolution through the action of the president; he saw but one chance to save it, and that was to drive out the moderates who now composed the president's cabinet and fill their places with ex-Senator Chandler, of Michigan, and other sound Republicans "of the old sort," and thus to place the party on its feet again.

Some allowance must be made for the feelings of officials who had spent years in building up the party in the South as a pledge of the permanence of the Union and in securing to freedmen the full fruits of the war. In a few instances these alien officials gained the favor of the people and were retained in office or found a permanent home in the South; but generally they returned to their former residences in the North, leaving the negroes to their fate. Having been transformed by political patronage of the whites from industrial agents into political agents, the negro officials showed a reluctance to return to their former employments. The colored editor of a religious journal lamented the fact that he had made over two thousand five hundred speeches for the Republican party and had gone through ordeals which had made him prematurely an old man, only to be compelled to admit that the party was now dead.[1]

Blaine, in executive session of the Senate, claimed that President Hayes could not disavow Packard without invalidating his own title, since both were

[1] *Independent*, May 3, 1877.

passed upon by the same board in Louisiana.¹ The charge was frequently made; but the administration of Hayes in Washington was easily and peaceably maintained, while that of Packard in Louisiana could have been sustained only by the permanent use of troops. No construction of the Constitution could warrant a state supported solely by force of arms: it would mean a demoralization of the entire system of government and practically a renewal of the war in the South. From the stand-point of practicability as well as of statesmanship, there was nothing for Hayes to do except to withdraw the troops.²

The action of Hayes really benefited the Republican party. Although it disappeared from the South and became practically a sectional party, it thereby gained vantage ground for the long fight against the "solid South" and for its efforts to detach states from that combination and add them to itself. The removal of the troops deprived many freedmen of their political rights; but it enabled them to enjoy civil rights previously denied them — the right to live peaceably, to earn a living, to educate their children, and to accumulate property. And they enjoyed these rights under a stable state government such as they never experienced in the turbulent days of reconstruction by force. A legal tribunal declared Hayes elected president; to refuse to be inaugurated would have been to repudiate its forma-

---

[1] *Cong. Record*, 45 Cong., 1 Sess., 21.
[2] Wise, *Recollections of Thirteen Presidents*, 136.

tion and finding, as well as to invite political anarchy and industrial chaos. Even Tilden, although the Democratic House resolved in the midst of the dispute that he had been duly elected, and although for years he reiterated in public speeches his belief that he had been defrauded, never thought seriously of testing by force the decision of the commission that Hayes was the president.

CHAPTER VII

REPUBLICAN DISSENSIONS
(1877-1878)

RECONSTRUCTION passed away so quietly that few realized when the unfortunate but inevitable drama was ended. The removal of the troops was the result of processes long going on; the Republican state governments which Hayes "deserted" were mere shadows; the number of soldiers actually withdrawn by his final orders was insignificant; and the number of states from which they were removed was only two out of the eleven in which they were originally stationed. But as affecting the Republican party, as indicative of the end of federal interference in the South, as the termination of the radical interpretation of the constitutional guarantee of each state to a republican form of government, the action was tremendous in its significance. To the old-time extremists of the party it meant a criminal abandonment of the agencies under which the great party had been built up since the close of hostilities. The stability of each Southern state was to be intrusted to the variable will of its own constituents. Impeachment of Hayes, if it could have been secured, would have been welcomed by many Republicans as a fit punishment for what they considered desertion of party and dereliction of duty.

Yet the dissension between President Hayes and his party leaders, which followed his removal of the troops, must not be attributed entirely to that decision. The legislative branch of the federal government, called on to support a war for the defence of the Union, to repair the political mischiefs of secession, and to provide against a return of that heresy, had gained a prestige hitherto unknown; and from 1860 to 1875 Congress was practically the Republican party. The slowly increasing party arrogance and party dictation culminated in the impeachment of President Johnson [1] for purely party reasons; it failed in its purpose; but to restore the balance between the two branches of government required many years and a fall of the party from power. At the time that Hayes became president, the executive had not recovered from the loss of prestige and dignity it had sustained at the hands of Johnson. Executive patronage rested in good part on congressional recommendation; and a president who ignored this condition did so at his peril, for it was thought to be still possible to "Johnsonize" a recalcitrant executive.[2]

The independence which Grant exhibited in the

[1] Dunning, *Reconstruction* (*Am. Nation*, XXII.), chap. vi.
[2] Fish, *Civil Service and Patronage*, chap. ix.

choice of members of his first cabinet was, it was supposed, not to be expected from Hayes, who was regarded as an "easy" man. Ex-Confederates were now plentiful in both House and Senate; but none of them except Attorney-General Akerman, of Georgia, appointed by Grant in 1870, had as yet found his way into the cabinet.[1] Hayes was willing to make good his promise of a policy of reconciliation by selecting some former secessionist as an adviser. Soon after the election he horrified a caller from Indiana by suggesting General "Joe" Johnston, formerly of the Confederate army, as a possible secretary of the navy. "Great God! Governor," cried the astonished visitor, "I hope you are not thinking of doing anything of that kind." [2] In the end, Hayes did select for postmaster-general a former officer of the Confederate army, David M. Key, of Tennessee.

Key had been restored to citizenship by President Johnson in 1866, and made conciliatory speeches in the South during the excitement over the election of 1876, saying of the two sections, "It is time that we should have that confidence which would allow us to trust each other." [3] Unfortunately, he allowed the first-assistant, Tyner, a professional politician of the old style, to retain control of the patronage, and his conduct soon offended the civil service reformers.[4]

[1] *Frank Leslie's Newspaper*, XLIV., 2.
[2] Foulke, *Morton*, II., 480.
[3] *Appleton's Annual Cyclop.*, 1877, p. 422.
[4] *Nation*, XXIV., 261.

As an earnest of a new policy towards the South, the radical Republicans would have selected not an ex-Confederate, but a loyal southern Republican. Nor was the appointment of Carl Schurz, former senator from Missouri, to the head of the interior department more agreeable: he was pronounced by straight-out members of the party to be a political trimmer and not a trustworthy Republican. "He has been equally at home with all parties and in all classes," said a prominent Republican in the House. "By turns he has been everywhere and has espoused and deserted every party. . . . Inconsistent in everything else, he has ever been constant to his trade, that of politics." [1]

The remaining appointments, although not so offensive, were not more in accord with the wishes of the party leaders. William M. Evarts, of New York, selected for secretary of state, was said to be the second man chosen for that position in a quarter of a century who had never been in the United States Senate. Nor did McCrary, of Iowa, as secretary of war, Devens, of Massachusetts, as attorney-general, or Thompson, of Indiana, as secretary of the navy, better represent the predominant party element.[2] Senator Cameron, of Pennsylvania, was insistent that his son should be a member of the cabinet, and when Hayes refused to heed the request, Cameron resigned his Pennsylvania senatorship and,

[1] *Cong. Record*, 45 Cong., 2 Sess., 2001.
[2] Mosher, *Executive Register of U. S.*, 221, 222.

by methods only too familiar in that state, actually handed over the senatorship to the younger man as a consolation prize. Angered by being ignored and by rumors that the troops were to be withdrawn, the party chieftains awaited an opportunity of venting their wrath on Hayes.[1]

The nominations made by Hayes were delayed in the executive session of the Senate which immediately followed the inauguration,[2] and a policy of obstruction devised which resulted in Hayes having more nominations rejected by the Senate during his four years than was experienced by any other president of the half-century.[3] The session fell into a sectional debate on the admission of certain southern senators, during which Blaine attempted to commit Hayes by calling upon him to deny the rumors that he intended to desert Packard. He insisted that he would not consent to see the remnant of the brave men who had borne the flag and endured the brunt of battle in the southern states, against persecutions unparalleled, now retired for the country's good. "I will stand," he cried, "for southern men of both colors, and when I cease to do that in public or in private let my right hand forget her cunning, let my tongue cleave to the roof of my mouth." Urged on by manifestations of applause in the galleries of the Senate, he made a strong plea for the protection of

---

[1] *Nation*, XXIV., 170; *Frank Leslie's Newspaper*, XLIV., 34.
[2] *Independent*, March 15, 1877.
[3] Fish, *Civil Service and Patronage*, 204.

the Republican party wherever it might be found between the Potomac and the Rio Grande.[1]

The executive session adjourned before the troops were withdrawn, and the radical spirits of the Republican party had to await some chance opportunity of venting their spleen on the head of the chief executive. The endeavor of Henry C. Bowen, editor of the *Independent*, to return to a sane observance of the Fourth of July brought together a vast crowd of people annually at Woodstock, Connecticut, who were addressed by the most eminent speakers to be obtained. In 1877 the chief orator was ex-Senator Chandler, of Michigan, prince of radicals, who had been chairman of the National Republican Committee in charge of Hayes's campaign. He took advantage of the occasion and the gathering to open the vials of his wrath on the peace policy of the president, going so far in his denunciation that some Republicans seated on the platform withdrew, refusing to countenance his words by their presence. He branded Hayes as a president who had climbed to his high seat over the dead bodies of hundreds of loyal men of the South; who had entered upon negotiations with those who were in arms against the loyal government of Louisiana in order that he might the more surely betray the friends who had trusted him and the cause he had sworn to uphold.[2]

Ex-Governor Chamberlain, of South Carolina, also

[1] *Cong. Record*, 45 Cong., 1 Sess., 21.
[2] *Nation*, XXV., 17 (July 12, 1877).

spoke, opening his budget of grievances, accusing Hayes of deserting the party, of exposing the brave Republicans of the South to danger of death, and branding him as unworthy of the effort his party had made to put him into office. In comparison with these speakers, Blaine, who spoke later in the day on the same forum, was moderate. He confined himself to sounding a cry of alarm lest the southerners once placed in power by the presidential policy should proceed to annex Mexico and thus overthrow the balance between the sections. To this preposterous fancy he added the time-worn aphorism: "The men who saved the Union should govern it."[1] These speeches were condemned by the moderate Republican press and the people generally.

Hayes was obliged to depend upon the people for vindication because he had antagonized his party leaders and could not hope for aid from his political opponents. The Democrats could not be expected to forget the manner in which he had gained his office, and were determined that he should not forget it. He was denounced in the Democratic press as a usurper, as "the fraud president," and as "president *de facto*."[2] Upon the day of his inauguration many flags were placed at half-mast to mark the passing of free government, or with the union reversed to denote the overthrow of the popular will. Many newspapers came out in mourning, and one New York print showed a cut of the new president

[1] *Independent*, July 12, 1877.   [2] Cox, *Three Decades*, 669.

with the word "fraud" marked across his brow. When he appeared in public after his inauguration, the motto, "Old Eight to Seven," greeted him, in reminder of the partisan vote of the electoral commission.

Congress met in early session, October 15, 1877, being called by President Hayes because the preceding Congress had failed to make an appropriation for the support of the army. In his message Hayes justified his action in removing the troops from the two states as "no less a constitutional duty and requirement, under the circumstances existing at the time, than it was a much-needed measure for the restoration of self-government and the promotion of national harmony." He insisted that the action was taken deliberately and with a solicitous care for the peace and good order of society and the protection of the property and persons and every right of all classes of citizens. Although the measure had been "subjected to severe and varied criticism," he declared it had brought progress to every part of that section of the country once the theatre of unhappy civil strife, a patriotic attachment to the Union, the resumption of southern industries, the restoration of state credit, and the disappearance of lawlessness.[1]

W. P. Kellogg, a Vermont carpet-bagger, who had been chosen senator from Louisiana by the repudiated Packard legislature, presented his creden-

[1] Richardson, *Messages and Papers*, VII., 459.

tials and was admitted to the Senate by a vote of 30 to 28.¹ Henry M. Spofford, elected by the Nicholls legislature, was rejected. This rebuke of Hayes's policy was followed by the reopening of the entire Louisiana case through the forgetfulness of the promise of immunity made by the Nicholls government to the Hayes investigating commission, and the consequent prosecution of the members of the returning board which had counted in Hayes and Packard. Thomas C. Anderson, one of the four Republican members, was charged with altering the official record of the vote of Vernon Parish, was tried, convicted, and sentenced to two years' confinement in the state penitentiary.² The defendants attempted to take their cases into the United States circuit court on a writ of *habeas corpus cum causa*, but their suit was denied by Justice Bradley because, as members of the state returning board they were officials of Louisiana and not of the United States. Later the verdict was reversed by the Louisiana supreme court on the ground that the act when committed did not constitute a crime known to the laws of the state. The prosecution of the other members of the board was then abandoned.

The presidential policy was the chief topic of congressional debate, because the entire situation

¹ At this time the full membership of the Senate was: Republican, 38, Democratic, 36, Independent, 1. McPherson, *Hand-Book of Politics*, 1878, p. 141; *Senate Misc. Docs.*, 46 Cong., 2 Sess., II., No. 79.
² *Appleton's Annual Cyclop.*, 1878, pp. 494–496.

in Louisiana turned upon it and upon the obligation presumed to rest upon the president of guaranteeing to every state a republican form of government and insuring it against invasion. This potent clause of the Constitution promised the protection of the United States against domestic violence in any state upon the application from the state legislature or from its governor. It was held by the critics of Hayes that the application issuing from Packard and Chamberlain for federal aid, supported by the laws of 1792 and 1795 authorizing the president to employ the military forces under such conditions, made it mandatory upon him to respond to the call and to retain the troops in the two states; and that he was consequently guilty of a culpable neglect of duty when he withdrew them.

His supporters replied that the application for aid came not from the legal governors of Louisiana and South Carolina, but from usurpers in office. They also pointed out that the militia laws of 1792 and 1795 were intended to be enabling but not mandatory; that the wording was, "whenever it may be necessary, *in the judgment of the president*, to use the military force hereby directed to be called forth," etc. For additional justification, they rested upon the indisputable fact that pacification by the bayonet had long since proven impossible, and that a true restoration of the Union could be accomplished only through generous treatment and impartial justice.

The radical Republican press was bitter in its denunciation of Hayes, and the Democratic press dared not defend him because it had pronounced him a usurper. *Harper's Weekly* and the *New York Times*, both important Republican organs in supporting Hayes in the campaign, accused him of treachery and hypocrisy. William E. Chandler, who was Hayes's counsel before the Florida canvassing board, now attacked him in a pamphlet bearing the striking title, "Can such Things be and overcome us like a Summer Cloud without our Special Wonder?" On the other hand, not all the extremists in the party joined in the criticism; Senator Conkling, of New York, who was ignored by Hayes in making federal appointments in that state, took no part in the denunciation. At a later time, Senator Morton, of Indiana, excused Hayes by placing the blame for the downfall of the Louisiana and South Carolina governments on his predecessor, Grant. Morton also thought Hayes wise to try to conciliate the Democratic House for the sake of securing future appropriations for the army. "Hayes simply used discretion," was the way he put it.[1] John Sherman approved of his course,[2] as did Senator Hoar.[3] Even Blaine, when writing of Hayes at a later time, moderated his criticism to "an unwise and unwarranted act on the part of the president to purchase peace

[1] Foulke, *Morton*, II., 487.
[2] John Sherman, *Recollections*, 586.
[3] Hoar, *Autobiography*, II., 12.

in the South by surrendering Louisiana to the Democratic party." [1]

The institution of the suit against Anderson and others in Louisiana thoroughly alarmed the Republicans for the safety of every member of the party in that state who had been connected with the Packard government. The blame was traceable directly to the presidential pacification policy. A senator from Wisconsin, Howe, imaginatively declared that poles had been erected at every cross-roads bearing flags inscribed "Presidential policy," and that self-appointed inquisitors lurked in convenient jungles to detect those who did not uncover to the flag.[2] Yet as soon as the Democratic majority in the House adopted a resolution to investigate the title of Hayes to the presidency, even his assailants were compelled to come to his rescue. To unseat Hayes and seat Tilden would mean ruin to thousands of federal office-holders.

The Republicans, consequently, refused to vote on the resolution under which the so-called Potter committee was appointed by the House, May 17, 1878. That committee examined over two hundred witnesses, and presented a majority report to the next session, signed by the seven Democratic members of the committee, which reviewed the conditions in Florida and Louisiana in 1876, the forged electoral certificates, and reached the conclusion that Tilden

[1] Blaine, *Twenty Years of Cong.*, II., 596.
[2] *Cong. Record*, 45 Cong., 2 Sess., II., 2000.

was elected president and not Hayes.¹ The Republican minority presented a report to the contrary.

The legislature of Maryland, under a provision of the act of February, 1877, that the electoral commission's finding should not necessarily be final, attempted to institute proceedings in the Supreme Court to invalidate the title of Hayes, and sent copies of its resolutions to Congress. The judiciary committee of the House reported on the resolutions that the remedy for frauds in the recent election lay in punishing the perpetrators in the courts; the House, by a vote of 215 to 21, agreed, June 14, 1878, not to reopen the question; and the various spasmodic attempts to put Hayes's title to some kind of a test led to no result.²

To offset these essays, and to prevent Tilden receiving the Democratic nomination in 1880 as a vindication, the Republicans made use of certain "cipher despatches," a part of thirty thousand telegrams forwarded during the campaign of 1876 by the Western Union Telegraph Company for both parties, and secured in January, 1877, through a subpœna by the Senate committee on privileges and elections. This committee, composed of Republicans, wished to prove by the telegrams that eight thousand dollars were offered by the Democrats for

[1] *House Reports*, 45 Cong., 3 Sess., II., No. 140; McPherson, *Hand-Book of Politics*, 1878, p. 186; John Sherman, *Recollections*, 654–656.
[2] McPherson, *Hand-Book of Politics*, 1878, p. 193; *Appleton's Annual Cyclop.*, 1878, p. 712.

an Oregon elector.[1] Before the despatches were returned to the company some one destroyed those relating to the Republican campaign methods, but abstracted and retained those supposedly incriminating the Democrats. During the summer of 1878, following the attempts to impeach the title of Hayes, certain of these despatches were made public through the *New York Tribune*. Many of them were directed to Mr. Tilden, and contained promises and offers to count in the Democratic electors in various southern states for money considerations. Apparently the negotiations were refused by Tilden and the votes were then given to Hayes.[2] Tilden issued a card, October 16, 1878, denying that he knew of the existence of the telegrams either in cipher or deciphered, and stating positively that no offer of any kind had been made to him by any person or persons.[3]

Upon demand of the Republicans the Potter committee investigated also these "cipher despatches," examined many witnesses, including Mr. Tilden, and incorporated the evidence in a majority final report favorable to Tilden. The Republican minority dissented. It was evident that each party had been used by unscrupulous men, who hesitated at no form of corruption; each contained leaders who at least

[1] *House Misc. Docs.*, 44 Cong., 2 Sess., No. 42.
[2] *Ibid.*, No. 31.
[3] *N. Y. Herald*, October 18, 1878; Bigelow, *Tilden*, II., 170–222; Haworth, *Disputed Presidential Election*, chap. xiii.

harbored plans for making the presidency vendible; and there the matter ended, with the public in doubt, but disgusted with the election of 1876, and willing to let it be forgotten. In the succeeding presidential election neither party could make capital of the election frauds of 1876.

Hayes won small gratitude among the masses in the South by his pacification policy, because they thought they had him driven into a corner where any other action was impossible. Nor could they forget that he was a Republican and in an office which seemed rightly to belong to them. Postmaster-General Key wrote an open letter to the people of the South, urging them not to make or to countenance further attacks on Hayes's title. The case was settled, he thought, by the preceding Congress and the electoral commission, and the recent Congress had no more right to unseat Hayes than Hayes had to send a file of soldiers into the House and unseat a Democratic member. However, the attacks on Hayes by the Democrats turned Republican criticism into Republican defence. The decrease of party strength in Congress [1] and the approach of another presidential campaign warned them that party dissension must not go too far. Gradually the Republican bitterness towards Hayes changed into profound contempt for "the old-woman policy of Granny Hayes," as the radicals called it. In the following election, Governor Hampton was re-elected

[1] See below, page 120.

in South Carolina, the Republicans making no nomination, and thus the last gap in the "solid South" was filled. Republican dissensions must be healed if the party was to meet this combination. The Democrats also aided in reuniting the Republicans by their persistent attacks on the various Republican measures known as the "election laws."

CHAPTER VIII

THE FEDERAL ELECTION LAWS

(1876–1881)

TO add to the difficulties under which Hayes labored, he was confronted by a Democratic majority in the House of Representatives during his entire term of office, and by Democratic control of the Senate during the latter half. It seemed incredible that the Republican hold on the national legislature, so firmly established by reconstruction acts, by amendments to the Constitution, by federal election laws, and by party patronage, could have been lost within so short a period. In 1870, when all the states were represented for the first time in ten years, the Republicans had 61 members of the Senate and the Democrats only 13; in the House, the Republicans numbered 172 and the Democrats 71. From these large majorities the Republican numbers dwindled, as the Democratic "solid South" was built up and as corruption in high Republican places was disclosed, until the "land-slide" of 1874[1] gave the Democrats control of the House for the first time in twenty years.

[1] Dunning, *Reconstruction* (*Am. Nation*, XXII.), chap. xv.

Variations in party strength in Congress during this period is shown in the following table:[1]

			SENATE			HOUSE		
			Rep.	Dem.	Ind.	Rep.	Dem.	Ind.
XLIII.	Cong.	(1873–1875)....	50	24		198	93	
XLIV.	"	(1875–1877)....	42	29	2	110	182	
XLV.	"	(1877–1879)....	38	37	1	136	156	
XLVI.	"	(1879–1881)....	33	42	1	130	148	15
XLVII.	"	(1881–1883)....	37	37	2	150	131	12
XLVIII.	"	(1883–1885)....	40	35	1	119	201	5

The Democratic majority in the House in 1877–1878 renewed their assault on what was to them the most obnoxious survival of the reconstruction machinery—federal control of presidential and congressional elections in the various states. Supervision of these elections had remained vested in the several states for more than seventy years, until the necessity of protecting the freedmen in their political rights called for federal action. Immediately after the Fifteenth Amendment was declared to be in force, Congress passed a series of drastic laws, prescribing penalties for preventing or intimidating a citizen from voting, giving jurisdiction to federal courts and authority to federal marshals in all such cases, and empowering the president to use force if necessary to secure civil rights to the freedmen.[2]

[1] Compiled from McPherson, *Hand-Book of Politics*, 1872–1884.
[2] See the statutes of May 31, 1870, February 28, 1871, April 20, 1871, and June 10, 1872; Dunning, *Reconstruction* (*Am. Nation*, XXII.), chap. xi.

Under these various statutes, two federal election supervisors of opposite parties were to be appointed by the circuit court in cities containing over twenty thousand inhabitants on application of two citizens, the court remaining open during ten days, including election day, for hearing cases under the act. The supervisors were required to attend the polls at congressional elections, to challenge suspected persons, to superintend registration lists, to count the ballots, and to return the election certificates. In addition the marshal for the district was authorized on application of two citizens to appoint special deputy-marshals to aid the supervisors, keep the peace, and bring arrested persons forthwith before a United States judge or commissioner.

Federal judges might exclude suspected persons from jury service, and require a test oath from jurors that they had not conspired to prevent exercise of the suffrage. The president was authorized to suspend *habeas corpus* under certain conditions, and to use the army and navy in enforcing all these acts; although the use of troops at the polls was understood to be authorized indirectly by the act of 1865, which prohibited their use except for keeping the peace. By a paragraph inserted in the civil appropriation bill of 1872, the system of federal supervisors and marshals was extended to every county and parish in the United States when ten residents thereof made application.[1]

[1] For these statutes, see *U. S. Statutes at Large*, XVI., 140, 433; XVII., 13, 348; *Nation*, XXVIII., 223.

Each political party assigned a different motive for the framing of these federal election laws. The Republicans lost New York from the ranks of Republican states in the election of 1868 through what they claimed to be extensive frauds in the naturalization laws, perpetrated by Tweed and his henchmen.[1] To prevent a recurrence of these frauds, the Republicans created the system of supervisors of elections, but the Democrats saw in it an attempt to place New York permanently with the southern states in the Republican ranks. "The very climax of radical attempts to obtain complete control of the United States" was the light in which it appeared to the Democrats.[2] The Republicans proclaimed their object to be to secure a free vote to all citizens both North and South. Blaine said it was unjust to accuse the party of demanding military aid with the remotest intention of controlling any man's vote; but the motive was to prevent votes from being controlled and voters from being driven from the polls.[3]

"In the south, one million Republicans are disenfranchised," said John Sherman, in supporting his statement that the Democrats in the Capitol would be in a pitiful minority if those elected by fraud and bloodshed were debarred. "We must have free elections. We are determined to assert the suprem-

---

[1] *North Am. Rev.*, CXXV., 193; *Nation*, XXXII., 355.
[2] *Cong. Globe*, 41 Cong., 3 Sess., App., pp. 127-132.
[3] Blaine, *Twenty Years of Cong.*, II., 643.

acy of the United States in all matters pertaining to the United States."¹ He would have given the control of the state elections also to the general government, if necessary to secure to all men their political rights.²

Within two years after the act went into force, district attorneys reported to the United States attorney-general that 501 persons had been arrested in South Carolina under the act, of whom 53 pleaded "guilty" and were sentenced, 220 were indicted but not tried, and the remainder not indicted. In North Carolina there were 37 convictions and more than 1000 indictments. Mississippi reported over 900 indictments and 30 convictions.³ Marshals and supervisors were equally active in the northern cities. The United States spent from sixty to one hundred thousand dollars on each congressional election between 1870 and 1878. John I. Davenport, the federal supervisor for New York City in 1868 arrested hundreds of persons who were trying to vote under naturalization papers granted to them by the state courts by Democratic judges. He claimed that the records of the courts were improperly kept, and that the papers were thus invalidated. By repeated arrests he reduced the number of these papers from 40,000 to 10,000 In 1878 one of these cases was brought before the circuit court of the

---

[1] John Sherman, *Recollections*, 750. [2] *Ibid.*, 873.
[3] *House Exec. Docs.*, 42 Cong., 2 Sess., No. 268, pp. 5-41; Dunning, *Reconstruction* (*Am. Nation*, XXII.), 271.

United States, and it was held that the records were valid and the actions of Davenport could not be upheld. The Democratic House in vain tried to have Davenport removed or impeached.[1]

The use of federal machinery in elections reached its climax in the election of 1876. Under the election laws, 4863 supervisors were appointed, at a cost of over a hundred thousand dollars; 11,610 deputy-marshals, to whom was paid a like amount; and in addition to these was the cost of chief supervisors and of commissioners. The total expense of federal supervision, aside from fees regularly paid to marshals, deputies, and attorneys, was $275,296, more than one-third of which was spent in New York City. Of the special deputy-marshals, 7000 were stationed at polls in the southern states, 2500 in New York City, and 1500 in other northern cities. The supervisors in the different states were so zealous in registering voters that those appointed by a Republican governor of Louisiana registered eight thousand more colored voters than were in the state when the United States census was taken four years later.[2] After the election the attorney-general was satisfied that "the United States marshals and attorneys acting in concert with the supervisors of elections under their instructions in New York, in

---

[1] *In re* Coleman, 15 Blatchford, 406; *House Reports*, 45 Cong., 3 Sess., No. 136; *in re* Davenport, 48 U. S., 531.
[2] *House Reports*, 45 Cong., 3 Sess., No. 120; Haworth, *Disputed Presidential Election*, 93.

Philadelphia, in Boston, in St. Louis, in Chicago, in New Orleans, and in several of the southern states, contributed materially to the preservation of the peace and to the securing of the citizens' freedom in the exercise of the right of suffrage."[1] A House committee investigated the elections in New York and Philadelphia, and made purely partisan reports.[2]

Such, in brief, were the federal election laws upon which the Democratic majority in the House opened war in 1876 by trying to put a "rider" on the appropriation for the support of the army, providing that no federal troops should be used to sustain the Republican government in Louisiana. At the next session they succeeded in attaching a "rider" to the army appropriation bill prohibiting the use of any portion of the army at the polls at any election. The Republican majority in the Senate refused to accept the proviso, and the Forty-fourth Congress adjourned without making provision for the army. Hayes inherited the deadlock, and was compelled to call the Forty-fifth Congress in extra session, October 15, 1877, payment to officers and men having been suspended from the end of the previous June.

The Democrats retained possession of the lower house, although with a reduced majority, and the Republicans held the balance of power in the upper house. Here began a four years' contest between Hayes, as a sacrifice to his party principles, and a

[1] *House Reports*, 44 Cong., 2 Sess., No. 20, p. 2.
[2] *Ibid.*, No. 218, I.

hostile majority in one or both branches of Congress, which added to the many difficulties under which he labored.[1] Of the twelve bills which he returned to Congress without his consent, eight dealt with the attempted abrogation of the federal election laws.[2] Under the leadership of Abram S. Hewitt, of New York, the House attempted to place on various appropriation bills "riders" calculated to emasculate the election laws; while the Senate, under the leadership of James G. Blaine, as persistently tried to retain control of the election machinery. At the special session, the Democrats eventually allowed the delayed army bill to pass without a "rider," November 21, 1877,[3] yielding to the law of necessity, and regarding their success of the previous session as a sufficient protest for the time being.

Hewitt and his followers opened the regular session of the Forty-fourth Congress, December, 1877, by attaching a proviso to the annual army appropriation bill, and commonly known as "Section 15," which made it unlawful to employ any part of the army as a *posse comitatus* for executing the laws, except as expressly authorized by the Constitution or by act of Congress. It also forbade the use of any part of the army appropriation for paying expenses of troops so employed, under penalty of fine and imprisonment. Under the text of the Constitution, troops could be used only "to execute the laws of the

[1] Cox, *Three Decades*, 630.   [2] Mason, *Veto Power*, 162-164.
[3] *U. S. Statutes at Large*, XX., 1.

Union, to suppress Insurrections and repel Invasions." The limitations imposed by the Constitution would consequently prohibit the use of troops by United States marshals, if this bill should pass. The Democrats were persistent; the Republican Senate and President Hayes were obliged to yield to save the army; and the bill became a law June 18, 1878.[1] The Democrats rejoiced that they had vindicated once more the inherited antipathy of the American people to the use of troops for civil purposes; yet they remembered that their work was only half accomplished so long as federal deputy-marshals and supervisors of elections could be used under the election laws.

The second session of the Forty-fifth Congress met in December, 1878. The congressional and state elections, which had taken place in the mean time, showed that the Democrats would have a majority in both houses of the next Congress for the first time in twenty years. It was their policy, consequently, to renew the war on the remaining "force bills" by attaching "riders" to the appropriation bills, which the Senate would oppose, and to force an early session of the Forty-sixth Congress, in which they would have a majority. This was done; the army appropriation bill again failed to pass with a "rider," and Hayes was compelled for the second time to call Congress in special session, March 19, 1879,[2] to provide

---

[1] *U. S. Statutes at Large*, XX., 152.
[2] Richardson, *Messages and Papers*, VII., 520.

for the deficiency. It was a situation without a parallel. In the previous history of Congress under the Constitution, covering a century, presidents had found it necessary only fourteen times to call a session of Congress in addition to the annual meetings required by the Constitution. The Civil War was carried on with only one extra session, reconstruction required only five. The cause in the present instance was the persistent effort of the southern people to regain self-government by regulating negro suffrage, and the repeal of the election laws was a prerequisite to controlling the elections.

The Republican losses in Congress were attributed by that party largely to the suppression of the colored vote in the southern states, notwithstanding the federal election laws. In Louisiana and South Carolina at large, and in certain congressional districts in other states, "the records of the elections seem to compel the conclusion," said Hayes, in his second message to Congress, "that the rights of the colored voters have been overridden and their participation in the elections not permitted to be either general or free." This was after "all disturbing influences, real or imaginary [*i. e.*, troops], had been removed from those states." He urged additional appropriations to the judiciary department, which was intrusted with the enforcement of the election laws.[1]

When the Forty-sixth Congress met, at the call of Hayes, March 19, 1879, the House contained 148

[1] Richardson, *Messages and Papers*, VII., 493.

Democrats, 130 Republicans, and 15 members of the Greenback or National party. The former Democratic speaker, Randall, was retained in the chair. The Republican minority gave their complimentary vote to James A. Garfield, of Ohio, evidently the coming man in the House. The Senate contained 42 Democrats, 33 Republicans, and 1 Independent. The turn of fickle public favor, first manifest in the "land-slide" of 1874, was continuing until it bade fair to work a complete reversal in national control. The Democrats now held a majority of more than thirty in the House, since the Greenbackers commonly voted with them, and also a safe majority of eight votes in the Senate.[1] They had so completely gained control of the southern states that only four Republicans were elected out of the one hundred and six congressional districts. This reversal may have been caused by the violent suppression of the colored vote in the southern states, as the Republicans claimed; or by a popular protest against the tyrannical actions of the opposite party, as the Democrats asserted. Account must also be taken of the tendency to desert the party in power at mid-administration elections. Resentment arising from the recent disputed election gave renewed vigor to the tendency to change, which otherwise must soon have spent itself. In time, the change might be expected to reach the presidential office.

[1] McPherson, *Hand-Book of Politics*, 1880, pp. 95-99.

Full thirty members of the Senate had been connected with the Confederate States government—among them Wade Hampton, ex-Confederate general, whom the withdrawal of the troops by Hayes in 1877 established as governor of South Carolina; Vest, of Mississippi, a former member of the Confederate Congress; Vance, of North Carolina, who had been refused admission to the Senate in 1870 because of "political disabilities"; and Williams, an ex-Confederate general from Kentucky. Removal by congressional leniency of the disbarments imposed by the Fourteenth Amendment opened up Congress to the real southern leaders. The growing number of ex-Confederates in Congress was indicative of the condition at the close of the century when the Senate contained more veterans of the Confederate than of the Federal army.

Having a majority in each branch, but not a two-thirds vote, the Democrats at once inaugurated two years of warfare upon the remaining "force bills." From the Republican stand-point the only change was the transfer of the duty of blocking their action from the Senate to the president. The first step was a proviso in the army appropriation bill, forbidding under heavy penalties any United States official from having at the polls any military force to preserve order or to keep the peace. It was vetoed by President Hayes, April 29, 1879, as unnecessary legislation, since existing laws, especially the clause

[1] Blaine, *Twenty Years of Cong.*, II., 639.

attached to the appropriation bill two years before, guaranteed the voter against interference by federal troops. "No soldier of the United States," said he, "has appeared under orders at any place of election in any state and no complaint even of the presence of United States troops has been made in any quarter." He also declared the "rider" to be the ingrafting of a new principle under the Constitution—viz., that one branch of Congress could deprive the executive of the qualified veto granted to him by that document.[1] The attempt to pass the measure over his disapproval by a two-thirds vote showed only 121 to 110 votes. The bill was passed again with the proviso in a modified form, forbidding any money appropriated by the act being used to preserve the peace at the polls. In this form, which was the equivalent simply to a re-enactment of the "rider" of the preceding year, Hayes acquiesced and the bill became a law.[2]

Congress next formed the essence of the vetoed "rider" into a bill prohibiting military interference at elections, by repealing all the "force bills." President Hayes returned it without his signature, May 12, 1879, holding it to be unnecessary and at the same time a barrier against the United States exercising its whole executive power in case an emergency demanded.[3] The attempt to pass this

[1] Richardson, *Messages and Papers*, VII., 523; Mason, *Veto Power*, 48.   [2] *U. S. Statutes at Large*, XXI., 35.
[3] Richardson, *Messages and Papers*, VII., 532; Mason, *Veto Power*, 162.

bill over the veto received the high vote of 128 to 97, but still lacked the required two-thirds.

To follow the legislative contest between Hayes and Congress is a tedious recital of attempts to place riders on the judicial appropriations and so prevent payment of special deputy-marshals; on the appropriation for United States marshals, with the proviso that deputies used in elections should not be compensated; and on the civil appropriation bill, forbidding payment to marshals and supervisors of elections.[1] The votes were strictly party alignments and the Democrats were never able to muster a two-thirds vote necessary to pass the disputed bill over the presidential veto. Each side was worn out, and, during the last year of Hayes, the triumph of the Republican party in the presidential election, and the tendency of the Supreme Court to undo the election laws, put an end to the war made by the Democrats upon them.

The various acts passed for securing their civil rights to the freedmen were potent factors in bringing to adjudication cases arising under the Fourteenth Amendment, and in clearing up the new relations between the states and the Union. Here was seen the full fruitage of the centralizing tendencies of the war period and the transfer of the unexpressed powers from the individual governments to the collective government. While the decision of the

[1] Mason, *Veto Power*, 162–164; McPherson, *Hand-Book of Politics*, 1880, pp. 55–64.

Slaughter Houses cases[1] in 1873 safeguarded the rights and immunities of citizenship in the United States from abridgment by a state, the verdict in the case of Strauder vs. West Virginia in 1879 went further and assured to the colored race all the political rights enjoyed by white persons, and bound the general government to maintain those rights.[2] In 1883 the courts held the civil rights act of 1875 to be invalid because it was not the function of the federal government to assure to negroes admission to theatres, accommodations in hotels, and transportation in cars upon an equality with white persons. Remedy for these private injuries must be sought in the state courts.[3]

What may be called the political rights of the negro, aside from the suffrage, which was given him by the Fifteenth Amendment, came before the Supreme Court in 1879, when it was held that negroes could not be excluded from jury service by a state law.[4] Another decision made state judges liable to prosecution by the general government for excluding negroes from juries even where no state law barred them.[5] The election laws received their first blow from the court in 1875 when it decided that a state may require a reasonable prerequisite, such as payment of a poll-tax, before a citizen is

[1] 16 Wallace, 36.
[2] Strauder vs. West Virginia, 100 U. S., 106.
[3] Civil Rights Cases, 109 U. S., 3; *Railway Gazette*, XV., 726 (November 2, 1883).   [4] *Ex parte* Virginia, 100 U. S., 339.
[5] Virginia vs. Rives, 100 U. S., 313.

allowed to vote at a congressional election.¹ This decision suggested the "Mississippi plan" of barring negroes from voting by requiring a prerequisite which many found impossible to meet.

The "federal election laws" came before the court in 1879. Five Maryland state judges of a congressional election held in the city of Baltimore, November 5, 1878, refused to permit the federal supervisors of elections and the deputy-marshals to examine the ballot-boxes, and some of the five were accused of inserting spurious ballots, a crime all too common to those days and known as "stuffing the ballot-box." Being convicted and sentenced in the United States circuit court, they petitioned the Supreme Court for release on the ground that the federal election law under which they were convicted was unconstitutional; that the state judges possessed exclusive control of elections held within the state, because there could not be two authorities exercising jurisdiction. The Supreme Court agreed that there could not be a joint sovereignty, but held that the state could not exclude the United States from exercising its proper functions. "Why do we have marshals at all," asked the court, "if they cannot physically lay their hands on persons and things in the performance of their proper duty? . . . If we indulge in such impractical views as these, and keep on refining and re-refining, we shall drive

¹ U. S. *vs.* Reese, U. S., 214; cf. Dunning, *Reconstruction* (*Am. Nation*, XXII.), 213.

the national government out of the United States and will relegate it to the District of Columbia or perhaps to some foreign soil." [1] The constitutionality of the law was thereby sustained.

At the same term of the court, the case of Clarke appeared on a similar petition. He had been convicted as an officer of a congressional election held in the city of Cincinnati of failing to deliver the ballot-box to the county clerk and of allowing it to be broken open. The court quoted its decision in the Maryland case, upholding the election laws and the jurisdiction of the circuit court. Justices Field and Clifford dissented from the majority of the court in these opinions, and held that the officer of a state cannot be punished for obeying the laws of the state.[2] In 1882 that part of the "enforcement acts" which forbade two or more persons to conspire to go on the highway or on the premises of another in disguise for the purpose of depriving him of his rights was declared unconstitutional because such regulation was of a private character and belonged to the state.[3] Thus shorn of all their agencies except the system of supervisors and deputy-marshals, the federal election laws became practically a dead letter, manifest in only one unpleasant incident at Cincinnati, Ohio, in the election of 1884, as related

---

[1] *Ex parte* Siebold, 100 U. S., 371; McPherson, *Hand-Book of Politics*, 1880, p. 22.
[2] *Ex parte* Clarke, 100 U. S., 399; McPherson, *Hand-Book of Politics*, 1880, p. 32.   [3] U. S. *vs.* Harris, 106 U. S., 629.

hereafter.¹ The days for federal interference in elections in northern cities were passed; the demand for local government had returned. In the South, the Ku-Klux Klan was dead; more subtle methods of controlling elections had been devised; and against these the federal election laws were powerless. The last vestiges were cleared from the statute-books by a Democratic administration in 1894.²

[1] See below, p. 346.
[2] Dunning, "Undoing of Reconstruction," in *Atlantic Monthly*, LXXXVIII., 437; *U. S. Statutes at Large*, XXVIII., 36.

CHAPTER IX

CURRENCY AND FISHERIES
(1877–1881)

FOR various reasons silver had fallen in value as compared with gold from 15 to 1 in 1860, to 16 to 1 in 1873, and to 17 to 1 before 1877. In a renewed effort to adjust the currency of the United States to these fluctuations, Congress in 1893 struck the standard silver dollar from the list of authorized coins and substituted a "trade dollar" containing a greater weight of silver, which, it was hoped, could compete with the heavy Mexican dollar in the Eastern countries. During the following year, a further discrimination was made against silver coins by limiting their legal-tender value to five dollars. These acts were in accord with those of other nations at the time, all tending to establish a gold standard of currency. The time was approaching for paying a large share of the national debt incurred in the Civil War, and a gold basis would insure its holders against payment in the cheaper metal—silver. On the other hand, resolutions appeared in Congress and in many state legislatures reciting that the bonds had been issued payable, if the government wished, in silver dollars containing 412½ grains each; and that payment in similar coins would not be a violation of the public faith nor an injustice to the holders of the debt. Consequently the resolutions demanded a restoration of the silver dollar with that over-valuation as measured by gold and the privilege of taking silver in any quantity to the mint and having it coined.

In 1877 the national debt consisted of $729,000,000 bearing interest at six per cent., and $708,000,000 at the rate of five per cent. The holders of this debt objected to what they considered "repudiation" by payment in silver, demanded payment in money of par value at the time of the discharge of the debt, and resisted the demand for free coinage of silver as likely to flood the country with cheap money.[1] Their opponents, the masses of people, located generally in the newer or borrowing part of the country, argued that needed reform in the currency should not be held back lest it might injure the interests of the men of wealth. It was the old line-up of the class against the mass. Besides the national debt, there were heavy private obligations incurred by the western farmers, mostly in farm mortgages, and the municipal bonds issued by many cities and villages in the newer regions for paving and lighting, for water-works and other public purposes, and the

[1] Dewey, *Financial Hist. of the U. S.*, 406; Richardson, *Messages and Papers*, VII., 463; see August Belmont's protest, in John Sherman, *Recollections*, 606.

vast issues of railroad bonds. These debts were held for the most part in the older states by banks, insurance companies, and private capitalists. Such were the conditions, added to the fact that certain western states were producing large quantities of silver, which prompted the attack on the "gold ring" and the demand for atonement for the so-called "crime of '73." [1]

The opponents of the proposed legislation pointed out the original purpose of the legal-tender law— viz., to secure to the man who lends the full purchasing power possessed by money at the time he loaned it. They refused to be a party to a legal justification of the debtor who wishes to discharge his obligation at ninety cents on the dollar. Whether gold had been forced up to a fictitious value, as some claimed, or whether silver had appreciated or depreciated, they believed in reckoning obligations at full face value in the highest standard. They declared any attempt to make the silver dollar, containing $412\frac{1}{2}$ grains of silver, permanently equal to the gold in a gold dollar impossible and futile. They ridiculed the argument that the restoration of this kind of a dollar would raise silver to its former value, for legislation never gave value to anything. The causes of the continued financial depression could not be found in any coinage system, they said, neither could it be relieved by any experiments.

[1] For earlier aspects of this controversy, see Dunning, *Reconstruction* (*Am. Nation*, XXII.), chap. xiv.

It was a natural result of the exhaustion of natural resources in the Civil War, and the unnatural and injudicious speculative craze which followed.[1]

As a guide to legislation, Congress by joint resolution, April 15, 1875, created a monetary commission to study the currency situation and to make recommendations. It consisted of Senators Jones, Bogy, and Boutwell; Representatives Bland, Willard, and Gibson; and three financial experts—Groesbeck, Bowen, and Chamberlain. It presented an exhaustive report March 2, 1877, giving a history of bimetallism, or the varying ratio between gold and silver, and advocating almost as many remedies for the present situation as there were members of the commission: some wished to give silver a permanent subsidiary relation to gold; others would keep it in this relation only until other nations could be persuaded to adopt both gold and silver as standard metals; still others advised a bold return to an arbitrary ratio of 15.50 grains of silver to 1 of gold, regardless of other nations; a few would return to the old ratio of 16 to 1, which had been in use up to 1873. Little was gained from the report.[2]

Generally speaking, the Republicans favored the gold and Democrats the silver standard, although sectional interests of East and West were too strong for strict party alignment. A Republican senator,

[1] *Cong. Record*, 45 Cong., 2 Sess., 644, 668.
[2] Report of the Silver Commission, *Senate Reports*, 44 Cong., 2 Sess., V., 703.

Matthews, of Ohio, introduced a resolution in the Senate, December 10, 1877, favoring the restoration of silver coinage, and was opposed by Senator Morrill, a Republican of Vermont, and Senator Bayard, a Democrat from Delaware. Of the 22 votes cast against the resolution when it passed the Senate, 15 came from Republican senators and 7 from Democratic senators.[1]

Hayes had long been known as a "sound money" man, having been thrice elected governor of Ohio on the joint issues of a return to specie money and the maintenance of a circulation of full value. In his message of 1877 he advised payment of the national debt in gold or its equivalent in value. "It is far better," said he, "to pay these bonds in that coin than to seem to take advantage of the unforeseen fall in silver bullion to pay in a new issue of silver coin thus made so much the less valuable."[2] He favored a resumption of silver coinage, but in a limited quantity, and he pronounced the popular expectation of any ease from an unlimited silver coinage to be a delusion. John Sherman, secretary of the treasury, had shown unusual ability as chairman of the House committee on finance, and had been intimately connected with the resumption act in Congress. He comprehended the intricacies of the money market, and possessed the confidence of

---

[1] McPherson, *Hand-Book of Politics*, 1878, p. 138; *North Am. Rev.*, CXXVI., 163.

[2] Richardson, *Messages and Papers*, VII., 463.

eastern capitalists. Although he had the reputation of wavering, he was regarded as "sound" for a gold basis.¹

Among the ardent advocates of a silver currency was Richard P. Bland, a representative from Missouri, who had spent several years in Nevada engaged in various silver-mining enterprises, and was familiar with all the arguments of the silver producer. As chairman of the committee on mines and mining in the Forty-fourth Congress, he introduced a measure and repeated it in later sessions, known as the "Bland silver bill." It proposed to require the unlimited coinage of legal-tender silver dollars weighing 412½ grains troy (the weight provided in the act of 1837 when the ratio was 15.62 to 1), to be coined from bullion purchased by the United States or brought to the mints by any person, on the same footing as gold. The Senate added an amendment proposed by Allison, of Iowa, striking out the "free and unlimited" feature and directing the secretary of the treasury to purchase not less than two million and not more than four million dollars' worth of silver per month for coining into silver dollars, provided the amount of money invested in bullion should not at any time exceed five million dollars.² Otherwise it was claimed that the United States must purchase practically all the silver mined in the United States at nearly one dollar an ounce. The House

---

[1] Dewey, *Financial Hist. of U. S.*, 375; John Sherman, *Recollections*, 618.   [2] *Cong. Record*, 45 Cong., 2 Sess., 671.

was obliged to accept the amendment or lose the entire bill. Bland said: "Let us take what we have and supplement it immediately on appropriation bills [*i. e.*, by riders]; and if we cannot do that, I am in favor of issuing paper money enough to stuff down the bond-holders until they are sick. I protest this bill while I vote for it under protest." [1]

The House vote on the original bill was 163 to 34, and on the amended bill 203 to 72. In the former vote 93 members did not take part; now only 17 were marked "no voting." In the Senate, the bill received 48 affirmative votes, almost exactly divided between Republicans and Democrats—a sharp contrast with later days, when "free silver" became purely a party question. Of the 21 negative votes, 14 were from Republicans and 7 from Democrats. Geographically, the lines were closely drawn between East and West: every senator from New England, New York, and New Jersey, placed himself on record against free silver; and only four votes of this kind came from states west of the Alleghany Mountains.

Encouraged by their success, advocates of "plenty of money" renewed their attempts to postpone the day set for the final redemption of the paper money through the resumption of specie payments. Under a clause of the resumption act of 1875,[2] the treasury was contracting the legal-tender notes to the amount of 80 per cent. of new national-bank notes, so that

[1] *Cong. Record*, 45 Cong., 2 Sess., 1251.
[2] See Dunning, *Reconstruction* (*Am. Nation*, XXII.), 250.

in 1878 less than $350,000,000 remained in circulation. To prevent the loss of more of these notes to circulation, the inflationists succeeded in getting an act passed in that year[1] prohibiting the further withdrawal of paper money in this manner.

Many of these inflationists were Greenbackers who seceded from the old parties in 1876 and demanded a repeal of the resumption act, the issue of legal-tender notes bearing interest not exceeding one cent per day on each one hundred dollars, the abolition of bank-notes, and the refusal to sell gold bonds in foreign markets. The sovereign right of issuing money must not be relegated by the government to corporations; but anything ought to be considered as money which bore the seal of the United States. A United States note was not to them a "promise to pay"; it was a payment in itself. The Greenback ticket in 1876 attracted only eighty thousand votes; in the congressional election of 1878 it reached a million; but in the presidential election of 1880 it fell to one-third that number, and disappeared after a feeble showing in the election of 1884, with Benjamin F. Butler as its candidate.[2]

Invested interests were greatly alarmed in 1878 by the repeated attempts to postpone the day of resumption and by the popular demand for "rag

---

[1] Act of May 31, 1878, see *U. S. Statutes at Large*, XX., 87; *Appleton's Annual Cyclop*., 1879, p. 766; John Sherman, *Recollections*, 658.

[2] Stanwood, *Hist. of the Presidency*, 367, 409, 423.

money." As many as thirteen bills were introduced into Congress in a single day in October, 1877, postponing the day set for resuming hard-money payments in the United States, but all failed to pass. During the following year a bill to repeal entirely the original resumption bill passed the House amid cries of "repudiation" from those who opposed payment of national obligations in paper. "The greenback is the most powerful enemy our country has ever encountered, slavery alone excepted," said Chittenden, a representative from New York.[1] "It is not money; it is a device." "I hold in my hands," retorted Davis, of North Carolina, "a ten-dollar bill issued in 1869. When issued it was worth $7.50. It is now worth $9.30, and yet is only a 'dirty rag,' a stain worth nothing in eyes prejudiced by gold." One side asserted that the repeal of the law and continuation of paper money were demanded by "loafers, gamblers, and bankrupts, the worst elements of society"; the other replied that "every millionaire, every man who owns two or three hundred dollars in government securities, is opposed to repeal and in favor of hard and grinding poverty for the debtor." The Senate refused to agree on the details of the proposed anti-resumption law as the House wished it, and preparations went on to begin specie payments on January 1, 1879.

Sherman began in 1877 to prepare for resumption by hoarding forty million dollars in gold and

[1] *Cong. Record*, 45 Cong., 2 Sess., 878.

by selling fifty million dollars' worth of gold bonds the following year.[1] A later sale of a similar amount brought the total coin reserve up to about $133,-000,000, on January 1, 1879, or nearly forty per cent. of the amount of notes to be redeemed.[2] By making the United States virtually a member of the New York Clearing-House, that body agreed to receive the government notes in payment of government drafts and checks, giving the former a standing and relieving the treasury from making payment in actual coin. Paper money was also made receivable for customs duties, and all remaining distinction between coin and paper currency was obliterated.

By taking these precautions, resumption day passed without excitement or friction.[3] Confidence had suddenly lifted the paper dollar to a par with silver and gold. Now that any one could exchange paper for coin, few wished to do so; only straggling demands appeared. Indeed, during the first year, less than twelve million dollars of paper were presented for redemption in gold. The importance of the occasion lay not in the amount but in the fact that the paper money, which in January, 1864, aggregated five hundred million dollars, and which in July, 1864, was worth only thirty-five cents on the dollar, had been redeemed and the national honor

---

[1] John Sherman, *Recollections*, 645-653.
[2] Dewey, *Financial Hist. of the U. S.*, 375.
[3] Bolles, *Financial History*, III., 297-303; John Sherman, *Recollections*, chaps. xxxiv., xxxvi.

saved. It was a great victory compared with the Continental paper money of Revolutionary days the remnants of which were redeemed under Hamilton's plan at the rate of 100 to 1.[1]

In the midst of hoarding his gold, Sherman was obliged to sell $5,500,000 worth of additional bonds to meet the award made by the Halifax commission to Great Britain. The century-long contest between that country and the United States over the joint use of the sea-fisheries about Newfoundland[2] brought the dispute before the joint high commission of 1871, where an agreement was reached by which the United States should have the right to take fish within the three-mile limit of the Gulf of St. Lawrence, for the period of ten years, during which time a joint tribunal should decide the amount of compensation due Great Britain for the privilege.[3] In 1875, Sir Alexander T. Galt was named by the queen and E. H. Kellogg was appointed by President Grant. By a blundering delay the United States was forced to accept M. Delfosse, Belgian ambassador at London, as third commissioner.[4] The intimate political and family ties existing between England and Belgium at the time persuaded the American people that Delfosse would be predisposed in England's favor.

The tribunal sat at Halifax, Nova Scotia, from

---

[1] *U. S. Statutes at Large*, I., 140.
[2] *Senate Docs.*, 56 Cong., 2 Sess., No. 231, pt. v., pp. 577-610, 615-630.   [3] *U. S. Treaties and Conventions*, 486-488.
[4] *Senate Exec. Docs.*, 45 Cong., 2 Sess., No. 44.

June to November, 1877, with a short intermission, hearing testimony from fishermen, fish-dealers, and owners of fishing-vessels, both British and American. The British counsel proved that about one thousand American vessels engaged annually in the inshore Canadian fishing, representing $7,000,000 American capital and employing sixteen thousand men. Every vessel earned gross about $5600 on every trip, to which was added the profit derived from the privilege of landing, transferring cargoes, establishing permanent stations, and the benefit of the protective service maintained by the British government. The latter was placed at $200,000 annually, and $12,000,000 total claimed for all these inshore benefits. The more distant cod-fisheries of Newfoundland were said to be used by American fishermen to the annual value of at least $240,000, or $2,880,000 for the period of twelve years covered by the treaty of Washington. Combining Canada and Newfoundland, the British claimed a total of $14,880,000 from the American government as the price of participating in the British fisheries during the twelve years.[1]

The American counsel tried to offset this sum by the advantages derived by British fishermen in the admission of free fish to America, amounting to $400,000 annually, by the inshore fisheries of the United States to which Canadian fishermen were admitted, and by the advantages derived by Canadian fishermen from contact with American fisher-

[1] Moore, *International Arbitrations*, 736–739.

men. In the end the damage award was scaled down to $5,500,000 in gold, and an agreement to this effect was signed by the British and the Belgian representatives, the American refusing to sign because the amount was excessive.[1] It was generally suspected that the large sum was due in part to the fact that of the $15,500,000 awarded to the United States against England for damages inflicted by Confederate cruisers more than two-fifths remained in the United States treasury in 1874 awaiting claimants, and a second court had to be established in 1882 to get rid of it.[2]

The Halifax finding aroused a storm of protest in the United States, and Congress came near repudiating it on the ground that the decision should have been unanimous to be binding.[3] A motion prevailed to give notice to Great Britain that the United States would terminate the agreement at the end of the ten years, July 1, 1885, and allow the matter of the fisheries to return to the status of 1818. Sound counsel finally prevailed over hasty impulse; Congress voted the sum and it was paid within the required twelve months, November 21, 1878. The draft was accompanied by a protest against accept-

---

[1] Moore, *International Arbitrations*, 740–742.
[2] *House Reports*, 43 Cong., 1 Sess., No. 628; *House Exec. Docs.*, 44 Cong., 1 Sess., No. 140; *House Reports*, 45 Cong., 2 Sess., No. 663.
[3] Henderson, *Am. Diplomatic Questions*, 518; Halifax Commission, *Documents and Proceedings, House Exec. Docs.*, 45 Cong., 2 Sess., No. 89.

ing the award as a just measure of the value of the fisheries to American citizens and insisting that the sum was paid solely in order to maintain good faith in treaties and to encourage the principle of arbitration between nations.[1]

Before the award was paid, the United States had an opportunity of retaliating. On Sunday, January 6, 1878, a number of Newfoundland fishermen attacked the crews of several American fishing-boats as they were drawing their seines along the inshore in Fortune Bay. To a demand for damages made by the United States, England replied that provincial law of Newfoundland forbade fishing on Sunday, and also that shore fishing did not permit landing to draw seines. America contended that no provincial law could impair or interpret a treaty. Hayes advised Congress, May 17, 1880, to clear up by legislation these disputed points in the treaty of 1871. Eventually Great Britain yielded, and the damages being reduced from $105,305.02, the amount claimed by the United States, to $15,000, was paid by Great Britain and distributed among the American fishermen who had suffered in the "Fortune Bay outrages."[2]

---

[1] *Senate Exec. Docs.*, 45 Cong., 2 Sess., No. 100; *Foreign Relations*, 1878, pp. 290, 316; *North Am. Rev.*, CXXVIII., 1; *Senate Docs.*, 56 Cong., 2 Sess., No. 231.

[2] Richardson, *Messages and Papers*, VII., 566, 590; VIII., 38; also see *Appleton's Annual Cyclop.*, 1880, p. 218; *Senate Exec. Docs.*, 46 Cong., 2 Sess., No. 180; *Foreign Relations*, 1880, pp. 555-573.

"With views unchanged with regard to the act under which the coinage of silver proceeds," said President Hayes to Congress in December, 1878, "it has been the purpose of the Secretary faithfully to execute the law and to afford a fair trial to the measure."[1] Purchasing silver to the minimum amount, two million dollars' worth a month, the secretary caused to be coined within the nine months following the passage of the bill almost twenty million silver dollars, of which about one-fifth was put in circulation and the rest retained in possession of the government. It was not deemed wise to put out the entire amount of silver coinage lest depreciation follow. By a year later, forty-five million silver dollars had been coined; but none of the disasters predicted by advocates of the gold standard followed. Such part of the coinage as was placed in circulation passed at par, for the reason that the silver dollar was in steady demand to make change and because the people had never become unfamiliar with fractional silver currency. It was also understood that the dollars would be exchanged for the paper notes at the time of resumption.

Thus it chanced that the silver measure and resumption offset each other; fear and uncertainty were anticipated by confidence and steadiness. In December, 1879, Hayes reported to Congress the complete success of resumption. As soon as the notes began to be redeemed in gold, they were re-

[1] Richardson, *Messages and Papers*, VII., 499.

ceived and paid out in all parts of the country as the equivalent of gold. A great revival of business followed. "With a currency equivalent in value to the money of the world," said Hayes, "we are enabled to enter upon an equal competition with other nations in trade and production. The increasing foreign demand for our manufactures and agricultural products has caused a large balance of trade in our favor. . . . Since resumption of specie payment, there has also been a marked and gratifying improvement of the public credit. The bonds of the government bearing only four per cent. interest have been sold at or above par."[1]

Hayes felt a pardonable pride in the fact that in the midst of the free-silver agitation and the efforts to postpone or disturb resumption, the work of refunding the national debt went steadily forward. Various forms of the debt, bearing the five and six per cent. interest which the government was obliged to pay to secure money during the Civil War, were now called in and replaced by new bonds bearing four and four and one-half per cent. In June, 1879, every dollar of redeemable debt had been refunded at a saving to the government of over fourteen millions annually in interest.[2]

The Allison amendment to the Bland silver bill,

---

[1] Richardson, *Messages and Papers*, VII., 558.
[2] Dewey, *Financial Hist. of the U. S.*, 352–354; Richardson, *Messages and Papers*, VII., 617; John Sherman, *Recollections*, chap. xxxvii.

which gives it the name of the Bland-Allison bill, provided for a conference of the powers of Europe and America by invitation of the president of the United States. It led indirectly to a meeting at Paris, April, 1881,[1] in which fourteen nations participated. The United States was represented by William M. Evarts, of New York, secretary of state under Hayes; Allen G. Thurman, recently a Democratic senator from Ohio; and Timothy O. Howe, until 1879 a senator from Wisconsin, who favored the double standard. No practical conclusion could be reached in this international monetary conference on the proper ratio of gold to silver, and no promises could be secured from European nations that they would join the United States in attempting to remonetize silver,[2] although the latter, at this time, was purchasing one-third the world's production of silver, to be turned into silver coin under the act of 1878; and the accumulation filled the storage space of the treasury building in Washington.[3] Meanwhile, other reforms besides that of the currency were demanding attention.

[1] *House Exec. Docs.*, 47 Cong., 1 Sess., No. 221.
[2] *House Misc. Docs.*, 49 Cong., 1 Sess., No. 396.
[3] Richardson, *Messages and Papers*, VIII., 133.

CHAPTER X

CIVIL SERVICE EVILS
(1877-1880)

PRESIDENT HAYES came into office in 1877 as the avowed champion of civil service reform, because it appealed to his ideals of good government. Elected on a Republican platform which demanded it, he gave first place in his inaugural address to its discussion. His first message contained a declaration of independence against the Senate, asserting the presidential right of appointment as the fundamental law in strict accord with the Constitution. Upon the Senate would devolve the duty of acting as impartial and disinterested judges of the merit of the appointments, while the House as a public censor would be invested with the prerogatives of investigation and prosecution in all cases of dereliction. He also promised that he would endeavor to reduce the number of changes in subordinate places usually made upon a change in the general administration.[1] Considering the attitude of Congress towards Hayes, it is not surprising that his repeated appeal for a revival of the appropriations for the civil service

[1] Richardson, *Messages and Papers*, VII., 466.

commission fell unheeded. The commission, formed under the act of 1871 but practically abolished by the failure of Congress in 1873 to continue appropriations for its support,¹ still had a kind of existence. Competitive examinations continued in some of the departments of the custom-houses with results sufficiently satisfactory to warrant a renewal or adoption of a complete merit-system.²

Unlike Grant,³ Hayes did not await the action of Congress but assumed the initiative in the good work. He indorsed a report of a commission appointed to examine existing conditions in the New York custom-house by saying, boldly: "No officer should be required or permitted to take part in the management of political organizations, caucuses, conventions, or election campaigns. Their right to vote and to express their views on public questions, either orally or through the press, is not denied, provided it does not interfere with the discharge of their official duties. No assessment for political purposes on officers or subordinates should be allowed." These sentiments he framed into an executive order June 22, 1877, announcing that "It should be understood by every officer of the General Government that he is expected to conform his conduct to these requirements." ⁴

[1] Dunning, *Reconstruction* (*Am. Nation*, XXII.), 193.
[2] Lambert, *Progress of Civil Service Reform*, 9.
[3] *North Am. Rev.*, CXXVI., 273.
[4] Richardson, *Messages and Papers*, VII., 450; McPherson, *Hand-Book of Politics*, 1878, p. 54.

Coming within six months after his induction to office, this order of President Hayes scattered consternation among party officials and their adherents, and gave additional excuse to members of Congress for venting the party wrath upon the head of the reforming president. Few believed that the lofty sentiments he had uttered on bettering the service were more than the usual platitudes, intended to catch the popular vote, and no more to be put into effect than the fine words on conciliating the South. Everybody was theoretically in favor of improving the civil service; no one wished to take definite steps. Consequently the order of Hayes was pronounced ill-advised and premature; its demands were said to interfere with the rights of the individual; and its emanation from the executive was declared to be an attempt to force the action of Congress.[1] It was argued that a more effective remedy would be the removal of the incentive to contributions by making the tenure of office more secure; the substitution of merit as the only basis of appointment, and the proof of incompetency or immorality as the only cause for dismissal. These changes should be made not by executive order, but by act of Congress.

Seeking to make good his words by still more definite acts, Hayes turned his attention to the New York City post-office and custom-house, both

[1] Lalor, *Cyclop. of Polit. Science*, I., 155; *Frank Leslie's Newspaper*, XLIV., 318.

of which had long been prime factors in conducting the party machine in that state. The former had already been cleansed by the appointment in 1873 of Thomas L. James, an open advocate of reform in the service, to the postmastership. His policy was given out in the statement that he and his associates could do more for the people of New York City by giving them "a good and efficient postal service than by controlling primaries or dictating nominations."[1] Hayes gave him hearty support and reappointed him to his position. The improved conditions which followed his introduction of the civil service rules into the New York post-office was an argument for extending the reform to the custom-house.

Through the port of New York passed three-fourths of the goods which came into the United States, and even a larger proportion of travellers. The unaccommodating service, which made a return to the United States the bugbear of a trip abroad, was due largely to the shield of political favor and partisan protection held over incompetent and not infrequently dishonest officials. Furthermore, each appointee acted with full knowledge, whatever his fidelity, that his term was measured by the supremacy of his party, or even of the president for the time being. When the Republicans came into national control in 1861, they changed 289 employés out of 690 in one division of the custom-house, and made a total of 1457 removals. The number of changes

[1] Richardson, *Messages and Papers*, VII., 511.

under Johnson and Grant aggregated 1678.[1] For six years prior to 1878, the office was under control of General Arthur, chief lieutenant of Senator Conkling and at the head of the Republican patronage bureau of the state. A commission in 1877, headed by John Jay, a strong civil service reformer of New York, reported gross errors and inefficiency in the custom-house, and called for the discharge of full one-fifth of the employés as an act of economy.

Hayes, with Sherman and other members of the cabinet, considered carefully the report and resolved to get rid of the highest officials for the good of the service. Arthur was opposed to any reforms, and even refused to take advantage of the suggestion made through a friend that he resign.[2] Cornell, the naval officer, was also chairman of the state and national Republican committees. When Hayes suggested that he resign these offices to divorce his position from politics, he also, backed by Conkling, refused to heed the suggestion, as involving a surrender of his personal rights; and Hayes boldly removed both him and Arthur, July 11, 1878.[3] For Arthur's position Hayes nominated James Roosevelt, a New York reformer and public-spirited citizen, but the Senate refused to confirm the appointment. At the subsequent session, Roosevelt being dead, he

[1] Lalor, *Cyclop. of Polit. Science*, III., 568; Fish, in Am. Hist. Assoc., *Annual Report*, 1899, I., 84.
[2] John Sherman, *Recollections*, 673-679; *North Am. Rev.*, CXXVII., 279.
[3] Richardson, *Messages and Papers*, VII., 511.

offered as a substitute E. A. Merritt, long connected with the custom-house, who was accepted by the Senate only after Sherman had appealed personally to many senators and had even threatened to resign his cabinet position.[1]

The removal of Arthur and Cornell was denounced by their friends as an indiscreet, unjust, and unwarranted interference on the part of the executive with New York politics. Hayes was said to have impeached his own declaration in his inaugural address, that an official should be held secure in his office "so long as his personal character remained untarnished and the performance of his duties satisfactory." The reports of the Jay commission and those of special agents were declared to be colored to accord with a preconceived verdict and intended to fill the purpose served by many "investigations" in previous years, which had always been made preceding a sweeping change of officials. Hayes was said to be under the influence of Evarts, Curtis, and other reformers, whose sole purpose was to overthrow Conkling and the "Stalwarts" of New York.

"The removal of Arthur and Cornell may lead to a severer test of the strength of Mr. Hayes's administration than did the removal of the troops from South Carolina and Lousiana," was a prediction freely made.[2] The system was stronger than sectionalism. Arthur defended his administration in

[1] John Sherman, *Recollections*, 681-686.
[2] *Nation*, XXV., 162.

several letters to the public and to Secretary Sherman, by showing that the percentage of removals during his six years of office was less than a thirtieth of the officials employed; while under the three preceding administrations of the custom-house the average had been a fifth.

When the appointment of Arthur's successor, Merritt, was confirmed by the Senate, Hayes wrote him an open letter equivalent to an executive order, February 4, 1879, desiring the office in New York to be conducted on "strict business principles" and "according to the rules of the Civil Service Commission." "Let no man be put out," said he, "merely because he is a friend to Mr. Arthur, and no one put in merely because he is our friend. The good of the service should be the whole end in view."[1] Hayes thus gratified the reformers although alienating himself further from his party by removing from office two of its most prominent members. That the party supported the removed officials rather than the president was manifest soon after, when Cornell was given the nomination for governor of New York, and Arthur that for vice-president of the United States.

Hayes thus dashed any hope he may have entertained of persuading the Republican members of Congress to heed the persistent appeals in his annual messages for a renewal of the appropriation for the civil service commission and the creation of a "merit system" of appointment and promotion. Nor could

[1] Richardson, *Messages and Papers*, VII., 549.

he expect aid from the regular Democrats, who had
no desire to place the Republican office-holders
permanently in place just when indications pointed
to continued Republican dissension and Democratic
victory in the coming presidential election. By his
efforts for reform, Hayes alienated himself still more
from many Republican leaders,[1] and this without
apparent results; but the good work was fairly
inaugurated and under strong leadership.

The civil service reform movement enlisted the
efforts of a number of courageous and persistent
men of public spirit, who risked the ignominy attaching to the word "reformer" for the sake of the
public good. The names of George William Curtis,
Carl Schurz, Andrew D. White,[2] John Jay, and
Dorman B. Eaton are prominent in the list. The
latter was appointed by Hayes to write a history of
the reforms accomplished in the civil service of Great
Britain.[3] Schurz, in the cabinet of Hayes, assisted
in extending the reform in his department. Jay was
appointed by Hayes to investigate conditions in the
New York custom-house, and was afterwards made
a state commissioner of civil service in New York by
Governor Cleveland. In 1877 a civil service reform
association was organized in New York, and was
extended to thirty-two other states. Four years

---

[1] *Cong. Record*, 47 Cong., 2 Sess., 246.
[2] Andrew D. White, *Autobiography*, I., 194–197.
[3] *Harper's Weekly*, XXIV., 2; Eaton, *Civil Service in Great Britain* (1880).

later a national civil service reform league was formed.[1] The propaganda was not allowed to languish: as many as a hundred articles appeared in the periodicals in a single year describing the evils existing in the service. Every prominent removal from office for political purposes was commented upon in the newspapers, where formerly such incidents were taken for granted and ignored.

If additional arguments were needed for a reform in the civil service, the campaign managers of both parties supplied it in 1880. The Republicans held the federal office-holders in their power because Hayes was not a candidate for re-election and officials must look to the next president for their positions after the 4th of March following. Under the pleasing fiction of "voluntary contributions," assessment lists were sent out by the Republican National Committee to all officials except heads of departments, specifying the sum each was expected to contribute—usually five per cent. of his annual salary. State committees in Republican states followed the example, and mulcted state office-holders for contributions to be used towards "the necessary expenses of the presidential campaign." In some instances, lists of federal officials refusing to be amerced, and names of those defaulting payment of instalments which they had promised from their meagre stipends, were mailed to the chiefs of departments for personal intimidation. Many of these

[1] *Harper's Weekly*, XXV., 578.

circulars were signed by T. C. Platt, Republican senator from New York, without his losing standing in public favor by his action.[1] Every contribution made by a subordinate employé of the United States to this fund was a violation of the law of 1876.

The Democratic campaign managers levied upon state officials in states which they controlled, and especially collected funds in New York City, the spoils in that city alone being reckoned at $90,000 to $125,000.[2] Prices were placed upon judgeships, seats in Congress, and aldermanic honors. Levies were made on policemen, firemen, and teachers in the public schools. Aldermen voted extravagant salaries to themselves upon the justification that they were subject to heavy political assessments.

With the growth of manufacturing and other corporate interests, it was inevitable that legislative favors should be desired. Exemption from overtaxation, acquirement of city franchises, rights of way, and prevention of unfavorable legislation brought the corporations into the lobby of Congress, into the state legislatures and the city councils. In return for favors received, the corporations made contributions to campaign funds. As the Republican party gradually assumed the championship of a protective tariff, sound money, and the rights of vested properties, it received larger campaign contributions than were made to the Democratic party, the advocate of low tariff and of silver money. It

[1] Lalor, *Cyclop. of Polit. Science*, I., 153.   [2] *Ibid.*

was foreseen that cutting off assessments from officeholders would result in heavier contributions from corporations; but this evil could be safely left to a later correction.

Conditions were not worse in the campaign of 1880 than in those of preceding presidential campaigns, except for increasing wealth, increasing possibilities of corrupt practices, and increasing boldness in levying upon individuals and corporations. The public was aware of these evils, and tolerated them with an easy patience; it needed a more impressive evidence of the iniquity of political assessments before the cry of the persistent reformers would grow into a national demand. Even when it transpired that Garfield, the Republican candidate in 1880, a man who had been associated in the popular thought with political reforms, was intimately connected with the iniquitous assessment system, the action was condoned by the thought that others were equally guilty of this polite brigandage.

CHAPTER XI

PRESIDENTIAL ELECTION OF 1880
(1880-1881)

THE principle of no third term for a president rests wholly on public sentiment, and is a strong tribute to the power of precedent within the limits of a written constitution. The proposition made in the Constitutional Convention to limit the presidential term to seven years without eligibility for a second election was rejected;[1] and Washington, the first president, was free to serve as many terms as public desire and his own judgment might dictate. "The spirit of the government may render a rotation in the elective officers of it more congenial with the ideas of liberty and safety," [2] he wrote to Madison in 1793, when contemplating retirement at the end of his first term. Having consented to a re-election because of the "perplexed and critical posture of our affairs with foreign nations," he rejoiced four years later that the condition of the republic no longer rendered "the pursuit of inclination incompatible

---

[1] McLaughlin, *Confederation and Constitution* (*Am. Nation*, X.), 267.   [2] Washington, *Writings* (Sparks's ed.), XII., 383.

with the sentiment of duty or propriety."[1] By declining a third term, Washington established a precedent resting entirely on the inclination of the incumbent.

President Jefferson first called public attention in 1807 to the danger lest, "if some termination to the services of the chief magistrate be not fixed by the Constitution or supplied by practice, this office, nominally for years, will in fact become for life; and history shows how easily that degenerates into an inheritance."[2] His determination to avoid this menace and to observe the "sound precedent of an illustrious predecessor" was praised in press and public meetings; rotation in office was declared to be the bulwark of freedom. No president between Jefferson and Jackson was sufficiently popular to put to the test this principle of "the unwritten Constitution," and Jackson had so persistently advocated in his messages to Congress the adoption of an amendment prohibiting a second term[3] that he could not think of accepting a third without stultifying himself. Later presidents made similar suggestions, and scarcely a session of Congress passed during many years without some proposition being introduced looking to a limitation of the presidential self-succession. Six presidents, from Jackson to

[1] Washington, *Writings* (Sparks's ed.), XII., 215.
[2] Jefferson, *Works*, V., 89.
[3] Ames, *Proposed Amendments to the Const. of the U. S.*, 90 et seq.

Lincoln, served but one term each; Lincoln was the first in twenty-five years to be elected for a second term.

The Republican organization, founded on northern participation and southern exclusion during the Civil War and Reconstruction, secured a second term for Grant, but could not prevent a revival of the old third-term fear as his second drew to a close. The cry of "Cæsarism" was raised soon after Grant's second election and continued until "no third term" became a shibboleth.[1] Consequently, Grant's name was not presented to the Republican convention of 1876.[2]

In May, 1877, ex-President Grant sailed from New York on a tour of the world, and returned three years later to be greeted with an outburst of popular enthusiasm which certain of his former leaders took to be a desire to have him return to the presidential chair, to resume the era of "strong" government.[3] The growing Democratic home rule in the southern states, the narrow escape from a Democratic president in 1876, the loss of both houses of Congress—all these apparently could be traced to the pacific policy of a "weak president." To save the day, Conkling brought New York into line for another term for Grant, Logan did the same for Illinois, Cameron

[1] McMaster, *With the Fathers*, 67; *House Journal*, 44 Cong., 1 Sess., 66; *Nation*, XXI., 393; XXII., 108; *Frank Leslie's Newspaper*, XLI., 265; cf. Dunning, *Reconstruction* (*Am. Nation*, XXII.), 299.   [2] Stanwood, *Hist. of the Presidency*, 368.
[3] *Nation*, XXIX., 236.

attended to Pennsylvania, and several minor states followed these leaders. Other names likely to come prominently before the Republican convention of 1880 were those of Senator Blaine, of Maine; John Sherman, of Ohio, secretary of the treasury; and Senator Edmunds, of Vermont.[1]

Many persons who had in 1876 opposed giving Grant a third term, in 1880 supported him on the ground that the precedent was against a third consecutive term, and that the four years which had elapsed since Grant left office removed this disability. The argument was plausible, but was declared by others to be against the spirit, if not the principle, of the "national habit." Grant's nomination, it was said, would revive the scandals of his administration, would therefore be detrimental to the party interests, and was likely to cost the Republicans the election. The alarming cries of four years before were revived; Cæsar, Cromwell, and Napoleon were instanced as examples of civic menace in a military hero. The self-denial of Washington, it was said, followed by that of Grant, would free America forever from the spectre of militarism. "No Third Term" leagues were formed, and "Young Scratchers" clubs were urged.[2] An "Anti-Third Term" convention was held in St. Louis in May, 1880, at which fourteen states were represented.[3] A majority of the Repub-

---

[1] *Nation*, XXX., 430; John Sherman, *Recollections*, 766.
[2] *North Am. Rev.*, CXXX., 197–236, 370, 417; *Nation*, XXX., 188.
[3] *Ibid.*, 362.

lican newspapers, judging from their editorials, were opposed to the experiment of a third term.

Grant's consent to be a candidate was afterwards explained in several ways by his friends. They pictured him chafing under the restraint of retirement after an active military life; and described his eagerness to return to America and get into military action, when he heard in England of the disorders growing out of the railway strike of 1877. Others suggested that Grant, in addition to his experience as a soldier, thought himself better prepared for national administration after the civic studies he had made during his extensive travels. The charitably inclined placed the responsibility on his friends and on the constant pressure from his family, eager to regain the social position they once enjoyed in the White House.[1]

The Republican convention assembled at Chicago, June 2, 1880. Conkling, lord of the day and chief promoter for Grant, lost his first battle when the convention agreed that after roll-call by states any member could demand an individual poll of delegates of his state, and that a divided delegation should be so recorded. This broke the attempt to introduce the Democratic custom of a "unit rule," under which the largest states would be held to Grant, according to their instructions.[2] On the first ballot, Grant secured only 304 votes, and never rose above 312 on

[1] Badeau, *Grant in Peace*, 319, 322.
[2] Becker, "Unit Rule in National Nominating Conventions," in *Am. Hist. Rev.*, V., 77–79.

subsequent ballots. Since 379 were required for a choice, there was evidently to be no third term for a president, even if it was not sequential.

In all the proceedings thus far General James A. Garfield, of Ohio, had been conspicuous. Rising from a birth sufficiently humble to win for him the fetching sobriquet of "canal-boat boy," resigning from the military service with the rank of major-general at thirty-two years of age to enter a congressional career, serving the famous "Western Reserve" of Ohio for many consecutive terms, candidate of the Republican minority for speaker, member of the electoral commission, senator-elect from Ohio, Garfield became by common consent the leader of those who opposed Grant and a third term. As chairman of the committee on rules in the Chicago convention, he reported the anti-unit rule, intended to destroy that throttling-machine which had been rejected by the Republican convention four years before and which now reappeared as the agency of Conkling and his associates. In a speech, which was the feature of the first few days of the convention, Garfield begged Conkling to withdraw a resolution that delegates who refused to be bound by the majority vote thereby forfeited their seats in the convention. Conkling somehow realized that the day for this high-handed manner of enforcing party discipline was past, and withdrew his motion.[1]

[1] Stanwood, *Hist. of the Presidency*, 403; Conkling, *Roscoe Conkling*, 593; *Chicago Tribune*, June 8, 1880; *Nation*, XXX., 449.

Although Garfield supported Sherman, of his own state, and refused to listen to Conkling's suggestion that he might be a "dark horse," he considered the candidate as a secondary matter compared with defeating Grant and a third-term movement.[1] For more than thirty ballots the convention sat in deadlock, 306 of Grant's delegates holding steadily together, and the other delegates scattering their votes. Conkling supposed that he could deliver the entire New York delegation to Grant; but nineteen of the delegates, headed by William H. Robertson, went over to Blaine. This gave to the man from Maine 284 votes on the first ballot, a number he could not increase on any subsequent ballot. Sherman reached his greatest strength, 119 votes, on the thirty-third ballot, being betrayed, as he believed, by Governor Foster's leaning towards Blaine.[2] On the thirty-fourth ballot, Wisconsin brought out the proverbial "dark horse" by going over bodily from Washburne to Garfield, who had received an occasional vote during the two days of balloting. Two ballots later the Blaine and Sherman delegations shifted to Garfield and secured his nomination.[3] As a solace to Conkling and the Grant supporters, they were allowed to name the candidate for second place. Seeking a vindication of Chester A. Arthur from the

[1] Brown, *Garfield*, 188.
[2] John Sherman, *Recollections*, 776–778.
[3] See tables in *Appleton's Annual Cyclop.*, 1880, p. 696, and McPherson, *Hand-Book of Politics*, 1880, p. 191.

shadow cast on his official life by his removal from the New York custom-house by President Hayes,[1] they nominated him.

The nomination of Garfield and Arthur closed most happily for the Republican party a difference which at one time threatened to become a breach. Garfield was an unexpected, but neither an unwelcome nor a forced candidate. Arthur had a large acquaintance from his service as quartermaster-general of New York during the Civil War, and in the New York custom-house; although his nomination was most objectionable to the reformers because he bore the reputation of being a "good fellow" and a spoilsman. However, they were willing to accept him in the second place because they had high hopes of Garfield in the appointing position.[2] With the two pivotal states of Ohio and New York represented on their ticket, the Republicans confidently awaited the nominations of the other parties.

The "Greenback" party met at Chicago, June 9, and nominated Weaver, of Iowa, and Chambers, of Texas, on a platform demanding that all money should be issued directly by the United States and not through banks; that legal-tender currency should be substituted for bank-notes; and that an unlimited coinage of silver as well as gold should be established by law. It also declaimed against con-

---

[1] See above, p. 159; John Sherman, *Recollections*, 886.
[2] Stanwood, *Hist. of the Presidency*, 407–409; *Harper's Weekly*, XXIV., 394.

vict labor, child labor, and the presence of "Chinese serfs . . . to brutalize and degrade American labor." A fortnight later, the Prohibitionists at Cleveland, on a platform setting forth their well-known principles, nominated Neal Dow, the temperance advocate of Maine, and Thompson, of Ohio.[1]

The Democrats assembled at Cincinnati, June 22, with a multitude of presidential possibilities and no predominating favorite. John Kelly, boss of New York City, had served notice that Tammany would not support Tilden again. Drawn out by a suggestion that he be given a vindication, that statesman wrote a public letter which was understood to be a declination; his health was known to be that of a valetudinarian. Nevertheless, a few of the faithful cast their votes for him because they thought a failure to renominate him equivalent to a withdrawal of the charge of fraud in the preceding election. It was also pointed out that Garfield, the Republican nominee, had been a member of the electoral commission, and his election would be a practical indorsement of that partisan decision. That the party had no factions was shown in the first ballot, when nearly twenty names received votes, among them being Bayard, of Delaware, Field, of California, Morrison, of Illinois, and Hendricks, of Indiana. On the second day's balloting Wisconsin bolted to General Hancock, and it resulted in his nomination.[2] For

---

[1] Stanwood, *Hist. of the Presidency*, 409-411.
[2] *Ibid.*, 411-415; *Harper's Weekly*, XXIV., 434.

vice-president, the nomination was given to William H. English of Indiana, who had served eight years in Congress during the Kansas controversy and had long been a Democratic leader in Indiana.

Hancock's appearance and bearing won for him the title, "Hancock, the Superb." Of an illustrious Pennsylvania family, he had served with distinction in the Mexican and in the Civil War. Modest but aggressive, courageous, genial, and dignified, he was an ideal standard-bearer. At first blush it would seem that a northern or "war" Democrat, one who had fought under a Republican president for the preservation of the Union, would not be acceptable to the southern voters; but they had a regard for a chivalric gentleman like Hancock, with lofty ideals and a clean record. He had endeared himself to them by his official conduct while in command of the "district" of Louisiana and Texas in 1867, under the congressional reconstruction acts, when he declared that "the great principles of American liberty still are the lawful inheritance of this people and ever should be."[1] Later he issued the famous "General Order No. 40," restoring civil justice to the regular courts and declaring that arbitrary power had no existence in the laws of Louisiana or Texas and could not be derived from acts of Congress.[2]

[1] Cf. Dunning, *Reconstruction* (*Am. Nation*, XXII.), chaps. vii., xi.
[2] Cox, *Three Decades*, 547; *Harper's Weekly*, XXIV., 437 (July 10, 1880).

He was so manifestly opposed to Republican methods of reconstruction that he was soon transferred to other duty; but he had won and carried with him the esteem of the Southern people.

During the campaign, the cool reception given campaign orators when attempting to revive sectionalism by waving the "bloody shirt," showed that the old animosity could no longer be made to serve the purpose of an issue. The speakers had to content themselves with attacks upon the "solid South," claiming that it dominated the Democratic national convention; they begged northern Democrats to "vote as they shot;" and argued that the party which saved the Union should continue to be intrusted with its care. They also laid special stress upon the protective tariff and national banks, describing the Democrats as playing into the hands of British traders and state repudiators. "A vote for the Republican ticket is a vote for protection to American industry and for good wages," was a war-cry destined to be heard in many subsequent campaigns. Hancock's record was beyond attack, but his unfamiliarity with public life and his unfitness for the high office were said to be shown by slips in the few speeches he made. For instance, he referred to the tariff as a "local issue," and one with which President Grant rarely cared to interfere.[1] The last breach in the Republican party was healed during the campaign, when Grant, the rival of Garfield in

[1] Stanwood, *Hist. o, the Presidency*, 415-418.

the convention, and Conkling, his manager, took the stump for the party candidate.¹

During the earlier part of the canvass, the Democrats tried to make an issue of Republican fraud in the campaign of 1876, but it smacked too much of the old sectionalism to make headway. Then they turned the campaign, most unfortunately and unwisely, into a series of personal attacks on Garfield. He had been a member of Congress in its most questionable days following the Civil War, when army contracts reduced the official conscience to its most vendible level. In 1875, before a congressional investigating committee, Oakes Ames, of Crédit Mobilier fame, testified that Representative Garfield, of Ohio, owned stock in that unsavory enterprise to the amount of one thousand dollars, on which he had been paid three hundred and twenty-nine dollars as a dividend. Garfield acknowledged having "borrowed" three hundred dollars from Ames in 1868 as a loan which he repaid soon after.² Another investigating committee in the same Congress found that Garfield had received five thousand dollars as attorney's fee during the paving-contract scandals of De Golyer, which had disgraced the city of Washington a few years before.³ The "Morey" letter was also sent out in facsimile, as described hereafter,⁴ to

---

¹ *Nation*, XXXI., 297 (October 28, 1880).
² *House Reports*, 42 Cong., 3 Sess., No. 77; Fuller, *Reminiscences of Garfield*, chap. xlvii.; *Nation*, XXX., 467; Dunning, *Reconstruction* (*Am. Nation*, XXII.), 232.
³ *Nation*, XXXI., 5.   ⁴ See below, p. 244.

prove that Garfield favored the admission of Chinese labor to California.¹ As usual, such tactics injured the accusers more than those whom they accused.

Thirty-eight states took part in the election, and proved to be evenly divided between the two parties; but the Republicans, as usual, carried the more populous northern states and secured a preponderance in the electoral college. Of a total of near ten million popular votes, the Republicans exceeded the Democrats by less than ten thousand—an ominous prophecy of the next election; but of the electoral votes, the Republicans had 214 against 155 gained by their opponents. The sectional alignment of states was significant. In any system of free government, the choice of a chief executive should be uninfluenced by sectionalism or anything which interferes with the consideration of the best man for the place. In the election of 1880, Garfield carried every state north of the old dividing line between slavery and freedom, with the exception of New Jersey; and not a state south of that line. In the extreme West he lost Nevada and five electors in California owing to the effect of the "Morey" letter. Opposed to this solid block of northern states carried by the Republicans was the Democratic "solid South." This was the heritage of civil war and reconstruction.²

Ten of these Democratic southern states were

[1] *Harper's Weekly*, XXIV., 722, 770; cf. Dunning, *Reconstruction* (*Am. Nation*, XXII.), chap. ix.
[2] Stanwood, *Hist. of the Presidency*, 417.

carried by the Republicans eight years before and three of them four years before.¹ Their loss was attributed by the Republicans to intimidation of colored voters and withdrawal of the federal troops; the Democrats attributed their gain to the restoration of franchise privileges to the whites, and to the indifference of the negroes, as well as the transfer of their allegiance from the Republican to the Democratic party after the forced abdication of the carpetbagger and the Freedmen's Bureau agents.

Many Republicans ascribed the existence of the "solid South" to the "milk-and-water" policy of Hayes, whose single term was now drawing to a close. He had announced in his speech of acceptance his "inflexible purpose, if elected, not to be a candidate for election to a second term." ² Few presidents had less prospect of being called at the end to serve a second term, although he left the party in as good if not a better condition than he found it. It regained, in the Congressional elections of 1880, the control of the House, which it had lost under Grant in 1875.

Coming into office at the dawn of the period of reform, Hayes failed to appreciate its meaning, or to respond to its demands. He lacked the domineering personality of the aggressive reformer, and did not possess the magnetism to attract a faithful band

---

[1] Stanwood, *Hist. of the Presidency*, 352, 383; *North Am. Rev.*, CXXXVIII., 47.
[2] McPherson, *Hand-Book of Politics*, 1876, p. 212.

of militant followers. He was in advance of his time in pleas for national pacification, and was met by sectional debates which retold old wrongs and revived old charges. A sincere churchman and the possessor of a live conscience, he could not bring his conscientious principles into every-day play on his fellows. To them he was simply a "goody-goody." He represented the old school of gentlemanly statesmanship, when the times were beginning to demand originality and aggressiveness. In his party relations he was a sacrifice to his advanced position; in his public relations he could not overcome worn-out traditions. During his four years, payment in specie replaced paper promises to pay; more than two hundred millions of the national debt was discharged; and over a thousand millions of the remainder was refunded at a lower rate of interest. By these achievements, by the progress made towards pacification, and by the industrial prosperity of the country, the administration of Hayes is to be measured, and not by personal popularity or by the worship of a party.[1]

Many of the excellent qualities shown by Hayes were shared by the woman who, beyond question, added to his limited popularity. Writers of the day compared her with Mrs. Fillmore as a model of domestic virtue and simplicity in a public station. They praised her for eliminating from Washington society the snobbishness which had grown up with

[1] *Harper's Weekly*, XXV., 162.

the accumulation of fortunes during the war. Army contractors flourished their often ill-gotten wealth, and "dirty politics" sullied the White House threshold until banished by the candor and simplicity of Mrs. Hayes. It is true that some of her reforms were injudiciously severe: in opposing the serving of wines at official dinners; she highly offended Secretary Evarts; with the result that the annual dinner to the diplomatic corps was omitted. However, for her stand in this matter, the "temperance women of the world" placed a portrait of Mrs. Hayes in the White House. Funds for the purpose were secured by giving "Lucy Hayes Tea-Parties" in various places, thus adding to the popularity of the first lady of the land. Her last Saturday reception was attended, according to newspaper reports, by no less than four thousand persons, while half as many more had been unable to gain admission when the doors were closed at the end of the hours assigned.[1]

The incoming Garfield family was praised as highly and its virtues extolled as widely as those of the outgoing Hayes family; and public interest was on the *qui vive* as the day of inauguration approached. The night of the 3d of March, 1881, saw the city of Washington buried beneath a blanket of wet snow which soon became slush, conditions not infrequent at that season of the year. All during the night could be heard the sound of martial

[1] *Independent*, March 10, 1881.

music as troops arrived to take part in the ceremonies.[1]

Notwithstanding the unfavorable weather, popular good-will was everywhere manifest. When the grudging sun at last came forth the following morning, nothing seemed wanting to make the occasion a complete success. In the rejoicing many were willing to grant that Hayes's pacification policy was justified by the manifest decrease of sectional animosity; that the reception recently accorded to a regiment of New York militia on a visit to New Orleans was sufficient evidence that the new era was really at hand.[2]

Regardless of party, the nation felt a sense of relief that the crisis of a presidential election was passed without a repetition of the uncertainty of four years before. The sentiment which attended the unexpected nomination of Garfield, which created a halo about the "canal-boat boy" in the campaign, was renewed at the inauguration when, after taking the oath of office, he turned to kiss his mother. The action was attributed to filial devotion and not to a striving after effect.[1] No administration was begun under more favorable conditions.

[1] *Harper's Weekly*, XXV., 180.
[2] *Frank Leslie's Newspaper*, LII., 61; Brown, *Garfield*, chap. xxvii.

CHAPTER XII

CIVIL SERVICE REFORM
(1881-1884)

GARFIELD was a party man, but, unlike Hayes, was unable and unwilling to rise above the party, and, consequently, was subject to all its vicissitudes. In its national aspect the Republican party was harmonious; but, as usual, New York had its factions. Senator Conkling headed the Stalwarts, or "machine" element, to which belonged vice-president-elect Arthur, Senator Platt, and Postmaster James. Opposed were the Half-Breeds, or "anti-machine" men, headed by Warner Miller. Before he left his home near Cleveland, Garfield sent for Conkling, apparently as the chieftain of the Stalwarts, to discuss the make-up of his cabinet. Conkling was willing to accept the selection of James as postmaster-general, although James advocated reforms in the civil service which Conkling opposed and despised; but he thought the post no sufficient recognition for the great state of which he was the political owner, and the interview, which caused much speculation at the time, terminated unsatisfactorily.[1]

[1] Conkling, *Roscoe Conkling*, 634.

According to a story then current,[1] Conkling again called on the president-elect soon after his arrival in Washington to demand the treasury portfolio for some New-Yorker. Garfield sat meekly on the bed in his hotel-room while Conkling vented upon him the vials of his wrath, his sarcasm, and his vituperation, under the approving glances of vice-president-elect Arthur and Senator Platt, who accompanied the irate Conkling on his call. The demand passed unheeded, and, after due consideration, Garfield selected for secretary of state, James G. Blaine, of Maine; secretary of the treasury, William Windom, of Minnesota; attorney-general, Wayne MacVeagh, of Pennsylvania; postmaster-general, Thomas L. James, of New York; secretary of the interior, Samuel J. Kirkwood, of Iowa; secretary of war, Robert T. Lincoln, of Illinois; secretary of the navy, William H. Hunt, of Louisiana.[2]

Levi P. Morton, of New York, received the important post of minister to France. With the appointment of James and Morton, Conkling might have been satisfied had not the first place in Garfield's cabinet been given to his dearest enemy, Blaine. Individual ambition and mutual jealousy were the fundamental causes of the enmity between the two; although Blaine had once contemptuously alluded to the New York senator as a "turkey cock." In a

[1] Andrews, *Last Quarter-Century*, I., 323.
[2] Mosher, *Exec. Register of U. S.*, 235, 236; *Harper's Weekly*, XXV., 194.

letter given out at a later time, Blaine stated his reasons for accepting a place in Garfield's cabinet to be the "shower of letters" he had received urging him thereto; the eighteen years of intimacy between Garfield and himself; and the belief that he could make himself useful to the country, the party, and to the president. Nothing but the inordinate conceit of Blaine, which was his master weakness, could have persuaded him to say that next to Garfield himself, he (Blaine) could make his administration eminently successful, judging from "the political forces which have been at work in the country for the past five years and which have been significantly shown in two great national conventions." [1]

The Senate was called in executive session March 4, 1881, to consider the presidential appointments. The terms of twenty-five senators had expired with the preceding session, and in filling their places the Democrats lost five, so that there were now 37 Republicans, 37 Democrats, and 2 Independents in that body. Blaine had been notified, it is said, that Conkling would ruin the administration if Garfield admitted Blaine to the cabinet. He persuaded Garfield to throw down the gauntlet to the New York dictator by sending the list of nominees to the Senate without consulting either of the New York senators. Among the appointments was that of Robertson, Conkling's sworn enemy, for the desirable collectorship of the New York custom-house. The battle was on.

[1] *Appleton's Annual Cyclop.*, 1881, p. 845.

In vain a number of Republicans, known as the "committee on conciliation," tried to avert the war between the administration supported by the Half-Breeds, and Conkling aided by the Stalwarts.[1] Party harmony went to the winds. In an endeavor to discredit Garfield and make him "bite the dust," Conkling gave out a letter written by Garfield during the campaign, virtually attempting to mulct government employés for campaign expenses.[2] It was simply additional light on a discreditable practice, went far towards bringing on the reform which Conkling opposed, and fell far short of the desired effect.

Meanwhile the attempt to organize the Senate resulted in a deadlock, the two Independents, Davis, of Illinois, and Mahone, of Virginia, taking no part. At the end of two months a truce was declared in order to consider the nominations sent in by the president. It was presumed that Conkling would allow the appointments he favored to be acted upon and then secure an adjournment of the Senate. To prevent this *coup*, Garfield withdrew all the New York appointments except that of Robertson. Finding himself powerless to prevent Robertson's confirmation, Conkling petulantly resigned his senatorship and sent a letter of explanation to the governor of New York.[3] His fellow-senator, Platt, joined him

[1] Andrews, *Last Quarter-Century*, I., 324.
[2] *Nation*, XXXII., 216, 344 (March 31, May 19, 1881).
[3] For the letter, see Conkling, *Roscoe Conkling*, 638; *Appleton's Annual Cyclop.*, 1881, pp. 644–646; *Nation*, XXXII., 341–345; *Harper's Weekly*, XXV., 368, 390.

in this trial of strength with the administration, thereby gaining from the cartoonists of the day the sobriquet of "Me Too." The two attacked Garfield because he had taken a high stand in his inaugural address for eliminating the spoils system, and had immediately removed the collector of New York to make room for Robertson as "a reward for his action as delegate to the national convention." Considering the senatorial right to "advise" as equally important with the executive power to "appoint" to office, they protested against the executive assumption of appointing without consulting. After the retirement of the New York senators, the Senate ratified the appointment of Robertson and adjourned, May 24.

With the eyes of the nation upon them, Conkling and Platt returned to New York, where the assembly was in session. They demanded re-election as vindication of their stand, and balloting was at once begun. "New York abounds in sons quite as able as we," they had said in their resignation manifesto, and the assembly showed a disposition to accept the proposition. On the first ballot, the names of the recalcitrant senators led, but they could not rally a sufficient number of votes to make a majority. After fifty-six ballots had been cast, Warner Miller and E. G. Lapham were elected to fill the vacancies.[1] Conkling felt keenly his fall from power and the results of his ill-judged action: he never

[1] *Appleton's Annual Cyclop.*, 1881, pp. 646–650.

reappeared in national politics; and Platt, who was also under the cloud of a personal scandal, retired from politics for several years. No senator has since tested his strength with an administration by the hazardous method of vindication.

With Conkling defeated and out of the way, with Blaine entering upon his active foreign policy, and with the national spirit aroused by the preparations for the Centennial celebration of the British surrender at Yorktown, Garfield's good-fortune seemed secure; but he had yet to reckon with an evil spirit which he himself had helped conjure up to aid in his campaign.

The inauguration of Garfield was attended by no reversal of political parties which would warrant a general proscription of office-holders. No charge of hostility could be made against the Hayes holdovers, since Hayes was not a candidate for re-election. Yet the thirst for office carried the expectations and demands for reward quite beyond the criterion of party; every active worker for Garfield in the campaign seemed to think himself entitled to an office. It was estimated that one-third the working time of the president was absorbed by applicants for office and that six-sevenths of his callers came upon the same errand. Candidates waylaid him when he ventured from the shelter of his official residence, and followed him even to the doors of the church where he worshipped. Contributors to the campaign fund, who sought a return, crowded his waiting-room and dogged his footsteps.¹ His service in the army and in Congress had made for him a wide acquaintance which now became a misfortune. If he had erred in adopting machine methods in the campaign, he must pay the penalty. During his four months' term of office he made 390 appointments, of which 89, or nearly a fourth, were to replace removals; Hayes, in his entire first year, made only 74 removals, or less than a tenth of his appointments.²

Additional evidence of the conditions existing in Washington and the need of reform was furnished by Thomas W. Brady, second assistant postmaster-general, who actually threatened President Garfield with exposure of his campaign methods if he did not call off a pending investigation into Brady's conduct in office. Brady was a hold-over from Grant's administration, in charge of the "star" routes, or those on which the mails were carried by private contract, the contracts bearing three groups of stars to signify special conditions of celerity, certainty, and security, under which the mails were to be transported. Rumors of corruption and fraud in this branch of the mail service had long been current; but neither Hayes nor his postmaster-general had courageously investigated them.

When James, the reformer, became postmaster-general, he declared that he would do "his whole

[1] Brown, *Garfield*, 211; *Harper's Weekly*, XXV., 246.
[2] Richardson, *Messages and Papers*, VIII., 147.

duty" in the investigation of these rumors. "It is a hard task," said he, "but it shall be pushed fearlessly, regardless of whom it may strike."[1] The words deserve to be handed down with those of President Grant, who said, in connection with the whiskey-ring scandals, "Let no guilty man escape." It was found that Brady, with various treasury and other clerks essential to the plan, had conspired with Senator Dorsey, of Arkansas, and other contractors, to increase the compensation on many of the two thousand star routes, dividing the profits among themselves. In the competitive bidding they secured one hundred and thirty-four routes, for which they were entitled to receive $143,169; but this sum they raised by supplementary agreements for "increase and expenditure" to $622,808. To cover their tracks, the conspirators devised hundreds of petitions for the extension of new star routes. One of these added routes ran through a thinly populated region of Dakota and cost the United States $6133.50 for service during one year, when the receipts were only $240.[2]

True to his threat, Brady published a letter from Garfield to "My dear Hubbell," who as chairman of the Republican congressional committee in 1880 levied the two per cent. "voluntary contribution" on the government clerks. The letter was similar to that given out by Conkling earlier in the spring. It expressed the hope that Brady would give them

[1] Andrews, *Last Quarter-Century*, I., 340.
[2] *Appleton's Annual Cyclop.*, 1882, p. 753.

all the assistance possible and inquired how the departments generally were doing.¹ It could be interpreted in no other way than as extorting a contribution from government employés. Sherman had warned Garfield at the beginning of the campaign that the public sentiment in favor of reform in the civil service could not be ignored, although politicians attempted to ridicule and belittle Hayes's efforts in that direction.²

The disgust of the people was increased by the events of the Brady and Dorsey "trial." Political influence was manifest at every turn, every obstacle known to astute political minds was cast in the way of the prosecution, and statements were openly made that no jury could be found in the city of Washington to convict these high and influential men. Partisan newspapers were persistent in minimizing the offence and in applying the party whitewash. On the other side, charges of jury-bribing were investigated and the foreman indicted; and five government employés, including the marshal of the District of Columbia, were dismissed from office for meddling in the case. Making use of technicalities and the law's delay, all the accused eventually escaped punishment except one small offender who was probably the least guilty.³

¹ *Nation*, XXXII., 325.
² See Sherman's letter to Garfield, in John Sherman, *Recollections*, 779.
³ *Appleton's Annual Cyclop.*, 1883, pp. 163, 177; *Nation*, XXIX.-XXXVII., passim; Andrews, *Last Quarter-Century*, I., 336-341.

In the midst of these exposures, with the clamor for office filling his ears, and with the party leaders in New York contending for supremacy, President Garfield was assassinated under conditions which pointed directly to the spoils system as the cause. Accompanied by Secretary Blaine, he planned to leave Washington on a visit to his *alma mater*, Williams College, July 2, 1881. As the two entered the Pennsylvania Railroad station in that city, one Charles J. Guiteau fired two bullets into the president's back. The wounded man slowly succumbed and passed away September 19.[1] For the second time within two decades the people of the United States faced the unwelcome fact that even a free government is no warrant against fanaticism and assassination. The shock was doubly severe because of the recent murder of the czar of Russia, which had brought an expression of thankfulness from the American people that they dwelled in a land of prosperity and content.[2]

The oath of office was taken by Vice-President Arthur at his home in New York, September 20, and repeated a few days later in Washington. "Men may die," said the new incumbent on the latter occasion, "but the fabrics of our free institutions remain unshaken."[3] Garfield's murderer in public

---

[1] Richardson, *Messages and Papers*, VIII., 14, 18, 20, 25; Andrews, *Last Quarter-Century*, I., 329-333; *Harper's Weekly*, XXV., 482.

[2] *Senate Exec. Docs.*, 46 Cong., 3 Sess., No. 2; *Harper's Weekly*, XXV., 197, 210, 226.

[3] Richardson, *Messages and Papers*, VIII., 33.

statements declared that he "removed" the president as a "political necessity," because party dissensions demanded it. He had been by turns preacher, editor, reformer, and politician, had allied himself with the Republican campaign managers, and had been a persistent office-seeker since the inauguration. "Mr. Conkling resigned," said he, "on Monday, May 16, 1881. . . . I was thinking over the political situation, and the idea flashed through my brain that if the president was out of the way everything would go better. . . . As the result of reading the newspapers the idea settled on me that if the president were removed it would unite the two factions of the Republican party and thereby save the government from going into the hands of ex-rebels and their Northern allies." Guiteau was arraigned in the courts of the District of Columbia, pleaded not guilty, was pronounced sane by medical experts,[1] found guilty, and was executed in Washington, June 30, 1882, lacking two days of a year from the date on which the crime was committed.[2]

The prolonged illness of President Garfield raised for the first time the question to what degree the disability of the president must extend before the vice-president may assume his duties. Whether mental incapacity constitutes disability, how long the impairment must continue before the office de-

[1] "Insanity as a Defence for Crime," *Appleton's Annual Cyclop.*, 1881, p. 429; Brown, *Garfield*, chaps. xxviii.–xliv.
[2] *Appleton's Annual Cyclop.*, 1881, p. 381; 1882, p. 809.

volves on the vice-president, whether the consent of the president is essential, whether, in case the incapacity prove temporary and the president recover, each man resumes his former station, or whether the vice-president is entitled to serve out the four years' term—these points gave rise to many and learned discussions in the press of the day. It was generally agreed that in case of physical disability the president might decide whether to continue in office, and in case of mental incapacity the question might properly be left to a judicial tribunal. As to whether the vice-president really became president or simply acted as president, and whether inability and disability were synonymous terms, a variety of opinion was found. No official action was taken, and the matter remained to be tested in some future emergency.[1]

Conditions existing at the time of Garfield's assassination called attention not only to the evils of the demand for office, but also to the necessity of providing a more dependable succession for the presidency. If some assassin had removed Arthur during the first months of his administration, the United States would have been without a legal head. The Constitution leaves Congress to arrange a sequence beyond the vice-president; by act of 1792 [2] it was provided that the president *pro tem* of the Senate and the speaker of the House of Representa-

[1] Richardson, *Messages and Papers*, VIII., 65; "Inability or Disability," *Appleton's Annual Cyclop.*, 1881, p. 414; *Harper's Weekly*, XXV., 583. [2] *U. S. Statutes at Large*, I., 239.

tives should follow the vice-president in order; and this was deemed sufficient. But the special session of the Senate of 1881 failed to choose a temporary presiding officer, owing to the political deadlock,[1] and the House had no speaker because the forty-sixth Congress adjourned March 3, 1881, and the next Congress would not assemble until the following December. Although the hazard of the situation at this time was admitted, nothing was done until the "presidential succession" act of 1886,[2] which provided a further succession of members of the cabinet in order, beginning with the secretary of state.

Against the murder of a president no certain remedy could be provided; even a motive was difficult to find. "Southern conspiracy" had to serve in the case of Booth, and the "spoils system" for the act of Guiteau.[3] If the death of Lincoln brought healing results which the most pacific policy he could have adopted might have failed to secure, the death of Garfield was followed by reforms in the civil service which would probably not have been gained during his administration. The commission appointed by Grant in 1871[4] had long been dormant. A bill to regulate the service directly instead of intrusting the reform to commissioners was introduced into Congress in 1880 and reappeared in suc-

[1] See above, p. 185.
[2] *U. S. Statutes at Large*, XXIV., 1; Dougherty, *Electoral System of U. S.*, 264, 265.
[3] John Sherman, *Recollections*, 817.
[4] See Dunning, *Reconstruction* (*Am. Nation*, XXII.), 193.

cessive sessions. It secured a favorable report in 1882 from the Senate committee on civil service,[1] the chairman of which was George H. Pendleton, a Democratic senator from Ohio. The report described the executive mansion as besieged if not sacked by applicants for office, its corridors and chambers crowded each day with the ever-changing but never-ending throng. It went so far as to say that "more than one president is believed to have lost his life from this cause."

The bill indorsed by this report was drawn by the civil service reform league, which, since the failure of the law of 1871, had been active in attempting to arouse public sentiment to demand a new and more effective law. Few proposals were subjected to more bitter attacks. Placemen, senators, party lieutenants, and other spoilsmen went as far as their fear of public wrath permitted. Its supporters were described as "holier than thous," as "goody-goodies," and its *raison d'être* was attributed to a maudlin sentiment. Many Democrats joined in the abuse, derisively nicknaming it "snivel service," and giving to Pendleton the sobriquet of "Gentleman George." They feared lest their opponents be placed irrevocably in office if the measure became a law, and all incentive to recovering national control would be lost to them.[2]

[1] *Senate Reports*, 46 Cong., 3 Sess., No. 872.
[2] *Cong. Record*, 47 Cong., 2 Sess., 247, 357-360, 463; *North Am. Rev.*, CXXXIII., 379.

While the proposition to reform the civil service was before the people, the congressional campaign of 1882 came on and demonstrated anew the need of some check upon political assessments. The Republican congressional committee, through its chairman, a congressman from Michigan, the "My dear Hubbell" of the Garfield letters,[1] mailed a circular, May 15, 1882, to each federal employé, stating the precise sum it was expected the incumbent would "esteem it both a privilege and a favor" to contribute. At the head of the letter appeared the names of the committee, including Senators Allison, Hale, and Aldrich, and it stated that they were "authorized" to say that such voluntary contributions from persons employed in the service of the United States "would not be objected to in any official quarter." Not satisfied with the amount of tribute received, the committee sent out a second circular in August, suggesting two per cent. of the annual compensation of each official as a suitable offering for "those most directly benefited by success."[2]

None were spared; government clerks, scrubwomen, enlisted men in the army, common laborers on works of public improvement, pages in Congress, janitors in public buildings—all were levied on to meet campaign expenses.[3] The only excuse made

[1] See above, p. 189.
[2] "Political Assessments," in *Appleton's Annual Cyclop.*, 1882, p. 693.
[3] *North Am. Rev.*, CXXXVI., 201; *Harper's Weekly*, XXVI., 530, 675.

by Senator Hale for this unworthy undertaking was that the Democrats were accustomed to levy national assessments before 1861 and that the circular sent out by the committee was a copy of those mailed by the Republicans in 1878 and in 1880, "which were submitted to and approved by the then civil service reform president, Hayes." [1]

The civil service reform league, through George William Curtis, Everett P. Wheeler, and William Potts, notified every federal employé that he laid himself liable to the law of 1876 if he contributed: for that act made it a misdemeanor for an executive officer or employé of the United States to request, to give, or to receive money for political purposes.[2] The league also proposed to prosecute the congressional committee for sending out the circulars; but Attorney-General Brewster gave an opinion that senators and representatives were not officers or employés of the United States within the meaning of the statute. The league further aided in the prosecution of General Curtis, a treasury official stationed in New York City and chairman of the State Republican Committee, who was charged under the law of 1876 with receiving political contributions from government employés.[3] Being convicted in the United States circuit court, and sentenced to pay

[1] *Cong. Record*, 47 Cong., 2 Sess., 141–143.
[2] *U. S. Statutes at Large*, XIX., 169.
[3] *Appleton's Annual Cyclop.*, 1882, p. 694; *Harper's Weekly*, XXVI., 467.

a fine of one thousand dollars, he appealed to the Supreme Court, and on December 18, 1882, a decision was rendered upholding the constitutionality of the act of 1876 as in keeping with acts passed in 1789, in 1812, in 1863, in 1867, in 1868, and in 1870, regulating federal employés. All such acts, it was held, conduced to the public good and were within the just scope of legislative power. The New York state Republican Committee voted a sum sufficient to pay the fine assessed,[1] and the case furnished one more argument for the need of reform.

To the surprise and delight of the reformers, President Arthur proved an earnest advocate of improvement in the service. He offset the Republican circular by a public announcement that employés of the government would not be affected in any way by their refusal to contribute. In December, 1882, he urged appropriate legislation which would protect the hundred thousand employés of the government, and at the same time relieve the president from the burden of their appointment.[2]

Led by these favoring conditions, the civil service reform bill passed the Senate, December 27, 1882, by a vote of 38 to 5, the minority being all Democrats. Of the 33 marked "not voting," 14 were Republicans and 19 Democrats. The bill passed the House, January 4, 1883, by a majority composed of 102 Republicans, 49 Democrats, and 4 Nationals; the

[1] *Appleton's Annual Cyclop.*, 1882, p. 604.
[2] Richardson, *Messages and Papers*, VIII., 145.

minority vote was made up of 7 Republicans, 39 Democrats, and 1 National; 87 "not voting."[1] The large number of "dodgers" in both House and Senate demonstrated the power of public sentiment and the fear of public disapprobation. It was a victory for the people over apparently hostile legislators, such as begets fresh confidence in representative government. The president signed the bill and it became a law January 16, 1883.[2]

This act "to regulate and improve the civil service of the United States" was not mandatory, but authorized the president to appoint three commissioners (not more than two from the same party), who should classify all employés of the government into grades. The conditions were left to the president's discretion, except that appointment and promotion to these grades when formed should be made from a list of eligibles prepared after competitive examination; and a period of probation must precede a permanent appointment. Congressional influence was checked by the injunction that recommendations for place by members of Congress must not be received. The evils of assessments were met by a positive prohibition of political assessments, political coercion, and contributions of anything of value. Appointments to public service in Washington were to be apportioned among the states and territories according to population, and soldiers and sailors

---

[1] McPherson, *Hand-Book of Politics*, 1882, pp. 8–18.
[2] *U. S. Statutes at Large*, XXII., 403.

with honorable records received a preference in filling places. Common laborers and employés not in the executive branch of the government were exempt from classification. No removal must be made for refusing to contribute to party campaign funds.

The administration of the needed reform was intrusted to Dorman B. Eaton, long the persistent advocate of public service purification, who had served on the old commission under President Grant. Associated with him were John M. Gregory, sometime president of the University of Illinois, and Leroy D. Thoman, editor of an Ohio newspaper and writer on civil service reform.[1] Government employés of the city of Washington whose salaries ranged from $900 to $1800, being 5517 out of 5652, were classified. In eleven of the largest customs districts, 2573 employés were classified and placed under the protection of the law. In twenty-three post-offices, 5699 officials were given the same benefit. In all, 13,924 government employés were within the first year permanently sheltered from political assessments and the fear of dismissal.[2] This number was increased by nearly two thousand through extension and growth during the remainder of President Arthur's administration.[3]

The prime purpose of the law was to demonstrate

---

[1] For rules adopted by the commission, see Richardson, *Messages and Papers*, VIII., 161.   [2] *Ibid.*, 186.

[3] For later extensions, see Dewey, *National Problems* (*Am. Nation*, XXIV.), chap. ii.

the principle stated by Webster, as early as 1835, that offices were not created for the benefit of those who are to fill them, but for the public convenience. It guarantees appointment and promotion for merit only, and takes away the temptation to remove an official, inasmuch as a vacancy cannot be filled at pleasure but only from a list of those qualified. If rewards and punishments are not within the power of a party chieftain, then a levy of assessments for party purposes would have no coercive power. It makes efficiency and honesty sole requisites for business positions, and neither of these qualities has any dependence upon political affiliations. The act did not cure all the evils. Naturally, party highwaymen, cut off from levying on individuals, would turn more and more to corporations for funds in return for legislation. The good work must be extended to state and municipal employés, and hesitating executives must be made to feel the weight of public opinion. Later needs could be met by later measures; an excellent beginning had been made by the reform bill of 1883. During the same year New York passed a civil service law, and Massachusetts soon followed the example.

CHAPTER XIII

THE ISTHMIAN CANAL

(1877-1885)

SCARCELY a decade of American history has passed without adding a chapter to the story of the isthmian canal project. The period which includes 1880 saw a transition in American public thought from the canal as a great international highway, constructed by capital collected from any source and under the protection of brotherly love, to the idea of an American canal built at least by an American company, and to some extent under American control. The ideal of a canal to be constructed exclusively by the United States government was evolved at a still later time. The change in sentiment about 1880 was due largely to the fear that a European company would succeed in an enterprise which Americans had long contemplated but had delayed in consummating. Granted that no monopoly or even official control of the canal was contemplated by its French promoters, American pride could not without disquietude see a foreign company appropriate an enterprise in which they were vitally interested.[1]

Remembrance of the depredations committed in the Pacific by Confederate cruisers because the federal navy could not readily pass from the Atlantic to the Pacific gradually died out as the war time receded; and the project of a canal across the American isthmus faded again from public thought. The opening of the Suez Canal, November 17, 1869, not only aroused fresh interest in inter-oceanic canals but affected America by opening a direct way between the Mediterranean and the Pacific coast without making the Cape of Good Hope passage. A canal across the American isthmus would prolong this route to the Atlantic and place a girdle of transportation about the globe. Rumor said that Ferdinand de Lesseps, promoter and builder of the Suez Canal, intended turning his attention next to making a vast inland sea of the Sahara Desert, and at the same time proposed attacking the American canal problem.

The *Société Geographique* of Paris, an organization of French scientists and engineers, made a careful study of the various routes proposed for the American canal, and indorsed that by Panama as the most feasible. In 1875 De Lesseps began what purported to be a most careful survey of this route

[1] For earlier stages of canal diplomacy, see Garrison, *Westward Extension*, chap. xviii.; Smith, *Parties and Slavery* (*Am. Nation*, XVIII.), chap. vii.

by means of money obtained by subscription in France. It is significant that a board of United States engineers was making a survey of the route at the same time, while other engineers had recently completed a survey of the Nicaraguan route.[1]

In 1878 Lucien Buonaparte Wyse, of the French navy, in command of the French scientific surveying expedition, and director in the International Interoceanic Canal Association of Paris, secured from the republic of Colombia (which had succeeded the former republic of New Granada) a concession[2] granting to a company which he might organize the exclusive right to construct a canal and accompanying railroad from ocean to ocean across the Isthmus of Panama. Canal and terminal ports were to remain neutral; in the event of war, troops were to be transported only by permission of the Colombian authorities. Grants of land were made to the company, and in return Colombia was promised five per cent. of the gross tolls collected. The canal must be opened within eighteen years, and the concession would terminate ninety-nine years after the opening. This grant, it was claimed, would not conflict with the provisions of the treaty of 1846 between Colombia (then New Granada) and the United States,[3] because that concession guaranteed the neutrality of the

---

[1] *Senate Exec Docs.*, 45 Cong., 3 Sess., No. 75.
[2] *House Exec. Docs.*, 46 Cong., 2 Sess., No. 1, pt. i., p. 243.
[3] Garrison, *Westward Extension* (*Am. Nation*, XVII.), chap. xviii.

transit only, and secured to the United States no monopoly of the route. Such had been the non-restrictive policy of the United States in 1846. Nevertheless, the Wyse concession now made special provision for sharing all its advantages with the United States if the latter so desired.

Upon returning to France, Wyse made over his concession to De Lesseps, and the latter entered upon his great plan of making the canal an international enterprise. Through the *Société Geographique* of Paris he arranged an International Congress of Geographic Sciences which assembled in Paris, May 15, 1879.[1] It was attended by seventy-eight representatives from twenty-five nations, including the leading scientists and engineers of the world. The United States was represented officially by Rear-Admiral Daniel Ammen, and by Engineer E. G. Menocal, of the navy; they were instructed to take part in the discussions but not to commit their government to any fixed policy concerning a route or pertaining to the construction of the canal. In all, fourteen *projets* were presented, involving seven different routes as finally considered by the technical committee of the congress. These included all crossings of the Isthmus generally considered feasible for a ship canal.

The Tehuantepec route, from the Bay of Vera Cruz to the Gulf of Tehuantepec, was 148 miles long

[1] *Senate Exec. Docs.*, 46 Cong., 2 Sess., No. 112, p. 84; *Appleton's Annual Cyclop.*, 1879, p. 503.

and required 120 locks. Although the alluvial soil on each slope made excavation easy, and although this route offered the shortest way between New York and San Francisco, the length of time required for a vessel to pass through the canal, estimated at twelve days, and the frequency of earthquake disturbances in that portion of the Isthmus were strong objections to the route. The Nicaraguan route, from the mouth of the San Juan River through Lake Nicaragua and thence to the Pacific Ocean, was 180 miles in length, and needed 17 locks. But it required an actual construction of only 60 miles of canal because of existing rivers and lakes, and was favored by many of the engineers in the congress. On the other hand, the utilization of the rapid and crooked San Juan River presented most serious difficulties.

The Panama route was located at the narrowest portion of the Isthmus, being only forty-five miles in length, but it had very little natural waterway available on the route. The valley of the Chagres River, along which the canal must pass for at least thirty miles from the Atlantic side, would require a vast aqueduct, or the river must be diverted from its course by an enormous dam. Although the pass of Culebra, which the Panama railway utilized in crossing from Colon to Panama, was the lowest crossing of the Cordilleran backbone on the Isthmus, a canal through it would require a cut of 285 feet to bring it down to sea-level. The decision between a tide-water and a lock canal must turn largely on the possibility of trenching the Culebra divide. Near the Panama route was another way, much less favorably known, which started from the Bay of San Blas on the Atlantic side and terminated near Panama on the Pacific side.

Still another possible crossing had been found near the South American mainland, along the Atrato River, a tributary of the Gulf of Darien, and the Napipi River, which flows into the Pacific. The space between the two rivers was not great, but was occupied by a lofty mountain range which must be pierced by a tunnel, and consequently, in the opinion of most of the engineers who took part in the proceedings of the Paris congress, was an insurmountable barrier against a canal. After full discussion, a motion prevailed to indorse the plan presented by De Lesseps, which was based on the Panama route under the Wyse concession. A *Compagnie Universelle du Canal Interoceanique* was immediately granted a charter by the French government, with a capital stock of six hundred million francs; and books were opened for a popular subscription at fifty francs each. Soon the number of subscribers reached six hundred thousand.[1]

Aside from granting the charter, the French government apparently took no part in the scheme. Nevertheless, the launching of a company in France

[1] *House Exec. Docs.*, 46 Cong., 3 Sess., No. 1, pt. i., p. 485; *Appleton's Annual Cyclop.*, 1881, p. 714; for the agreement of the Company, see *North Am. Rev.*, CXXX., 144.

to build a canal in America caused both alarm and indignation in the United States. Rumor was persistent in saying that the French government, whose connection with the enterprise of Maximilian during the Civil War had not been forgotten, was secretly backing De Lesseps. Even if this were not true, the enterprise was headed by a French engineer, was under the direction of a French company, the funds were subscribed largely by French people, and its legal questions would be solved in French courts. It would be an easy task for France to make excuse of one of the disputes likely to occur in the South American zone of political disturbances and to assume control of the canal in order to protect French interests.

The French canal company was under a ban in the United States in its early days. American representatives to the Paris congress charged De Lesseps with duplicity. "The calling of the scientific congress in Paris and the decision at that congress," said Rear-Admiral Ammen, in testifying before a House committee,[1] "was brought about entirely in conformity with a contract which had been made by seven individuals between themselves, two of them holding commissions from the Colombian government. They entered into this contract previous to the meeting of the congress. . . . De Lesseps was

---

[1] *House Misc. Docs.*, 46 Cong., 3 Sess., I., 16; Menocal, "Intrigues at the Paris Canal Congress," in *North Am. Rev.*, CXXIX., 288; *Nation*, XIX., 71.

deserted there by every engineer of the society of civil engineers of Paris—a very distinguished body."

To counteract this rumor and also to encourage subscriptions in America, De Lesseps came to this country and appeared before a House committee, March 18, 1880, where he testified that the French government had no official connection with his company, aside from having granted it a charter; and that he would look more naturally for protection to a powerful nation like the United States, which was most interested.[1] In a magazine article, De Lesseps explained that the company had been chartered in France rather than the United States because the French laws were more stringent and afforded better protection to the stockholders than did the American laws. As to control of the company, he showed that the American stockholders, if sufficiently numerous, could maintain supreme control. He attributed the opposition in the United States towards the canal to the Pacific railway companies, which thus attempted to throttle competition. The United States had been officially represented in the Paris congress, and her representatives at the time had made no protest and could not have been deceived. He contrasted the open methods of the Paris congress with the secret conferences of the interoceanic canal commission of 1872, whose report had never been made public. The United States had spent five million dollars, he said, on surveys of the various routes,

[1] *House Misc. Docs.*, 46 Cong., 3 Sess., No. 16, I.

and thus far without results; why not co-operate with the French company and share in its success?[1]

The visit of De Lesseps worked a wondrous change of feeling in certain quarters towards his project. Banking syndicates found reason for sudden faith in the enterprise; newspapers experienced a conversion; and many members of Congress were led to oppose any American intervention at Panama. Subscriptions were announced in liberal numbers. Suspicion was aroused that public opinion had been influenced by a liberal dispensation of stock if not of cash, and these rumors were strengthened when the corrupt methods employed by the company were revealed at a later time. When R. W. Thompson, secretary of the navy, upon whom would have rested the burden in a naval war with France, resigned from Hayes's cabinet to accept the chairmanship of the American branch of the De Lesseps company, the action aroused a storm of criticism and brought out a number of charges.

The more aggressive Americans saw immediate war with France as the only possible result of the French beginning work on the American isthmus. The attempt of the United States to establish a coaling station near Panama, a project long contemplated and in accord with a policy adopted soon after the Civil War, was accepted as an indication of immediate hostilities. Senator Bayard said: "Every

[1] De Lesseps, "The Interoceanic Canal," in *North Am. Rev.*, CXXX., 1; also *ibid.*, CXXIX., 288.

counsel of wisdom, therefore, exhorts us to 'seize the day' and in time of peace prepare for war; for it is the surest mode to avoid it," and the words were widely and favorably quoted. It was pronounced a method superior to strategy, fraud, and human butchery.[1]

In order to anticipate the French company in beginning work on the Isthmus, several moribund Panama companies, which held shadowy concessions from the Colombian or New Granadian government, petitioned Congress for aid. Other promoters wished to checkmate the French by constructing a rival canal, and an interoceanic transit company asked a subsidy from Congress for the Nicaraguan route. A new Marine Canal Company of Nicaragua asked Congress to guarantee its capital stock in return for free transportation of troops and mails, as had been done for the "land grant" railroads. The precedent of the Bolivian Steam Navigation Company, to which Congress in 1870 gave a charter for placing a line of steamers on the Amazon River in Bolivia, was considered in point. Ex-President Grant headed a Nicaraguan canal company and contributed articles to the press describing the advantages of that route.[2]

Captain Eads, who had solved the problem of clearing the sediment from the mouth of the Mississippi River, appeared before Congress with a plan to construct a ship railroad across the Isthmus of Tehuantepec. A report of the survey of the Panama

[1] *Nation*, XXX., 762.   [2] *North Am. Rev.*, CXXXII., 107.

route in 1875 by Commander Lull, and of the Atrato-Napipi route by Lieutenant Collins in the same year, were printed by Congress.[1] The House, May 29, 1880, asked the president for the report of the surveys made by the interoceanic canal commission of 1872, which had been submitted in 1875,[2] but, as De Lesseps pointed out, was never made public. It recommended the Nicaraguan route as being the most feasible.

The Monroe Doctrine had been in storage since 1870, when President Grant returned it after the Santo Domingo annexation failure.[3] Senator—formerly General—Burnside, of Rhode Island, offered a resolution in the United States Senate,[4] June 25, 1879, that the United States could not view without disquietude the trespass of any power on the Isthmus, rendered neutral by the Monroe Doctrine, and would not consider it other than a manifestation of unfriendly disposition towards the United States. Other attempted resolutions[5] pledged the United States to aid any worthy Nicaragua canal company, and authorized the president to call a congress of South American states and the United States to consider what steps were necessary for their mutual safety and protection against the political systems of the governments of Europe.

[1] *Senate Exec. Docs.*, 45 Cong., 3 Sess., No. 75.
[2] *Ibid.*, 46 Cong., 1 Sess., No. 15.
[3] Dunning, *Reconstruction* (*Am. Nation*, XXII.), chap. x.
[4] *Cong. Record*, 46 Cong., 1 Sess., 2312.
[5] *Ibid.*, 2 Sess., 12, 14, 1392, 1709.

The House appointed a committee of eleven on an interoceanic canal, December 19, 1879, which heard testimonies, including that of De Lesseps, and presented several reports, including a resolution, on March 8, 1880,[1] to the effect that the establishment of any form of a protectorate by any European power in America would be contrary to the Monroe Doctrine; and that the United States was entitled to control and govern solely any Isthmian canal. Further, the president was authorized to terminate any treaty conflicting with these principles. Although this resolution was called up a second time, March 3, 1881, it failed to pass.[2]

The Clayton-Bulwer treaty of 1850 with England,[3] against which the last clause of the House resolution was directed, lay during a half-century a repressive weight on American initiative on the Isthmus. While it checked the supposedly ambitious designs of Great Britain upon the Central American coast, by pledging each party not to colonize or exercise dominion in that part of the world, it kept the United States from constructing an isthmian canal at Nicaragua by its provisions for a joint guarantee of neutrality, and its pledge that the canal should be open on like

---

[1] For report of the testimony, see *House Misc. Docs.*, 46 Cong., 3 Sess., No. 16; for the resolution, see *Cong. Record*, 46 Cong., 2 Sess., 1392.

[2] *House Reports*, 46 Cong., 3 Sess., 390.

[3] *U. S. Treaties and Conventions*, 440–444; Garrison, *Westward Extension* (*Am. Nation*, XVII.), chap. xviii.; Travis, *Clayton-Bulwer Treaty*, chap. i.

terms to other powers choosing to enter the partnership. The prospect of a wholly American canal was still further impaired by the provision of the treaty that in time of war between Great Britain and the United States, each party should have free use of the waterway. By extending the international partnership to "any other practicable communication between the two oceans," the hands of the United States were tied at Panama as well as at the other prospective crossings. In order to break these bonds and to anticipate the French, impetuous Americans would disregard the six months' notice required by the Clayton-Bulwer treaty and annul it on the ground that it had been broken by Great Britain in persistently refusing to vacate the Mosquito Coast after 1850, and in turning Belize into a British colony.[1]

Another possible way of checking the French company might be found in the treaty of 1846,[2] between the United States and New Granada (now Colombia), in which the former guaranteed "positively and efficaciously" to the latter the perfect neutrality of the Isthmus, with the view that the free transit from the one to the other sea might not be interrupted; and in consequence the United States guaranteed the rights of integrity which New Granada possessed over her soil. Under this guarantee, the Panama railroad had been constructed and was now being operated; troops had been landed

[1] Smith, *Parties and Slavery* (*Am. Nation*, XVIII.), chap. xviii.
[2] *U. S. Treaties and Conventions*, 205.

at various times to protect it. Would not the construction of a French canal interfere with the perfect neutrality of the Isthmus? Was Colombia empowered to give even the concession of a right of way over soil guaranteed to her by the United States? In other words, could she alienate the sovereignty of any part of her domain? Granted that she could give the right of way, and that the canal would be built by the De Lesseps company, must not the United States under the guarantee of 1846 resist with war any attempt of France to assert authority over the canal? Or in case of a revolution on the Isthmus, when the United States would interfere to protect the railway and France to safeguard the canal, might not serious complications follow?[1]

De Lesseps dismissed all these complex questions of international guarantees by saying that the concession given by Colombia to his company guaranteed the neutrality of the canal. He insisted that his project was in strict accord with the Monroe Doctrine; that he held letters of welcome from the authorities of Colombia and of Panama; that the canal would be a benefit to them; and that the best interests of the South American states would be served by the construction of the canal, and their best interests formed the very essence of the Doctrine.[2]

[1] *Nation*, XXX., 762.
[2] *North Am. Rev.*, CXXIX., 288; *Harper's Weekly*, xxiv, 162.

Amid this confusion of counsels and this uncertainty of written language, one clear American word came from President Hayes. He took advantage of the request of the Senate, March 8, 1880, for copies of all diplomatic correspondence in connection with the isthmian canal to express a growing conviction of the American public. "The policy of this country," said he, "is a canal under American control. The United States cannot consent to the surrender of this control to any European power or to any combination of European powers. . . . No European power can intervene for such protection without adopting measures on this continent which the United States would deem wholly inadmissible. An interoceanic canal across the American isthmus will essentially change the geographical relations . . . between the United States and the rest of the world. It would be the great ocean thoroughfare between our Atlantic and our Pacific shores, and virtually a part of the coast-line of the United States. No other great power would, under similar circumstances, fail to assert a rightful control over a work so closely and vitally affecting its interest and its welfare." [1]

Here was decidedly advanced standing compared with the message of President Taylor in 1849, when announcing a new treaty with Nicaragua, whereby that power and the United States would jointly pro-

---

[1] Richardson, *Messages and Papers*, VII., 585; *Am. Hist. Leaflets*, No. 4, p. 27; Travis, *Clayton-Bulwer Treaty*, 205; *House Docs.*, 46 Cong., 2 Sess., No. 57.

tect any company undertaking a canal along the Nicaraguan route. "All other nations," said he, "are invited by the State of Nicaragua to enter into the same treaty stipulations with her; and the benefit to be derived from such an arrangement will be the protection of this great interoceanic communication against any power which might seek to obstruct it or to monopolize its advantages." If constructed under a world guarantee and control, the canal would become, in Taylor's estimation, a bond of peace instead of a subject of strife between the nations of the earth.[1] Hayes, on the contrary, would stand for the principle for which Seward and Fish had contended—the assumption by the United States of the sole responsibility for the canal as a part of the coastline of the United States.

The new spirit of a purely American canal was manifest also in the documents which Hayes sent with his message. In one of them, Secretary Evarts concluded an historical review of the canal project with the significant statement that the United States had a "paramount interest" in any canal constructed across the Isthmus, and, as a territorial question, must exercise a potential control.[2] Essential to this control was, on the one hand, the modification or abrogation of the Clayton-Bulwer agreement; and, on the other, the assurance that the French govern-

[1] Richardson, *Messages and Papers*, V., 15.
[2] *Senate Exec. Docs.*, 46 Cong., 2 Sess., No. 112; see also *Foreign Relations*, 1879, p. 339.

ment was not the official sponsor for the De Lesseps company. The correspondence submitted by Evarts included an inquiry put by him to M. Outrey, French minister at Washington, and the repeated assurances of the latter that the French government was in no way concerned in the De Lesseps enterprise and in no way intended to interfere or to give it any support, either direct or indirect. The French cabinet proposed to let it remain an essentially private matter.[1]

Diplomatic assurance that the French enterprise was a private undertaking could not allay the fears nor lessen the indignation of the American people in February, 1881, when seventy French engineers, superintendents, and workmen landed on the Isthmus of Panama preparatory to inaugurating work on the canal. They laid out camps along the proposed line, erected hospitals and other buildings, and made preparations for a prolonged stay. The route as planned by De Lesseps from Limon Bay, near Colon, on the Atlantic side to the end of the Pacific extension near the island of Naos, south of Panama, was about forty-seven miles in length. At a distance of six miles from its Atlantic terminus the route entered the valley of the Chagres River, which it followed for twenty-four miles to Obispo, and passed thence through the crest of the divide at Culebra to the Rio Grande, which it followed to the Pacific. For the most part, the canal lay in

[1] *Foreign Relations*, 1880, p. 387.

alluvial soil. Owing to the shallow harbors at the termini, long breakwaters would be necessary to carry the canal out to deep water.

De Lesseps at first planned a tide-level canal, the difference in the height of tides in the Atlantic and Pacific being corrected by tide-gates. The vast volume of water discharged by the Chagres River during the wet season was to be held in check by a high dam across the valley above the point where the canal left it, the water to be finally discharged through a tunnel into one of the oceans. Since the canal route was paralleled by the Panama railroad, crossing and recrossing it, De Lesseps purchased the railroad for $17,000,000, expecting to use it in carrying material for constructing the canal. Its capital stock was only $7,000,000; but because it frequently paid as high as twenty per cent. dividends, its shares of stock were held at a high figure.[1]

Machinery was brought at large expense from Europe and the United States; workmen were found among the native negroes and Indians, or imported from Jamaica, China, and Europe; and excavation was begun at several elevated points, the plan being to reduce them all to the same high level and then to bring the whole to the required sea-level. The company's engineers had estimated the cost of the canal at 843,000,000 francs, but De Lesseps reduced the estimate to 600,000,000 francs ($120,000,000),

[1] *Appleton's Annual Cyclop.*, 1882, pp. 107, 814; *Foreign Relations*, 1884, p. 121.

and even issued invitations for the ceremonies of opening the route, which he set for 1888.[1]

The beginning of work on the Isthmus was almost coincident with the inauguration of Garfield and the installation of Blaine as secretary of state. In his inaugural address, Garfield quoted Hayes's message of 1880, but modified his strong words by the statement that "we will urge no narrow policy nor seek peculiar or exclusive privileges in any commercial route."[2] However, Blaine found the situation at Panama fitted exactly into his plan for a vigorous South American policy. He had not long to await an opportunity to open the entire canal question, and especially its relation to the Clayton-Bulwer treaty. The attempts of the Colombian Congress to alter or abrogate the treaty of 1846,[3] and the persistent rumors that Colombia was making overtures to certain European powers to assume a joint guarantee over the De Lesseps canal, caused Blaine to send an identical letter to the American ministers in Europe, June 24, 1881,[4] asking them to serve notice that "any movement in the sense of supplementing the guarantee contained therein [*i. e.*, the treaty of 1846] would necessarily be regarded by this government as an uncalled for intrusion into a field where the local and general interest of the United States of

---

[1] Rodgers' report, in *Senate Misc. Docs.*, 48 Cong., 1 Sess., No. 123.   [2] Richardson, *Messages and Papers*, VIII., 11.
[3] *Ibid.*, 41; Tucker, *Monroe Doctrine*, chap. v.
[4] *Foreign Relations*, 1881, p. 537.

America should be considered before those of any other power save those of Colombia alone." He went so far in a new doctrine of American guarantee of the canal as to say that in the event of war in which the United States or Colombia might be engaged, the passage of a hostile war-vessel through the canal would no more be permitted than the passage of an armed force over the railway lines in the United States connecting the two oceans. Consequently any agreement in Europe for a joint guarantee of the canal would be regarded in America as an indication of an unfriendly feeling and would be viewed with the greatest concern.

These declarations were in exact contravention of the Clayton-Bulwer treaty, the second article of which provided that in case of war between the United States and Great Britain the canal should be free from blockade, and vessels en route through it should be free from capture for a fixed distance from each end. Consequently, Blaine followed this letter a few months later by a proposition,[1] made through Lowell, the American minister at St. James, to modify the partnership so that the United States would have a right to fortify a Nicaraguan canal and to retain its political control; but he promised that the sites necessary for military and naval stations would not be considered as acquisitions of territory. He also wished to annul that part of the

[1] *Foreign Relations.*, 1881, p. 554; Henderson, *Am. Dipl. Questions*, 144.

agreement which extended it "to any other practicable communications" between the two oceans, and thus leave the United States free to construct a canal by another route or to interfere with the French at Panama without consulting England.

To these propositions Lord Grenville replied, January, 1882,[1] that his government was also a New-World power, interested equally with the United States in the construction and neutrality of the waterway and equally entitled to participate in its political control. He could not conceive how any Central American republic would allow the United States to fortify and garrison a canal in its territory, as Blaine proposed. In view of these objections, he thought the peace of the world and the prosperity of the western hemisphere would best be served by continuing to act on the principle that the canal would be a world highway and that all nations were entitled by invitation to share in its benefits and in its guarantee of neutrality.

How England regarded the neutrality of a "world's highway" was exemplified, in American opinion, by her acquisition of the control of the Suez Canal. Originally opposed to its construction, because it opened a short road between France and British India, she resolved after its completion to command it. Of the 397,438 shares issued by the Compagnie Universelle du Canal Maritime de Suez, the khedive

[1] *House Exec. Docs.*, 47 Cong., 1 Sess., I., pt. i., 549; *Foreign Relations.*, 1882, pp. 271-282, 302-314.

of Egypt owned 176,602. These England purchased in 1875. Added to the shares privately held in that country, they gave to her a controlling majority of stock. Taking advantage of a rebellion of natives against foreign interference in Egyptian finance, England bombarded Alexandria, July 11, 1882, landed troops in Egypt, and used the canal at will for military purposes, regardless of the protests of De Lesseps.[1] The tactics by which England thus obtained financial and political control of the Suez Canal could easily be repeated in any Central American republic. England already possessed control of too much of the world's commerce and its pathways; she must be prevented on the American Isthmus by the dissolution of the Clayton-Bulwer convention, and the construction of the canal by American capital and under American guarantee of neutrality. This was the policy of Blaine.

Aside from the canal, Blaine had occasion to use a brisk American policy when Count Lewenhaupt, umpire for a commission on arbitration of claims of American citizens against Spain contracted during the Cuban rebellion, decided in 1881 that a Cuban-born claimant, Buzzi, was not a naturalized citizen of the United States, although he held a certificate which he had obtained in Baltimore in 1869. The certificate was issued without the required previous term of residence, and, in the opinion of the

[1] Woolsey, *Am. Foreign Policy*, 136-141; *Harper's Weekly*. XXVI., 477.

umpire, for fraudulent purposes. Blaine instructed the American counsel before the commission to say that no more cases would be submitted for trial on these principles.[1] He also took a firm stand against the growing tendency of Germany to claim military service from former subjects, who had become naturalized citizens of the United States and who returned temporarily to their native land.[2] England also gave opportunity for vigorous diplomatic language by questioning the United States citizenship of certain persons charged with Fenian dynamite outrages in England.[3]

Especially Blaine cherished an ambition to enlarge the limited sphere of United States influence in South American affairs both by attracting trade, which went to Europe, and by acting as arbiter in the numerous disputes characteristic of the South American people. His predecessor, Evarts, had attempted in vain to arbitrate the territorial war between Peru, Chili, and Bolivia, in October, 1880.[4] Blaine renewed the effort, and especially sought to prevent the absorption of the Peruvian and Bolivian coast by Chili. He even sent a special envoy, Trescot, of South Carolina, December, 1881, to the three countries for this purpose.[5] Trescot was also in-

[1] Moore, *International Arbitrations*, 1019; *Senate Exec. Docs.*, 46 Cong., 2 Sess., No. 86.
[2] *Foreign Relations*, 1881, p. 449; 1882, p. 186.
[3] *Ibid.*, 1882, p. 192.
[4] *Ibid.*, 1880, pp. 121, 487; *Senate Exec. Docs.*, 46 Cong., 3 Sess., No. 26.   [5] *Foreign Relations*, 1881, p. 54.

structed to visit Brazil and other South American states with the object of calling eventually a full and free conference for the consideration of New-World matters.[1] Immediate fruits of Blaine's efforts were prevented by the difficulty of ascertaining the legitimate heads of the contending factions in the uncertainty of South American politics; by differences among the American ministers to these countries; and by his own retirement from office after the death of Garfield. For Blaine could not remain permanently in the cabinet of Arthur, the bosom friend of Conkling. However, Blaine lived to renew his policy in the cabinet of President Harrison.[2]

Blaine's successor, Frelinghuysen, continued the correspondence with England on the Clayton-Bulwer treaty and the isthmian canal question. He brought out the Monroe Doctrine which Blaine ignored, and charged England with violating the agreement at the time she made a dependency of the Mosquito Coast, and by that action freed the United States from the terms of the covenant. This revived the old controversy and led to nothing.[3] Frelinghuysen did not press Blaine's plan of a pan-American congress. Finally, in 1884, to put the strength of the

---

[1] *Foreign Relations*, 1881, p. 64; *Harper's Weekly*, XXV., 895.
[2] Cf. Dewey, *National Problems* (*Am. Nation*, XXIV.), chap. xiii.
[3] *Senate Exec. Docs.*, 47 Cong., 1 Sess., No. 194; *ibid.*, 48 Cong., 1 Sess., No. 26; Henderson, *Am. Dipl. Questions*, 152-158; Latané, *Dipl. Relations of U. S.*, 203-212; *Foreign Relations*, 1883, pp. 418, 477, 529.

Clayton-Bulwer treaty to a test, he made a treaty with Nicaragua for the construction of a canal over that route entirely under American control in return for a guarantee of the integrity of the territory of Nicaragua,[1] but it was withdrawn from the Senate by President Cleveland,[2] who entered office while it was pending.

The return of the canal question to the *status quo* is attributable in part to the death of Garfield and the retirement of Blaine, who would probably have forced an issue with England on the Clayton-Bulwer compact. The subsidence of public indignation was due to the growing conviction that the French company would not succeed in its enterprise. One witness before the House committee of eleven predicted in 1880, before work was actually begun: "Let De Lesseps spend all the money that he wishes. There is not the slightest chance of his success." By 1884 loan after loan had been secured from the French people, interest charges were accumulating, and apparently little progress had been made on the gigantic task. A special commission of American engineers visited the works and reported to President Arthur in 1884 [3] that the estimated cost, $120,-000,000, had already been exceeded by nearly $10,-000,000, with no immediate prospect of completion.

[1] *Senate Reports*, 55 Cong., 2 Sess., No. 1265, p. 20; *Independent*, December 25, 1884; cf. Dewey, *National Problems* (*Am. Nation*, XXIV.), chap. xiii.
[2] Richardson, *Messages and Papers*, VIII., 327.
[3] *Senate Exec. Docs.*, 48 Cong., 1 Sess., No. 120.

The $17,000,000 which the company agreed to pay for the Panama railway was not yet paid. "The whole undertaking is so gigantic," said one of the commission, "that one cannot believe that it will soon be finished, but I am impressed with the fact that the French are thoroughly in earnest and that if they fail to finish the canal on account of the lack of funds, the work done by them will be well done, and will be so extensive as to always give this route great advantages over any other."

In 1889 the last chapter in this brilliant undertaking was written. The company was bankrupt, its scandals disclosed, its promoters sentenced to prison, and eight hundred thousand French stockholders left with no prospect of returns. Less than one-fifth of the necessary excavating had been done, much of the work completed was going to ruin, and a plant worth not less than thirty million dollars was rusting and decaying in idleness. The course of events had saved the American isthmus from European invasion and preserved it for American initiative, without armed intervention or even official use of the Monroe Doctrine. But the French attempt wrought a change of public sentiment in the United States. "An American canal, built by American capital or by the National Government, under American control, and subject to rules announced by the American people" was to be the future slogan. Temporarily a change of administration would bring a return of the policy of a decade before, but the Spanish-American War and the sensational voyage of the *Oregon* around Cape Horn in 1898, duplicating the exploit of the *Monadnock* in the Civil War, would transform American sentiment into action on the Isthmus of Panama.[1]

[1] Latané, *America the World Power* (*Am. Nation*, XXV.), chap. iii.

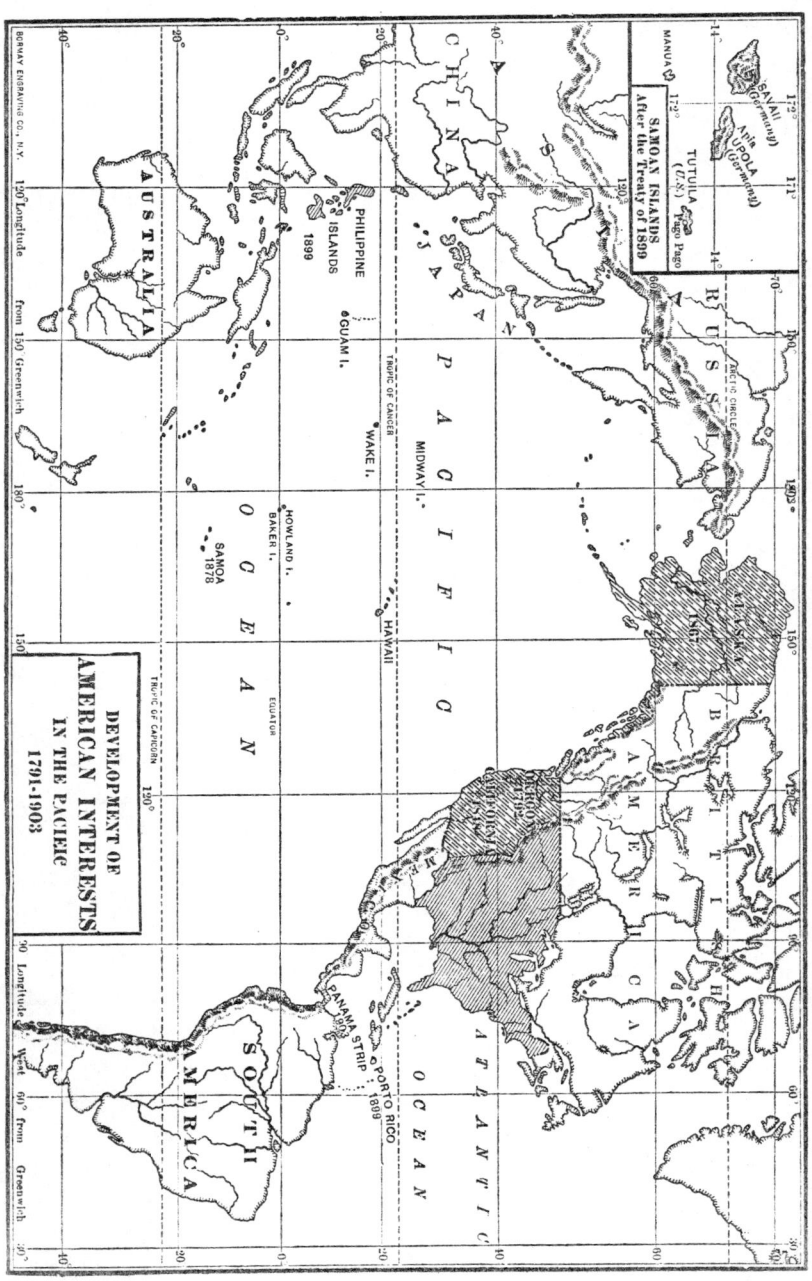

CHAPTER XIV

THE CHINESE QUESTION
(1879–1885)

AN act to prohibit the coming of Chinese laborers to the United States for the ensuing ten years became a law May 6, 1882. In the process of amalgamating the various elements which have contributed to the peopling of the United States, three races have presented hard problems, each from a different stand-point. In the case of the Indians the dispute has been territorial; in that of the negroes it has been political; and in connection with the Chinese it has been industrial.[1] The Indians were prior occupants—tenants at will on the national domain; the negroes were inherited from the British colonies; the Chinese were aliens, late comers, and subject to restrictive laws. It was possible to shut the doors against them only.

The first federal statute relating to immigrants was an act of March 2, 1819,[2] which simply required a statement of the number of passengers brought on each ship. Even when the number of immigrants

[1] Cf. Hart, *National Ideals* (*Am. Nation*, XXVI.), chap. iv.
[2] *U. S. Statutes at Large*, III., 488.

increased from 8385 in 1820 to 669,431 in 1881, no restraining legislation was passed, not even during the American or Know-nothing agitation of 1854 to 1856,[1] which looked to the safeguarding of American-born citizens. The homestead act of 1862 was calculated to attract immigrants; and an act of July 4, 1864,[2] was intended to encourage immigration by providing a bureau for their protection on arrival. During the agitation for free labor coincident with emancipation, various states passed new laws intended to attract immigrants and to secure to each its share of them.

Such was the situation at the dawn of the industrial era, when laborers began to organize for improvement of conditions and the advance of wages. Their success must depend largely upon the removal or debarment of workers who would not or could not conform to the rules they established for themselves. A uniform wage presupposes some uniformity of expenditure and a similar scale of living. It naturally follows that organized labor must be hostile to a man or a race willing to work a greater number of hours for a less wage or under unfavorable conditions; whose pleasures are cheaper and whose wants are fewer; who spends too little or who saves too much; and who carries no burden of a dependent family. These objections applied precisely to the Chinese, and caused an agitation against their com-

[1] Smith, *Parties and Slavery* (*Am. Nation*, XVIII.), chap. x.
[2] *U. S. Statutes at Large*, XII., 392; XIII., 385.

ing before demand for similar restriction was made against other alien laborers.

The time when the first Chinese came to the United States is in doubt. So inconsiderable was their number prior to 1850 that no separate account of them was made in the census of that year. The demand at that time for labor in San Francisco was extreme, because the rush to the gold-fields had left the city stripped of servants and common laborers. A large part of domestic work had to be done by men; under these conditions the coming of the first Chinese coolies was hailed by employers as a godsend. Engaging as cooks and launderers in the cities, the overflow found its way to the gold-fields, where the hardships attending placer-mining, the labor of panning, cradling, and sluicing, made white labor difficult to procure. With a stolidity characteristic of a race inhabiting an over-populated country, they toiled long hours, subsisted on scanty food, and accepted wages which Caucasian workmen scorned.[1] They possessed the desirable qualities of temperance, frugality, and industry; but they were not actuated by any desire to improve their surroundings. In a census of California taken in 1852, almost ten thousand Chinese appeared among its cosmopolitan inhabitants; and before the national census was taken in 1860 this number was increased almost four times by fresh arrivals.[2]

[1] McNeill, *Labor Movement*, 454.
[2] U. S. Ninth Census. 1870, I., 8.

Before the demand for common labor in the goldfields slackened with the introduction of machinery, and before the reflux had set in towards the cities, the construction of the Pacific railways, begun in 1862, called for an unlimited number of patient and cheap laborers. The Chinese seemed unusually qualified for this arduous work, and were imported in large numbers under the direction of Leland Stanford and other Pacific railroad magnates. In 1866 the Pacific Mail Steamship Company established a regular line of subsidized steamers between San Francisco and Hong-Kong, with joyful demonstrations on the part of the Americans. Representatives of the Six Companies, as the Chinese monopolies controlling emigration were called, were given dinners at which complimentary speeches were made by prominent citizens of San Francisco. Measures were taken to try to persuade the Chinese authorities to be more liberal in permitting coolies to leave for America. Those Chinese who returned from California carried glowing accounts of the beauties and possibilities of the land which they called by a Chinese word signifying "Gold Hills." In 1859 the discovery of the Comstock lode in the territory of Nevada caused the Mongolians to spread to that region.

Up to this time the Chinese in America could appeal to no express treaty for protection, since the treaties and trade conventions made between the two countries in 1844 and in 1858 guarded Americans living in China but was not reciprocal. In 1868, Anson Burlingame, former minister of the United States to China, arrived in San Francisco at the head of a Chinese embassy authorized to make a new treaty with the United States. The party was received with enthusiasm, and a treaty was ratified at Washington, July 28, 1868,[1] concerning "trade, consuls, religious toleration, and emigration." It recognized the "inherent and inalienable right of man to change his home and allegiance, and also the mutual advantage of the free migration and emigration of their citizens and subjects respectively from the one country to the other for purposes of curiosity, of trade, or as permanent residents. Citizens of the United States visiting or residing in China shall enjoy the same privileges, immunities, or exemptions in respect to travel or residence as may there be enjoyed by the citizens or subjects of the most favored nation; and, reciprocally, Chinese subjects visiting or residing in the United States shall enjoy the same privileges, immunities, and exemptions in respect to travel or residence as may be enjoyed by the citizens or subjects of the most favored nation." The treaty was received with every manifestation of favor by the American people.

The completion of the first overland railroad to California in 1869 worked a reversal of feeling on the Pacific coast, because it brought laborers from the eastern states who found themselves in competition

[1] *U. S. Treaties and Conventions*, 179.

for the first time with the Chinese. They were compelled to acknowledge that the Mongolians were formidable rivals, not so much because of bad as of good economic qualities. They would work any number of hours, under intolerable conditions; would eat the cheapest food, dwell in the most undesirable abodes, and through it all preserve a cheerfulness which was most exasperating to their Caucasian neighbors. As to wages, they secured as much as they could; but they would always accept, if necessary, less than the white man considered essential to maintain life itself.[1]

When laborers began to arrive in large numbers from both directions, California bade fair to have an over-supply. In 1869 alone, more than twelve thousand Chinese came to America, finding employment almost exclusively on the Pacific coast. According to the federal census of the following year, nearly one-half the Chinese in the United States were employed in personal service, chiefly as laundrymen and servants. Almost as many were classified as engaged in manufacturing or mining, including for the most part cigar-makers, carpenters, fishermen, and miners. About five per cent. were employed on the railroads as laborers, and another five per cent. were engaged in agriculture. Out of a total of 56,000 only 467 were found east of the Rocky Mountains.[2]

[1] *Cong. Record*, 45 Cong., 3 Sess., 794-798.
[2] U. S. Ninth Census, 1870, 704-715.

The inhabitants of the older states were as yet undecided concerning the desirability of the Chinese as immigrants; the people of the Pacific section rapidly developed an anti-Chinese sentiment. When employed in gold-mining or in railroad construction in the early days, encounters between Chinese and whites were not infrequent, and the Chinese were usually worsted. If the two disputed over the possession of a mining-claim the affair generally ended with the whites in possession. Chinese were frequently "run out" of a community, but no serious riot occurred until that of Los Angeles, California, on the night of October 24, 1871, which resulted in the hanging of fifteen Chinamen and the shooting of six others by a mob. The grand jury, when investigating the deplorable affair, placed the blame upon the city police, who made no determined effort to rescue the victims from the hands of the mob.[1]

With the increase in number of the Chinese and the opportunity of ascertaining their habits, they were seen to be diametrically opposed to the American ideal. "Chinatown," as that portion of the city of San Francisco which they appropriated was called, was declared to be a menace to the health of the remainder of the city. In addition to habitual gambling and opium smoking, the Chinese brought in numbers of Chinese women for immoral purposes. In 1874, President Grant said to Congress: "The great proportion of the Chinese immigrants who come

[1] *Am. Annual Cyclop.*, 1871, p. 92.

to our shores do not come voluntarily to make their homes with us and their labor productive of general prosperity, but come under contract with headmen, who own them absolutely. In a worse form does this apply to Chinese women. Hardly a perceptible percentage of them perform any honorable labor, but they are brought for shameful purposes."[1] Others charged that the Chinese in California constituted a "vast secret society,"[2] whose ways were past finding out; that a murder, blackmail, or any crime could be secured for pay; and that these crimes were traceable to a sworn band, to whom was given the term of "Highbinder," a term long synonymous in the eastern states with "ruffian."[3] In fine, the habits, manners, and customs of the Chinese would forever preclude them from amalgamating with the mass of Americans, as the Germans, Irish, and other European races had done.

Were Chinese admissible to citizenship? When extending the naturalization laws in 1870[4] to include "aliens of African nativity and to persons of African descent," effort was made in the Senate by Sumner to throw open the gates of citizenship to all nations; other senators wished to include the Chinese in terms; but the proposition was lost through the efforts of the senators from the Pacific coast, aided

[1] Richardson, *Messages and Papers*, VII., 288.
[2] Address adopted by public meeting in San Francisco, May, 1876, *Appleton's Annual Cyclop.*, 1876, p. 85.
[3] *House Reports*, 46 Cong., 2 Sess., No. 572, p. 8.
[4] *U. S. Statutes at Large*, XVI., 254.

by the Democrats and absentees.[1] In 1878 a decision was rendered in the Pacific circuit of the United States courts by Judge Sawyer, holding that the Chinese were not eligible to citizenship because they were under discussion when the law was framed and were intended to be excluded by the wording of the law.[2] A similar answer was given in a federal court in New York to the application of Chinese for privileges of citizenship.

In 1876 each political party in California placed anti-Chinese planks in its platform; the state Senate investigated the conditions through a committee; and public meetings were held in the streets of San Francisco. The United States Senate sent a committee of investigation to the Pacific coast, which made an exhaustive report in February, 1877,[3] charging that the Chinese accepted sordid wages, used no public schools, had no family life, and brought social and moral evils which overcame all advantages derived from their presence as laborers. It repeated the frequently made suggestion that the Burlingame treaty be revised to embrace only commercial relations with China, and thus make possible the exclusion of her subjects.

During the disorder attending the railway strike of 1877,[4] the ill feeling against the Chinese culminated

[1] *Cong. Record*, 41 Cong., 2 Sess, 5122, 5155.
[2] *In re* Ah Yup, 5 Sawyer, 155.
[3] *Senate Reports*, 44 Cong., 2 Sess., II., 689.
[4] See above, p. 73.

in California in mobs and rioting. A "workingman's" party was formed with the purpose of "ridding the country of Chinese cheap labor." Night after night crowds assembled to hear their orators on a tract of unimproved land in central San Francisco known as the "sand lots." Their leader was Dennis Kearney, a shrewd agitator-politician, who ended every harangue with the edict: "The Chinese must go." Banners were borne through the streets with the motto, "Four Dollars a Day and Roast Beef." Three thousand men waited on the mayor of the city for relief, declaring that otherwise they must steal; law-abiding citizens organized a League of Four Hundred; a "Pick-handlers' Brigade" also appeared, ostensibly to maintain order, but really to make war upon the Chinese. Almost nightly attacks were made on the Chinese quarter. Strong measures had to be taken to suppress the disorder: the state legislature passed laws against inciting to riot; Kearney was arrested, carried to jail, released by the state supreme court, and given an ovation by his people. An attempt was made to remove the mayor of the city, a Kearney man, but without success. Eventually factions arose in the working-man's party which disrupted it, merged it again in the national parties in 1880, and Kearneyism was at an end.[1]

These disorders, extending over a considerable length of time, drew general attention to the Chinese

[1] *Nation*, XXIX., 139.

question. It had been thought unlikely that Chinese labor ever would be a menace to labor in the older states; but in 1870, during a strike of workmen in a shoe-factory at North Adams, Massachusetts, a number of Chinese shoemakers were brought from California to break the strike.[1] In 1877 Chinese were imported from California to replace striking workmen in a cutlery works at Beaver Falls, Pennsylvania.[2] These incidents gave to the Chinese question a new aspect among the laboring men of the eastern states. It was presupposed that the Chinese would introduce the cultivation of silk, rice, and tea industries, which enabled China to support an enormous population; but it soon transpired that only unskilled coolies came to America. If barred from the mines and railroad construction, they turned cook and launderer, or with unusual aptitude they learned some trade.[3] Investigation showed that Chinese were employed in San Francisco in making a coarse kind of shoes and carpet slippers, and in the manufacture of cigars. Some restriction must be placed upon them.

Besides mobbing the Chinese, the people of the Pacific coast resorted to legal enactments both state and municipal, intended to repress the undesirable race; but all such efforts were subverted by decisions of the federal courts. In 1876 an ordinance

[1] McNeill, *Labor Movement*, 431; *Harper's Magazine*, XIV., 468, 493.
[2] *Lippincott's Magazine*, XIX., 708; Powderly, *Thirty Years of Labor*, 413.
[3] *Senate Reports*, 44 Cong., 2 Sess., No. 689, pp. 312, 342.

passed by the city of San Francisco requiring the hair of all prisoners to be cut within three inches of the scalp was declared unconstitutional by a federal judge, as being class legislation and a cruel and unusual punishment.[1] In 1874 the state commissioner of immigration seized twenty-two Chinese women arriving in San Francisco under the law forbidding the importation of women for immoral purposes. Through writs of *habeas corpus* they secured a respite at every stage of their prosecution. The state courts ordered them back to China, but they appealed to the federal circuit court and were freed by Judge Field[2] on the plea that the state did not possess the right of deportation among its police powers, and that the United States alone could deny right of ingress to aliens.

In 1879 a new state constitution gave the California people opportunity to strike an effective blow at the hated Celestials.[3] Provisions were inserted requiring the legislature of the state to impose various conditions under which objectionable persons might reside in the state, and to delegate the power of regulating Chinese to cities and towns. In conformity with these instructions the state legislature passed many regulations for the Chinese which were, for the most part, set aside by the United States courts. For example, in 1880 a state law which

[1] Ho Ah Kow *vs.* Nunan, 5 Sawyer, 552.
[2] *In re* Ah Fong, 3 Sawyer, 157; also Chy Lung *vs.* Freeman *et al.*, 92 U. S., 275.   [3] *Nation*, XXVIII., 328.

prohibited a corporation holding a state charter from employing Chinese was held to be discriminative legislation and therefore void.[1] The same court had previously held that an act of the Oregon legislature prohibiting the employment of Chinese on state contract work was contrary to the Fourteenth Amendment and in violation of the Burlingame treaty: "The right to reside in a country implies the right to earn a living," said the court.[2] Acts regulating conditions under which Chinese might maintain laundries and compelling Chinese to live within certain limits were also nullified by federal court decisions for similar reasons.

If California suffered from the failure of the eastern states to appreciate fully the Chinese question, she atoned by her ability to change readily her political complexion. Each party was encouraged to believe that it could capture her electoral vote in the presidential campaign of 1880. A bill was accordingly introduced in the Democratic House, January, 1879, by the representative from Nevada, which required captains of vessels bringing Chinese into the United States to register at the port of entry a list of Chinese passengers and forbade a vessel to bring more than fifteen Chinese on any voyage. An amendment was added in the Senate, requiring the president to notify the government of China that the sections of the treaty which provided

[1] *In re* Tiburcio Parrott, 100 U. S., 401; *Nation*, XXX., 224.
[2] Baker *et al. vs.* Portland, 5 Sawyer, 566.

for the free interchange of citizens would be considered null and void on and after July 1, 1879, the day the proposed exclusion was to go into effect.

Being brought to a vote in the House after a debate of one hour, January 29, 1879, the restrictive act received 155 affirmative votes—108 Democrats and 47 Republicans; 72 negatives—54 Republicans and 18 Democrats were recorded, with 61 absentees. In the Senate 18 Republicans, mostly from the western states, supported the measure, together with 11 Democrats. The negative vote was composed of 18 Republicans and 9 Democrats. Ingails, of Kansas, was the only senator from a state west of the Mississippi who dared to declare himself opposed to the measure. After a Senate amendment was added requiring the abrogation of the treaty, the House vote on final passage showed a stronger party alignment, the Republicans being opposed to barring the Mongolians and the Democrats in favor of it.[1]

President Hayes returned the bill to the House, March 1, 1879, with the objection that while Congress had a right to declare a treaty null and void, it had no power to encroach on the executive by ordering him to abrogate a treaty or any part of one. In only one instance, that of France in 1798, had Congress declared a treaty abrogated, and that because of its repeated violation on the part of France. China, on the contrary, had observed the Burlingame treaty so faithfully that Hayes doubted even whether

[1] McPherson, *Hand-Book of Politics*, 1880, pp. 39–41.

an unquestioned abrogation by Congress would be justifiable. He was unwilling, by withdrawing the protection which the treaty afforded to Chinese in America and to Americans in China, to expose each to the fury of the mob. He would prefer the "proper course of diplomatic negotiations" to remedy the conditions of which the Pacific coast states reasonably complained. A motion to pass the bill over the objections fell far short of the required two-thirds; indeed, the affirmation was less than on the original vote.[1]

Aroused to the urgent situation in the West, and desirous of justifying his sentiments concerning the sacredness of a treaty, Hayes immediately despatched James B. Angell, of Michigan, John F. Swift, of California, and William Henry Trescot, of South Carolina, to China as ministers extraordinary to modify the Burlingame treaty or to form a new one. At Pekin, November 17, 1880, they secured from the Chinese representatives a modification of the Burlingame treaty which permitted the United States to "regulate, limit, or suspend," but not absolutely prohibit, the coming of Chinese laborers, whenever their coming or their residence affected or threatened to affect the interests of this country, or to endanger the good order of the country or any locality within it. The United States was made sole judge of the

[1] McPherson, *Hand-Book of Politics*, 1880, pp. 41–45; Richardson, *Messages and Papers*, VII., 514; Mason, *Veto Power*, *Appleton's Annual Cyclop.*, 1879, pp. 218–226.

time when it might be necessary to apply the restriction. Other subjects of China—teachers, students, merchants, or travellers from curiosity, together with their servants, and such laborers as were then in the United States, were not to be restrained. Unusual measures of protection were also promised them.[1]

News of the result of the mission reached America in time to influence the elections favorably for the Republicans. An attempt was made to offset this result by the publication in facsimile in a New York paper called *Truth*, a few hours before the election, of the following letter, supposedly written by the Republican candidate, Garfield.[2]

> "*Personal and Confidential.*
> "HOUSE OF REPRESENTATIVES,
> "WASHINGTON, D. C., *January 23, 1880.*
>
> "DEAR SIR,—Yours in relation to the Chinese problem came duly to hand.
>
> "I take it that the question of employees is only a question of private and corporate economy, and individuals or companies have the right to buy labor where they can get it cheapest.
>
> "We have a treaty with the Chinese government which should be religiously kept until its provisions are abrogated by the action of the general Government, and I am not prepared to say that it should be abrogated until our great manufacturing and corporate interests are conserved in the matter of labor.   Very truly yours,
> "H. L. MOREY,   "J. A. GARFIELD."
>   "Employers' Union, Lynn, Massachusetts."

[1] *U. S. Treaties and Conventions*, 182.
[2] *Nation*, XXX., 352; Andrews, *Last Quarter-Century*, I., 314; *Appleton's Annual Cyclop.*, 1880, p. 576; see above, p. 176.

Although the letter was easily proved to be a forgery, so strong was the anti-Chinese sentiment on the Pacific coast that the Republicans secured only one of the nine electors in California and Nevada. In Oregon, the letter failed to have an appreciable effect.[1] At this time there were about one hundred and five thousand Chinese in the United States, four hundred of whom lived in Denver. During the campaign an anti-Chinese riot occurred in that city, in which one Chinaman was killed and Chinese property destroyed to the value of fifty thousand dollars.

Possessing, under the treaty of 1880, the power to "regulate, limit, or suspend" the coming of Chinese laborers, Congress in 1882 inserted a clause in an act to execute the stipulations of the treaty, by which the coming of Chinese laborers was prohibited for the twenty years following the passage of the act. It passed the Senate by a vote of 28 Democrats and 8 Republicans, as against 1 Democrat and 14 Republicans. The House vote stood 164 in the affirmative—96 Democrats, 62 Republicans, and 6 Independent; 66 negative—4 Democrats and 62 Republicans.[2] The Democratic platform of 1880 declared unequivocally for "No more Chinese immigration, except for travel, education, and foreign commerce," while the Republican platform demanded restriction of Chinese immigration by "just,

---

[1] Stanwood, *Hist. of the Presidency*, 416.
[2] McPherson, *Hand-Book of Politics*, 1882, p. 94-96.

humane, and reasonable laws." The restrictive act just mentioned, whether just, humane, and reasonable, was a Democratic measure, inherited from the preceding Democratic Congress, and one for which the Democratic party would claim due credit. The Republican votes which the measure received came almost entirely from the western states.

President Arthur returned the bill to the Senate, April 4, 1882, with his objections and certain accompanying documents. He held that the provisions of the proposed act were in violation of the recent treaty, which allowed the United States to "regulate, limit, and suspend" the immigration, but did not permit a total suspension for a period so long as twenty years, virtually a generation. "A nation is justified," said he, "in regulating its treaty obligations only when they are in conflict with great paramount interests. . . . It needs no argument to show that the policy we now propose to adopt must have a direct tendency to repel Oriental nations from us and to drive their trade and commerce into more friendly lands." [1] Accompanying documents showing the history of the treaty negotiations illustrated the true meaning of the phrase "to regulate." On a motion to disregard the objections of the president, only 7 Republican senators voted with 22 Democrats, while 21 Republicans voted in the neg-

---

[1] Richardson, *Messages and Papers*, VIII., 112; Mason, *Veto Power*, 58; McPherson, *Hand-Book of Politics*, 1882, pp. 96-102.

ative, so that the required two-thirds was not obtained.¹

Arthur suggested that a "shorter experiment" of the exclusion policy might be wiser; and Congress took him at his word and framed a second bill, which reduced the time of suspension to ten years, during which period no Chinese coolies, including "both skilled and unskilled laborers and Chinese employed in mining," were to be permitted to enter the United States. The law was to go into effect ninety days after passage. Any Chinese laborer leaving the United States after the expiration of that time must secure from the collector of customs of the port of departure a certificate which would entitle him to re-enter the United States. Chinese other than laborers coming to the United States must present a certificate from the Chinese government specifying that the holder was entitled to enter under the treaty provisions. Both state and federal courts were forbidden to confer citizenship on Chinese. This first Chinese exclusion act received the president's signature May 6, 1882, and went into effect on August 5, following.² The constitutionality of the law was upheld by the federal courts because the act was an incident of sovereignty.³

Each political party took to itself the credit for the protective measure, although its inefficiency

---

[1] McPherson, *Hand-Book of Politics*, 1882, p. 102.
[2] *U. S. Statutes at Large*, XXII., 58.
[3] Wong Wing *vs.* U. S., 163 U. S., 235.

soon became apparent. The certificates of identification proved useless, because all Chinese looked alike to the inspectors; and a wholesale trading of certificates went on in China between those returning and those wishing to come. Smuggling laborers across the Canadian border caused additional complaint, especially when the attorney-general of the United States, Brewster, gave an opinion, December 26, 1882,[1] that between forty and fifty thousand Chinese coolies whose contracted term of service in the West Indies was about to expire, and who wished to pass through the United States in returning to China, could not be barred under the treaty or required to secure certificates. Passing through at various times and in various places, it was feared that many of these coolies would take advantage of the opportunity to take up residence furtively while en route.[2]

Complaint came from the governor of California that the federal authorities of the port of San Francisco were lax in enforcing the law. "With that cunning and persistence which no one will deny them," reported a member of the House from California,[3] the Chinese were adopting ways and means of evading the law. In response to the many complaints, Congress passed a second Chinese restriction

---

[1] *Senate Exec. Docs.*, 48 Cong., 1 Sess., No. 62, p. 13.
[2] *Appleton's Annual Cyclop.*, 1882, p. 391; *Senate Exec. Docs.*, 48 Cong., 1 Sess., No. 62.
[3] *Cong. Record*, 48 Cong., 1 Sess., 3752.

law, approved by the president July 5, 1884,[1] as amendatory of the first, which limited the meaning of the word "merchant," provided additional requirements of identification for "visitors" to America, and placed more stringent requirements on masters of vessels bringing Chinese. The debates brought out no new points, and the votes were distributed as on the first bill, the number of "absent" members being increased. All later attempts to negotiate with China were vitiated by the passage of the Scott act of 1888, cutting off the privilege of returning, and by the Geary act of 1892, which extended the suspension for another ten years.

The hostility towards the Chinese as laborers proceeded in large part from the growing influence of labor organizations, and included laborers coming from other lands as their number increased. In 1880 the total number of arrivals was 327,371, and in the following year it rose to 669,431—a figure never reached in any preceding year. Among the new factors of population arriving in 1881 were 112,712 Canadians and 1500 Russian Jews, the latter flying from religious persecution. The introduction of these new elements created a demand for some general restriction which would apply to others than the Chinese. It was claimed that foreigners were willing to work for lower wages and would ultimately drive natives out of work; that they embraced the criminal class, the illiterates, and the paupers of

[1] *U. S. Statutes at Large*, XXIII., 115.

Europe; and that they tended to corrupt local government in the United States. A restrictive act was passed by Congress, August 3, 1882,[1] barring paupers, criminals, convicts, and the insane, and requiring them to be returned at the expense of the owners of the vessels in which they came; a poll-tax of fifty cents was imposed upon all for the relief of the needy; and enforcement of the act was intrusted to the secretary of the treasury in connection with state officials. Three years later, February 25, 1885, was passed the first of a series of laws to bar laborers coming under contract, a species of legislation which belongs to the later industrial period.[2]

[1] *U. S. Statutes at Large,* XXII., 214.
[2] Dewey, *National Problems* (*Am. Nation,* XXIV.), chap. iii.

CHAPTER XV

THE FAR WEST

(1876-1888)

AS has been shown in the preceding chapter, the Chinese question was a western problem, because the Pacific slope was the only part of the country which keenly felt the yellow peril. The far West had many other difficulties to meet, one of which was the incessant rivalry between the farm and the cattle-ranch. Before the white men had finished their conquest of the aborigines, they inaugurated among themselves another warfare as persistent and vindictive, although not so bloody, for possession of the land they had won. Ranchman fought ranchman, and miner contended with miner, for spoils that rivalled a king's empire in power and wealth. The inherent predatory instinct of man, unchecked by the restraints of law, turned might into right. The story of Morgan and Dampier and their fellow-buccaneers near the Spanish Main in colonial history was duplicated by the land buccaneers of the Golden West. While the trapper gathered the last tribute from stream and woodland, the impatient hunter pressed his lingering steps to take the great game from plains and mountains. As the buffalo disappeared from the grazing-lands, the cattle of Texas, adapted by breeding, came to replace them under the ranchman. The ranch, with its novel system of branding, its picturesque cow-boys, its marvellous "drives," and its unique "round-up," formed a panorama which will long delight the painter, the poet, and the novelist.[1]

Life on the ranch was one long watch against the thieving "rustler," who altered cattle brands and stole horses in reckless fashion. Vigilantes made short shrift of these land pirates, and it was said that they hanged and shot more men in Montana, Wyoming, and Nebraska during the decade between 1876 and 1886 than have been legally executed since in any six states.[2] On the other hand, the rancher contended with English syndicates and eastern capitalists who, through the land offices and territorial legislatures, sought to deprive him of what he considered two inalienable rights — free grass and free water-fronts. Later he had to resist in Montana and Wyoming the invading sheep-rancher; and still later entered the hopeless lists against the farmer, who stretched long lines of wire fence across the grazing-lands and turned them with the plough.

Among the cattle kings of New Mexico in the late seventies were the Chisholm brothers, of the Pecos Valley, in Lincoln County, whose ranch and herds

---

[1] *Harper's Weekly*, XXIV., 637; Andy Adams, *Reed Anthony, Cowman.*   [2] Hough, *Story of the Cowboy*, 283.

were coveted by a band of freebooters under "Billy
the Kid." The partisan war inaugurated between
the two embroiled the people of fully one-third the
territory, in which an occasional robbery of the mail-
coaches and passengers formed a diverting side
feature. President Hayes issued a proclamation
October 7, 1878, warning the combatants to desist
and to disperse peaceably to their several abodes.[1]
General Sherman was ordered to enforce the command with the federal troops, and eventually succeeded.

In 1881 lawless bands of men calling themselves
"cow-boys" infested southern Arizona, making frequent raids into Mexico for pillage. President
Arthur, in December, 1881, asked Congress to frame
laws necessary to enable him to use military force
to subdue these lawless men, if asked by the governor
of the territory;[2] and to be allowed to use the army
as a *posse comitatus*, a use which had been forbidden
by a rider in the army appropriation bill of 1878.[3]
The following May, Arthur issued a proclamation
commanding the desperadoes to disperse.[4] Gradually American home-makers invaded the great West,
as they had swept over the wild land farther east;
law and order were established in the territories;
and violence no longer reigned as when the elements
of states were rounding into form. The United

[1] Richardson, *Messages and Papers*, VII., 489.
[2] *Ibid.*, VIII., 54. [3] See above, p. 127.
[4] Richardson, *Messages and Papers*, VIII., 123.

States troops were withdrawn from the most thinly populated portions to be concentrated in the vicinity of large cities—the future danger points; many of the military reservations were handed over by the department of war to the department of the interior to be thrown open to sale and settlement.[1]

The Great West owed its fame and its solidarity to its remoteness; when invaded and settled it speedily lost its individuality and its picturesqueness; then it disappeared. The completion of the first Pacific railroad in 1869 marked the beginning of the end of primitive conditions. It followed the central of three great routes pronounced practicable by government surveyors. The southern, commonly known as the thirty-second parallel route, which was rejected by Congress in 1862 in favor of the central route, was taken up a few years later by the Atlantic and Pacific Company, a subsidy of public land was secured from the United States, and December 1, 1881, the last spike was driven near El Paso in a rail connection between New Orleans and the Pacific Ocean, which subsequently became known as the "Southern Pacific Railroad." Work was also begun on the most northerly of the three routes, with an eastern terminus at Duluth, which would tap the Great Lakes. A branch was constructed to St. Paul, and a western terminus established at Portland, Oregon, with a branch northward to Puget

---

[1] For a list of abandoned military reservations, see Commissioner of General Land Office, *Report*, 1900, pp. 138–156.

Sound. Its construction involved the most difficult feats in engineering, and its necessary deviations in crossing the Rocky Mountains caused a longer mileage than either of the other routes. It crossed the Cascade Range at an elevation of 6560 feet. In 1883 trains bearing guests from Chicago and from Portland met at a point in western Montana where a spike was driven to mark the completion of the Northern Pacific Railroad, as the line was called.[1]

Three months prior to this celebration a similar ceremony marked the end of construction on a fourth trans-continental line, the Atchison, Topeka & Santa Fé, which started in Kansas, due west of St. Louis, but soon dropped to the thirty-fourth parallel route and passed around the southern end of the Rocky Mountains, through desert regions which many official surveyors had pronounced impassable. Its original terminus was Guaymas, on the Gulf of California, but was changed to Los Angeles before the road was completed in 1883.

Without the aid of the federal government, the building of the Pacific railways must have been delayed until private capital was sufficiently accumulated to undertake their construction.[2] Between 1850 and 1872, Congress passed acts granting public land to no less than 108 companies for constructing

[1] Henry Villard, *Memoirs*, II., chap. xli.
[2] Hart, *Practical Essays in Am. Govt.*, chap. x.; Sanborn, *Congressional Grants of Land in Aid of Railways* (University of Wisconsin, *Bulletins*, Economics, Pol. Sci., and Hist. Series, II., No. 3); Donaldson, *Public Domain*, 273.

railroads, which called for 155,000,000 acres when the roads were completed. By 1880 the roads had constructed 15,430 miles with the aid of the land grants and had claimed and received 45,647,347 acres.[1] Part of the vast donation lapsed because the roads did not fulfil the conditions; and part was never patented.

Although the railroads were intended to carry prospective purchasers of land to their new homes and to return their products to market, these enormous gifts of land were regarded as robberies of the individuals. While the railroads in twenty years, ending in 1872, secured 155,000,000 acres as a *douceur*, the people were permitted to purchase at prices varying from 12½ cents to $2.50 an acre only 170,000,000 acres in nearly a hundred years. Between 1862, the date of the homestead law, and 1880, nearly 470,000 applications were filed by settlers seeking western homes, about one-third of whom eventually complied with all conditions and received the land.[2] In 1880 there were 179 military reservations, embracing nearly 3,000,000 acres of land, scattered through the West, most of which would be thrown open to the public as the troops were gradually withdrawn, to guard against the future danger of outbreaks in the cities. Timber, stone, coal, and mineral lands could be acquired on special terms. Under the law of 1877, "desert" land—that is, land which cannot be

[1] Donaldson, *Public Domain*, 208.
[2] *Ibid.*, 350.

cultivated without irrigation, could be obtained at twenty-five cents an acre by irrigating it and cultivating it for three years.[1]

These were the attractions of the great West, which rendered the task of restraining the eager settlers doubly hard; which brought forth a presidential proclamation in 1880; which usually precipitated the Indian wars; and which peopled a wilderness within a shorter time than any in recorded history. The settlement of the West wrought many economic changes in the older states. As the buffalo, long the source of food, disappeared, the prairie upon which he fed was turned into grazing-lands for domestic cattle, and then into corn and wheat fields. The surplus grain from the thinly populated regions found its way over the railroads to the older states, and beyond by ocean transit to feed over-populated Europe. As early as 1878 breadstuffs to the value of nearly $200,000,000 were exported from the United States, part of the harvest which was estimated that year to be three times the amount needed for home consumption. During the preceding year Illinois and Iowa alone raised 346,000,000 bushels of Indian-corn, while Kansas took her place among the grain-producing states by yielding 15,000,000 bushels of wheat and 103,000,000 bushels of corn. The surplus wheat crop of Oregon was estimated at 5,000,000 bushels. Between 1870 and 1880 the number of farms in Kansas and Dakota

[1] Donaldson, *Public Domain*, 415.

increased ten times, and in Nebraska five times. In other trans-Missouri states and territories they doubled and trebled. This surplus breadstuff found its way to Europe and attracted in return laborers to till the fields in which it was produced. Germans and Scandinavians predominated among these immigrant agriculturalists. During the decade ending in 1880, Dakota led the states of the Union in the increase of foreign born over native born citizens, followed by Oregon and Colorado.[1]

The independent and often defiant spirit of the West was shown in its highest degree by those people in Utah who were organized in a social, religious, and political body known as the Church of Jesus Christ of Latter-Day Saints. Man is always in search of Utopia, and a place where individualism may assert itself unhampered by the masses. As Puritan, Pietist, and other non-conformists early turned to the remote and extended American colonies to find asylum against persecution by the tyrannical majority, so these later advocates of individualism migrated to the West, trusting to find some place so remote that they might lead unmolested the special life to which they felt themselves called by God. In Missouri and in Illinois, previous to 1846, the Mormons suffered the persecution which commonly befalls the separatist in democratic America, partly because of the doctrine of polygamy already put forth by Joseph Smith and finally announced by

[1] U. S. Tenth Census, 1880, I., p. xl.

Brigham Young soon after the hegira of the Mormons to Utah in 1847.[1]

Polygamy was abhorrent to the mass of people in the United States—a noxious plant which must be eradicated by the strong hand of the law and not left to mobs and lawless persecution. When the Mormons reached the supposed haven of Salt Lake, they set up the provisional state of Deseret, but in 1850 were included in the limits of the territory of Utah. They officially adopted the doctrine of "spiritual marriages" by an ordinance of 1851, which incorporated the Church of Jesus Christ of Latter-Day Saints. The transition into a territory did not affect polygamy, because the church had sufficient strength to control the offices and acts of the territory. In 1855 an act to revise the laws in force, duly passed by the territorial legislature and signed by the governor, Brigham Young, also prophet of the Mormon church, openly permitted polygamy as a legal practice. After an armed resistance to the United States authorities ended, in 1858,[2] Congress began to consider the problem, and July 1, 1862, passed an act to punish the practice of "bigamy" in the territories of the United States, annulling all acts tending to establish, maintain, protect, or support the doctrine of polygamy.[3] The law was diffi-

---

[1] Linn, *Story of the Mormons*, 282.
[2] Smith, *Parties and Slavery* (*Am. Nation*, XVIII.), 328.
[3] *U. S. Statutes at Large*, XII., 501; Linn, *Story of the Mormons*, 540.

cult to enforce because of the remoteness of the region.

After the distractions of the Civil War ceased and the completion of the Pacific railroads opened Utah territory to public inspection, it was ascertained that polygamy was extensively practised, notwithstanding the law of 1862. To check the growth of Mormonism, the secretary of state made an effort, August 9, 1879,[1] to persuade foreign governments to discourage the teaching of Mormonism or to forbid the emigration of Mormon converts, but with small results. Occasionally polygamous marriages were punished in the United States courts under national laws, and leading Mormons were sometimes indicted; but testimony was difficult to obtain. The act of 1862 specified that it must not be construed as affecting the right to worship God according to the dictates of conscience, and under this proviso the Mormons shielded the practice of polygamy as part of their doctrine. "Because of the peculiar difficulties attending its enforcement,"[2] Hayes was compelled to acknowledge, in 1879 that the law, although on the statute-books for seventeen years, was practically a dead letter.

By act of June 23, 1874,[3] Congress reorganized the territorial courts of Utah and retained additional

---

[1] *Foreign Relations*, 1879, II., 349–964 passim.
[2] Richardson, *Messages and Papers*, VII., 560; Linn, *Story of the Mormons*, 595.
[3] *U. S. Statutes at Large*, XVIII., pt. iii., 254.

supervision over the acts of the territorial legislature; writs of error were allowed, to bring a person convicted of bigamy from the territorial supreme court to the United States Supreme Court. Under this law, a case appeared in the latter court and a decision in 1879 disposed of the argument that federal interference with polygamy was an infringement on freedom of religious worship. Nevertheless, difficulty was encountered in prosecuting persons accused of bigamy under the law of 1862 because a wife could not be compelled to testify against her husband. Prosecution was also delayed because the federal and territorial courts had not concurrent jurisdiction. Mormon lawyers claimed that the phrase "every person having a husband or wife living who marries another" did not cover a simultaneous marriage to two or more wives. Only three final convictions were obtained, it was claimed, between 1862, when the first anti-polygamy law was passed, and 1882, when it was amended to correct these deficiencies.[1]

The growth of Mormonism was a constant argument for stringent measures to check its pernicious practices. Since 1837, when Mormon missionaries were first sent abroad, they had penetrated every civilized part of the globe except Prussia and Austria, whose governments forbade their entrance. In 1880 they supported more than two hundred "elders" as foreign missionaries, and welcomed annually not less

[1] *North Am. Rev.*, CXXXIV., 328.

than two thousand converts to add to their number in Utah. There were at this time about one hundred thousand people in Utah territory, of whom the forty-four thousand foreign born were nearly all Mormon recruits. The greatest number came from Great Britain, followed in decreasing order by the Scandinavian countries, by Germany, and by Canada.[1] To offset the Mormon doctrines by religious and educational influences, the Presbyterian church maintained more than forty missionaries in Utah; the Congregationalists supported eleven; the Methodists eighteen; while the Episcopalians and the Woman's Home Mission Society supported schools, churches, and hospitals.[2]

The "Edmunds law" of March 22, 1882,[3] defined simultaneous marriages as bigamy, and prescribed loss of citizenship as an additional penalty for bigamists; it legitimated children born in polygamy before 1883; threw safeguards about the qualifications of jurors and the testimony of witnesses; and replaced by a commission of five the registration and election officers of the territory. Under this act the commissioners revised the registration of voters in the territory, appointed election officers, and supervised an election of a territorial delegate to Congress, November 7, 1883. Although they ex-

---

[1] U. S. Tenth Census, 1880, I., 531.
[2] *Appleton's Annual Cyclop.*, 1881, p. 860.
[3] *U. S. Statutes at Large*, XXII., 30; McPherson, *Hand-Book of Politics*, 1882, pp. 51–56; Linn, *Story of the Mormons*, 598.

cluded about twelve thousand men and women from voting because they practised polygamy, the Mormon delegate was elected over the Gentile by a vote of 23,000 to 4000.[1] The Mormons also carried the elections for local officers, although the officials elected were required to be monogamists. In 1884 the commissioners reported that polygamous relations had decreased in the cities of the territory but not in the country.[2]

Under supervision of this "Utah commission," a Gentile jury was formed by putting to every venireman the question, "Do you believe it right for a man to have more than one living and undivorced wife at the same time?" The Mormons unanimously replied "Yes," and were excluded for cause. Rudger Clawson was tried for bigamy before this kind of a jury in 1884; his second wife was compelled to testify; and he was sentenced to pay a fine of eight hundred dollars and to serve four years in the penitentiary. The prisoner was a bishop in the church, and among the witnesses were its chief officers. The trial caused intense interest throughout the country, and the decision of the supreme court of the territory, followed by that of the United States in 1884 confirming the sentence of Clawson, was a triumph for federal regulation of polygamy in the territorial courts.[3]

[1] *Appleton's Annual Cyclop.*, 1883, p. 812.
[2] *House Exec. Docs.*, 48 Cong., 1 Sess., No. 153.
[3] Clawson *vs.* U. S., 114 U. S., 477; *Appleton's Annual Cyclop.*, 1884, p. 792.

Another prominent Mormon, Angus M. Cannon, was sentenced under the Edmunds act by the territorial courts for the practice of polygamy; he appealed the case; and in 1885 the Supreme Court of the United States upheld the constitutionality of the act.[1] In 1888 the commission reported over a thousand convictions under the Edmunds act.[2] Damage suits against the commission, instituted by Mormons for depriving them of their political rights, were dismissed by the courts. The later steps taken to eradicate polygamy, the dis-incorporation of the church, and the attempts to bar polygamists from the United States Senate, lie beyond the limits of this volume.

[1] Cannon *vs.* U. S., 116 U. S., 55; see also U. S. *vs.* Snow, 4 Utah, 295, and U. S. *vs.* Clark, 6 Utah, 120.
[2] *House Exec. Docs.*, 50 Cong., 1 Sess., No. 447.

CHAPTER XVI

THE INDIAN QUESTION
(1877–1885)

THE Indians have been associated with the great West in public thought since 1834, when the policy of setting aside tracts of land in the trans-Mississippi region for their special use was inaugurated by the creation of the Indian territory.[1] In addition to removing the Indians from the older states to this and adjacent reservations, the nomadic tribes of the West were gradually confined to similar bounds to make way for the advancing whites. In the older states small reservations were occasionally made for tribes which had become sufficiently reduced in numbers or sufficiently civilized to cease to be a menace to their white neighbors. By executive order the required lands of the public domain were withdrawn from sale or entry and set apart for this particular purpose. In this way the United States reservation system for the Indians was developed.

After two hundred years of failure to subdue the

[1] MacDonald, *Jacksonian Democracy* (*Am. Nation*, XV.), chap. x.

savages by force, the more humane "peace policy" or the "missionary idea," as it is sometimes called, came into full practice during Grant's administration, although the idea of converting Indians to Christianity and of training them in agriculture and other industrial pursuits had been advocated by both Lincoln and Johnson. An organized system of Christian civilization was long urged by various religious denominations and by societies formed for this purpose. The basic idea of the peace policy is the progress of the individual.[1] In accord with this thought the old theory that each Indian tribe constituted a "domestic dependent nation," capable of diplomatic relations, was abandoned in 1871,[2] when Congress placed in the Indian appropriation bill a proviso forbidding "treaties" to be made with the Indians in the future. Nevertheless, "contracts" continued to be made, and the Indians were usually treated as members of a tribe with which the government dealt as a unit. The ancient fiction was also preserved in fact by permitting the more advanced "nations" to develop self-government, while the smaller and weaker tribes were allowed to be absorbed, if they wished, in the local government of their white neighbors.

With the rapid peopling of the West, as heretofore described, the demand for the good farming-lands of the reservation, uncultivated by the Indian sav-

[1] *U. S. Statutes at Large*, XVI., 566.
[2] *Senate Exec. Docs.*, 48 Cong., 2 Sess, No. 95.

age, made the task of preventing encroachment on Indian reservations exceedingly difficult. The discovery of precious metals frequently precipitated a "rush" of white men, to whom the sacred promises of an Indian treaty were no restraint. The federal troops, stationed in the West after the close of the Civil War, for the protection of the settlers from the savages, were frequently called upon to protect the savages from the white men. Gradually the spaces assigned to the Indians grew smaller as those allotted to their natural foemen increased in size.

The Nez Percés in the Northwest, for instance, with whom a treaty was signed in 1855,[1] promising permanent possession of a tract of land, saw with dismay an invasion of their reservation by gold-hunters during the Civil War, and the establishment of a town-site, Lewiston, on their lands. To accommodate the new conditions, a new treaty was drawn up in 1868,[2] ceding the desired portion of their reservation; but it was signed by only twenty chiefs out of the fifty-eight who had signed the former treaty thirteen years before. Among those refusing to participate in the new agreement was Chief Joseph, who with his band declined to leave the Wallowa Valley. President Grant yielded to his contention in 1873,[3] but two years later was persuaded by the governor of Oregon, by the territorial delegate, and

---

[1] *U. S. Statutes at Large*, XII., 927.   [2] *Ibid.*, XV., 693.
[3] Sec. of Interior, *Report*, 1878, p. 765.

by the impatient settlers, to rescind his former order and to throw open to settlement all that part of Oregon lying west of the Snake River.¹

Chief Joseph and six hundred of his people, evicted from the Wallowa Valley by federal troops, started on an aimless flight to escape their persecutors, and succeeded in dodging all the available federal forces sent in pursuit of them until they reached a point in Montana near the British border full thirteen hundred miles from the Wallowa Valley.² Cornered by the federal troops and defeated with heavy loss, Joseph surrendered and was removed to the far-off Indian territory, where his people speedily succumbed to the warmer climate and changed conditions. Nearly one-third their number died within the first two years, and they soon ceased to give their civilized guardians further cause for anxiety. In 1883 the remnant was removed to Idaho to join those Nez Percés who had not resisted the transfer eight years before.³

Appealing even more strongly to the sympathy of residents of the older states, who never came into contact with the troublesome Indians, was the case of the Poncas. In 1875 it was desired to push the

---

¹ Sec. of Interior, *Report*, 1878, p. 766; *House Reports*, 43 Cong., 1 Sess., No. 63.
² *Senate Exec. Docs.*, 45 Cong., 2 Sess., I., No. 14; *Appleton's Annual Cyclop.*, 1877, p. 40.
³ Young Joseph, "An Indian's Views of Indian Affairs," in *North Am. Rev.*, CXXVIII., 412; Howard, "True Story of the Wallowa Campaign," in *ibid.*, CXXIX., 53.

Sioux reservation eastward in order to wrest from them the gold-yielding Black Hills of Dakota;[1] but the way was blocked by the small reservation of ninety-six thousand acres occupied by the peaceful Poncas, which lay directly east of the Sioux in the southeast corner of Dakota. Here they dwelt under a treaty of 1855,[2] raised their crops, built their houses, opened schools, constructed a church, and prospered as much as the frequent raids of their neighbors, the Sioux, would allow. They represented probably the best results of the application of the peace policy to the savages, and it was once officially said of them that no Ponca had ever killed a white man.[3] Yet on the chess-board of inland diplomacy they must be shifted hundreds of miles to the Indian territory in order to allow the Sioux to occupy their position, and so make way for the miners and capitalists in the Black Hills. At the same time the Sioux, coming into possession of the tilled land, one hundred houses, and other property of the Poncas, would receive an impulse towards civilization. Congress at first made the consent of the Poncas a condition of their removal; but when this could not be secured from the intelligent Indians by the usual promises, Congress ordered their unconditional "removal and permanent location" in the Indian Territory.[4]

[1] *U. S. Statutes at Large*, XIX., 254.   [2] *Ibid.*, XII., 997.
[3] Sec. of Interior, *Report*, 1878, I., viii.
[4] *U. S. Statutes at Large*, XIX., 192, 287.

Yielding to the inevitable, these Indian farmers, with their families, about six hundred persons in all, journeyed for fifty-two days through the spring rains and over muddy trails to the territory, where they found a precarious lodging in tents on lands belonging to the Quapaws. During the first year 85 deaths were recorded officially,[1] the Indian count being 157. The survivors were now shifted to a new location on the Kaw River, where they must begin new improvements. Without tools or implements, devastated by death, and sick in spirit, small bands of the Poncas began stealthily to return northward to their old home in Dakota. They carried the bones of their dead to be interred in the land of their fathers. As the story of their wrongs spread through the public prints, a great storm of popular indignation broke upon the head of Secretary Schurz, the vicarious sacrifice of Congress in the removal of the Poncas.[2] Newspapers teemed with editorials and articles demanding the return of the expatriated Indians to their Dakota homes and the restoration of their lands.

Among the Ponca chiefs was Standing Bear, who, with twenty-five followers, disobediently left the Indian Territory and migrated to their friends, the Omahas, in Nebraska. They declared their inten-

---

[1] *U. S. Statutes at Large*, XX., 76; Sec. of Interior, *Report*, 1877, I., 492-498; *Frank Leslie's Newspaper*, July 28, 1877.

[2] *Nation*, February 24, 1881; Schurz, "Removal of the Poncas," in *Independent*, January 1, 1880.

tion of abandoning their tribal relations and becoming self-supporting. Nevertheless, they were arrested by Brigadier-General Crook on orders from Washington for having left their reservation without permission. Here was a new point in law. The prisoners were released on a writ of *habeas corpus* by Judge Dundy, of the United States district court of Nebraska, May 12, 1878, on the ground that an Indian was a "person" within the meaning of the laws of the United States, possessed of the inherent right of removing from place to place, and entitled to the privilege of *habeas corpus*. Evidently the Indian was rapidly passing, as the negro had done, from being the ward of the republic to a citizen thereof. Whether the new status in which the Indian was placed by the decision would have been upheld by the Supreme Court was unfortunately never determined, because Standing Bear gave no bond for his appearance in a higher court after the case had been appealed by a representative of the bureau of Indian affairs, and the whole controversy was dropped.

Standing Bear immediately toured the country with an educated Ponca girl named Bright Eyes, both addressing large audiences, organizing Ponca relief associations, and arousing public indignation with the story of their wrongs. President Hayes

[1] *Senate Reports*, 46 Cong., 2 Sess., VI., No. 670; *Senate Misc. Docs.*, 46 Cong., 3 Sess., I., No. 49; Sec. of Interior, *Report*, 1879 pp. 21, 77, 179.

freely acknowledged that enough of the responsibility for the wrong consummated on the Poncas attached to him to make it his particular duty and earnest desire to do all that he could to give them the redress which was required alike by justice and humanity.[1] He created a Ponca commission, composed of two army officers and two civilians, who visited the scattered Poncas and reported, February, 1881, that 521 were living contentedly in the Indian Territory and had no wish to return; and that about 150 were dwelling in Dakota and Nebraska, and desired to remain there.[2] This disposition was eventually made,[3] and the excitement subsided.

To recount the Indian wars in the period contemplated in this volume would be a tedious and harrowing recital; to describe their causes would be to show the whites almost invariably in the wrong. Encroaching settlers, miners, and prospectors; dishonest Indian agents and broken government promises; starving Indians and near-by herds of cattle; personal encounters in remote regions which grew into mutual charges of murder; forced removal from the path of progress to distant and undesirable lands—these and similar causes were responsible for the prolonged warfare which was to determine the survival of the fittest.[4] In 1878 the Bannocks, in

[1] Richardson, *Messages and Papers*, VII., 634.
[2] *Ibid.*, 630; *Senate Exec. Docs.*, 46 Cong., 3 Sess., No. 30.
[3] *U. S. Statutes at Large*, XXI., 422.
[4] *North Am. Rev.*, CXXXIV., 272.

Oregon, suffering from insufficiency of food, took the war-path. At nearly the same time the Cheyennes started from the Indian Territory without provocation on a pillaging expedition across Kansas, scalping and burning, and causing wide-spread alarm before they were subdued and returned. In 1879 the attempt of a Ute agent in Colorado to compel his charges to become agriculturalists or starve, backed by the presence of troops, caused the Indians to revolt and a war followed. Another tribe of Utes had to be removed from another part of Colorado, because precious metals had been discovered on their lands and the whites could not be restrained;[1] the inevitable Indian war followed. The Apaches of New Mexico, under Chief Victoria, dissatisfied with their treatment, left their reservation in 1879 and were pursued by troops across the Rio Grande and over one hundred miles into Mexico before the American forces were warned to desist by the Mexican authorities. Victoria was killed and his band almost annihilated. Another Apache war raged in Arizona and the Mexican border in 1882 and 1883. Sitting Bull, who led the war of the Sioux in 1876 to retain possession of the Black Hills, and fled to Canada for refuge, was persuaded to cross the Canadian line in 1880 and surrendered on promise of a pardon.

Indian wars between 1865 and 1880 cost twenty-

[1] *Appleton's Annual Cyclop.*, 1879, p. 46; 1880, p. 116; 1881, p. 117.

two million dollars and the lives of forty officers and five hundred and twenty-six men in attempting to carry out the peace policy and to keep the Indians on their reservations.¹ More than a hundred pages are required to print a list of engagements of the troops with Indians between 1868 and 1882.² "The Indians," said Hayes, in 1877, "were the aboriginal occupants of the land we now possess. They have been driven from place to place. The purchase money paid to them in some cases for what they called their own has still left them poor. In many instances, when they had settled down upon lands assigned to them by compact and begun to support themselves by their own labor, they were rudely jostled off and thrust into the wilderness again. Many, if not most, of our Indian wars have had their origin in broken promises and acts of injustice on our part." ³

Those who interested themselves in the wrongs of the Indians found additional ground for complaint in the manner in which the money appropriated by Congress to pay tribes for their lands or for their maintenance was diverted from its proper recipients by damage claims instituted against the tribe. These claims of white men for losses sustained in the Indian wars constituted a steady drain upon government payments. Some of them dated as far

¹ *Senate Exec. Docs.*, 46 Cong., 3 Sess., No. 15.
² Sheridan, *Record of Engagements with Hostile Indians.*
³ Richardson, *Messages and Papers*, VII., 475.

back as the War of 1812, although it was questionable whether the sins of one generation of Indians should be expiated by the next. These claims did not differ from others in their tendency to appreciate; and the federal court of claims found it necessary in many instances to cut off as much as forty per cent. of the sum originally demanded by the white men. In 1890 over eight thousand claims had been filed before the court, involving a total of more than twenty-five million dollars, some of them so large as to bankrupt certain tribes if allowed. No official report shows the activity of the claim agent in securing appropriations from Congress for the benefit of the Indians to be ultimately given to damage claimants, fifty per cent. of which sometimes found its way into his pocket.

That it was cheaper to feed idle Indians on reservations and allow them quietly to degenerate and to disappear than to exterminate them in warfare was the early underlying principle of the Indian reservation. Even this economy required expenditures of large sums of money. Between 1875 and 1885 the annual appropriations for the Indians varied from five to nine million dollars. Some of these Indian appropriation bills contained as many as one hundred and seventy-six different items for which money was specifically given, including permanent annuities to certain tribes, some of which Congress had been voting annually for nearly one hundred years; in-

[1] *Senate Exec. Docs.*, 52 Cong., 1 Sess., No. 117.

terest on tribal funds; money to purchase food, salt, medicine, iron, and steel; vaccination expenses; wages for Indian agents, carpenters, millers, teachers, physicians, and police; also for expenses of Indian delegations visiting Washington, and for conveying Indian children to and from schools.[1] Most of these payments, however, were simply instalments on purchase money for Indian lands, retained by the government as a guardian.

At various times, beginning with 1819,[2] the federal government made small appropriations to aid missionary schools established among the Indians of the eastern states by various religious denominations. About 1873, under the influence of the peace policy, Congress inaugurated a new method and appropriated twenty thousand dollars to be used directly by the government in educating the Indians, and increased the sums for this purpose annually until they passed the million-dollar mark within fifteen years.[3] The schools provided for in this manner were located for the most part on the different Indian reservations; but in 1878 seventeen Indians, who were prisoners in Florida, were sent as an experiment to a normal and industrial school for negroes which had been opened a decade before in the abandoned war barracks at Hampton, Virginia. The hope that the young Indians, when removed from the enervating influence of the reservation,

---

[1] *U. S. Statutes at Large*, XXIV., 459.   [2] *Ibid.*, III., 516.
[3] *U. S. Statistical Abstract*, 1900, p. 36.

would progress more rapidly in the arts of civilization, was well founded. Consequently, Captain R. H. Pratt was authorized to bring fifty more Indians from Dakota, and in 1879 an abandoned army post at Carlisle, Pennsylvania, was made into the United States Training and Industrial School for Indians.[1]

Other industrial schools were opened at Lawrence, Kansas, Chilocco, Oklahoma, and elsewhere. Boarding-schools were also established on the reservations, to which Indians were sent. In 1880 more than seven thousand Indian children were in school, and not less than twice that number of adults were engaged in useful labor, knowledge of which they had acquired in schools.[2]

Beginning with Madison in 1816, various presidents advised allotting the lands in the reservations to the Indians in severalty, with patents conferring fee-simple title, inalienable for a certain period; and, if any tribal land remained after that process, disposing of it for the common benefit of the tribe. This was to be done with the consent of the Indians, who were then to be placed on an equal footing with the whites in the protection afforded by the laws of the country. Indians were made eligible for a homestead on the public lands in Michigan by act of March 3, 1875,[3] and in other states by later acts; but in 1880 the number who had taken advantage of

---

[1] Sec. of the Interior, *Report*, 1879, p. viii.
[2] Richardson, *Messages and Papers*, VII., 623.
[3] *U. S. Statutes at Large*, XVIII., pt. iii., 420.

the opportunity to secure farms did not exceed a hundred.[1] Manifestly the tribal ties and the ease of reservation life would long keep the savage in the "blanket" stage.

In the Indian appropriation bill of 1875 it was provided that "for the purpose of inducing the Indians to labor and become self-supporting," the agent distributing supplies might require all able-bodied males between the ages of eighteen and forty-five to perform service upon the reservation to an amount equal in value to the supplies delivered. Owing to the natural antipathy of the savage to steady productive labor, this provision was carried out with great difficulty. Experience with it made the Indians still more reluctant to abandon their tribal relations and take lands in severalty. In his last message to Congress, December, 1880, Hayes announced that the Utes in Colorado had voluntarily surrendered their large reservation and agreed to hold the land in individual titles. "For the first time in the history of the country," said he, "an Indian nation has given up its tribal existence . . . to live as individuals under the common protection of the laws of the country."[2]

A remedy for the Indian troubles seemed to have been found at last. "We have to deal with the appalling fact," said President Arthur in 1881, "that though thousands of lives have been sacrificed and

[1] Donaldson, *Public Domain*, 243.
[2] Richardson, *Messages and Papers*, VII., 624.

hundreds of millions of dollars expended in the attempt to solve the Indian problem, it has until within the past few years seemed scarcely nearer a solution than it was half a century ago."[1] He recommended making the laws of the various states and territories applicable to the Indian reservations within their borders, and extending the laws of Arkansas over that portion of Indian Territory not occupied by the five civilized tribes, who were trying to establish self-government. He also advocated liberal appropriations for Indian schools and a general law requiring the survey of the Indian reservations and allotment of lands in severalty to those desiring it. Notwithstanding these repeated recommendations, Congress did not provide general laws for individual holdings and tribal disintegration until 1887.[2]

No official count of the wild or nomadic Indians was made for the census before 1890; but in 1870 an attempt was made through the various Indian agencies to form an estimate at least. It showed a total of 383,712 Indians living within the jurisdiction of the United States, including 70,000 in Alaska. Of these 25,731 were civilized or taxable Indians, having abandoned their tribal relations and being scattered through every state and territory except Delaware and the Indian Territory. They represented the broken bands and remnants of once pow-

[1] Richardson, *Messages and Papers*, VIII., 55–57.
[2] *U. S. Statutes at Large*, XXV., 891.

erful tribes, reduced by competition with civilization, and through no fault of their own, to a condition bordering on pauperism. In the Indian Territory dwelt nearly 60,000 Indians on reservations, and about 35,000 nomads. On the other reservations, located chiefly in the western states, were nearly 125,000 Indians, subsisting almost wholly on the provision of the United States. Their reservations embraced nearly 100,000,000 acres of land, or over 700 acres for each individual. The nomadic or wandering tribes were estimated to number about 235,000.[1]

In 1880 the total number of Indians had increased only 10,000, or four per cent., while the number of taxables or those having abandoned their tribal relations grew from 44,000 to 66,800, or sixty-six per cent. California contained the largest number of these civilized Indians, with New Mexico, Michigan, Wisconsin, and Washington following in decreasing order.[2] During the year Indian farmers cultivated half a million acres of land and grazed four hundred thousand head of cattle.[3]

Notwithstanding his progress in civilization and education, no Indian as yet possessed the right of citizenship unless he entered a homestead. Being originally only a "domestic subject" and not a

[1] U. S. Ninth Census, 1870, XVII. Estimates made by the army differ; see *Am. Annual Cyclop.*, 1871, p. 42.
[2] U. S. Twelfth Census, 1900, I., 488.
[3] *Appleton's Annual Cyclop.*, 1880, p. 28.

"white person," Congress occasionally conferred civil rights on individual Indians who abandoned their tribes;[1] but whether severance of tribal relations made an Indian a citizen under the Fourteenth Amendment was not decided until 1883. John Elk, a civilized Indian who had left the reservation and took residence in Omaha, Nebraska, brought suit against the election officers for debarring him from voting. A majority of the justices in the federal Supreme Court decided, November 3, 1883,[2] that an Indian was by birth an alien and dependant, and could not at will cast off the disbarment, but must have the consent of the United States. The Fourteenth Amendment, it was held, concerned the status of the negro only. Also the old barrier to representation—"excluding Indians not taxed"—remained in the Constitution and was an argument against Indian political equality. A minority of the court held that the Amendment included all Indians dwelling outside a reservation, and made them citizens of the United States and entitled to all privileges in the several states.

[1] As in the case of the Wyandots in Kansas in 1855; see *U. S. Statutes at Large*, X., 1159.
[2] Elk vs. Wilkins, 112 U. S., 94.

CHAPTER XVII

THE TARIFF OF 1883
(1873-1883)

IN 1874 there was a deficit of more than a million dollars in balancing the receipts and expenditures at the United States treasury; in 1882 there was a surplus of $145,000,000. A surplus of money in the treasury is as troublesome, although not so alarming, as a deficit; the attempts to avoid "a feast or a famine" have led to many financial adjustments and experiments. A distribution of the surplus among the several states was tried in 1837;[1] but commonly relief has been sought by raising or lowering the tariff duties.

The panic of 1873 was largely responsible for the deficit of the following year. Customs receipts declined nearly $30,000,000 within the year, and continued to fall until 1878, when they were $86,000,000 below the mark of 1872. Owing to the withdrawal of the special-license stamp, and corporate taxes in 1870, and removal of the income tax in 1872, the annual receipts from internal revenue decreased more than $200,000,000 between 1866 and 1874. On the

[1] Hart, *Slavery and Abolition* (*Am. Nation*, XVI.), chap. xx.

other hand, the expenditures were lessened annually from the half-billion mark of 1866 to $236,000,000 during the compulsory economy of 1878. Suddenly the tide turned and an era of good times raised the customs receipts from $130,000,000 in 1878 to $220,000,000 in 1882. The internal revenue receipts increased correspondingly from the consumption of liquors and tobacco; and they included a few odds and ends of the war taxes, which were taken off in 1883. Expenditures during this time of returning prosperity increased more slowly than the receipts, being kept below $300,000,000 a year by the rigid economy of Congress.[1]

These imposts were levied for the most part under the "war tariffs." Beginning with 1862, they had been extended and increased from time to time to meet the demands of the war, until the schedule included nearly every commodity in use by the American people. Duties on sugar, salt, molasses, manufactured iron and other metals, druggists' articles, every kind of wearing apparel, utensils, and select grocers' goods were increased from 10 to 30 per cent.; pig-iron was taxed $2 a ton, sugar 2 cents a pound, and salt 6 cents a hundredweight. An average of 5 per cent. on all manufactured goods was intended to be levied, although on articles which paid both as raw material and finished products the tax was not less than from 8 to 15 per cent. The necessity for these rates at the time they were im-

[1] Sec. of the Treasury, *Report*, 1882, pp. 12-19.

posed was generally conceded; according to the title of the early acts, they were only "temporarily" increased; but who could have imagined that the burden placed upon the shoulders of a reluctant people by the hard hand of war would have grown to be an attractive load borne willingly for twenty years, and not cast aside when opportunity offered?

These war taxes were imposed by the Republican party, which was in power. Although Stevens, Morrill, and others intrusted with framing the taxes were avowed protectionists, the party was not yet committed to the principle of a protective tariff. But if an excise tax is laid on an article, a corresponding addition should be made to the import duty; and consequently the excise became an entering wedge for a protective tariff. These excises and direct taxes acted as a counter-irritant to conceal the annoyance of exacting a duty; consequently they were removed whenever opportunity presented; but the corresponding tariff charges remained, for if both were removed the revenue might be too much diminished. Under these conditions a tariff for revenue, as it was in the thoughts of the people, grew into a tariff for protection. One result was the reduction of the public debt during the two decades between 1860 and 1880 from $78.25 to $37.74 per capita without resorting to direct taxation.[1]

New industries were occasionally instituted under the protection of the tariff—such as the manufac-

[1] *U. S. Statistical Abstract*, 1900, p. 24.

ture of silk in the years following the Civil War and the tin-plate industry of recent times; also the total manufactured products of the United States increased in value from $1,850,000,000 in 1860 to $4,232,000,000 in 1870, and to $8,000,000,000 in 1880. The manufacture of steel rails, for example, under an average protective duty of $28 a ton, grew from 30,000 tons in 1870 to 1,200,000 tons in 1881.[1] The average price of raw cotton fell from 43 cents at the close of the war to 10 cents in 1882; nevertheless, the high tariff was retained on manufactured cotton goods, and their total production increased between 1860 and 1880 from $115,000,000 to $192,000,000. When the consumers cried out against this tax and the profits reasonably supposed to accrue to the manufacturers, it was easy to demonstrate that their profits were shared by the workers employed. The opening of the industrial era and the organization of laborers, who had now a fixed vocation and could no longer look to agricultural occupation as a relief, brought a high scale of living and high wages in comparison with European workmen dwelling in densely populated countries, where there was more labor than demand and where very few resources remained to be developed. Any protectionist orator could prove that New York and Chicago workmen received three times the wages paid in France and Italy, twice those paid in England and Belgium, and one and one-half times those

[1] *Cong. Record*, 47 Cong., 1 Sess., 2697.

current in Scotland.¹ Thus the demands of the manufacturer, who had tasted the sweets of protection, were supplemented by the wish of the workingman, who thought his increased wage compensated for the increased cost of living under the tariff. The result was that the war tariff, instead of being removed in time of peace, was actually increased on wool in 1867, on copper in 1869, and on marble and nickel in 1870. On the other hand, the tax was taken from quinine, as a medicinal remedy, in 1869, and from tea and coffee in 1872.² Aside from this "tinkering," the tariff grew more and more difficult to change as the years advanced. On the one hand, in 1866 Congress refused to pass a highly protective tariff proposed by Mr. Morrill, and, on the other, a low schedule prepared during the following year by Mr. Wells.

The reduction made in 1872 took fifty-three millions from the customs receipts, yet left "the great industries intact," as the secretary of the wool manufacturers association said. Most of these eliminations were restored in 1875. In that year, tariff reformers claimed that there were more than four thousand articles on which the American people were compelled to pay a tariff tax, and only six hundred on the free list; but statistics showed that between 1867 and 1883 the tariff schedules never contained more than sixteen hundred enumerated articles, of which

---

¹ *Cong. Record*, 47 Cong., 1 Sess., 2820.
² Taussig, *Tariff Hist. of U. S.*, chap. iii.

nearly four hundred were free.¹ In the high tide of customs receipts, which was reached in 1881, nearly one-fourth the collections came from the tariff on sugar and molasses. Wool and woollen goods were next largest contributors, next iron and steel and their products, with manufactures of silk and manufactures of cotton following, and wines and liquors last of the large importations. Receipts at the customs-houses on these six classes of goods formed two-thirds of the whole tariff collections.²

The war tariff was not sustained all these years by the old Hamiltonian plea for the encouragement of infant industries, because most of the beneficiaries were well established before the war. Nor could the continuation be grounded upon the needs of the treasury, because there was a surplus of $10,000,000 in 1870,³ and another of $68,000,000 in 1880. This unused cash grew to $100,000,000 in 1881, and to $145,000,000 in 1882,⁴ at which figure it became a menace because it withdrew too much money from circulation. In order to return it to the people, in 1870 the secretary of the treasury purchased bonds in the open market as they fell due, or at other times by paying the price. Incurred at different times during the war, the debt in 1880, for instance, bore five different rates of interest and was redeemable

---

[1] Act of February 8, 1875, *U. S. Statutes at Large*, XVIII., pt. iii., 307; Stanwood, *Am. Tariff Controversies*, II., 197.
[2] *U. S. Statistical Abstract*, 1900, pp. 252-258.
[3] Dewey, *Financial Hist. of U. S.*, 401. [4] *Ibid.*, 429.

at seventeen different periods. These dates could not be anticipated except by payment of a high premium to the holders. In 1881 more than $600,000,000 of the war debt would be due; but more than $900,000,000 of the more recent four-per-cent. bonds would not be redeemable until 1891 and 1907.[1] When Congress failed to pass a refunding bill for the $600,000,000, the secretary of the treasury continued the debt by notifying its holders to bring in their bonds carrying five and six per cent., and receive others paying three and one-half per cent. interest, which could be called in at the pleasure of the government. Full ninety-seven per cent. of the debt was thus continued, the holders preferring to accept a lower rate covered by the security of a government loan.[2] The government was saved a large sum in the difference of interest; but the surplus in the treasury was not relieved, as it would have been if the bonds had been redeemed.

An overflowing treasury was a constant temptation, as President Arthur said,[3] to large expenditures. The sums necessary to be allowed annually for the civil and judicial list, for the diplomatic and consular service, for the post-office, the Indians, light-houses, and the army and navy in time of peace, had become wellnigh fixed through long years of experience. Even the occasional appro-

---

[1] McPherson, *Hand-Book of Politics*, 1882, p. 191.
[2] Richardson, *Messages and Papers*, VIII., 48.
[3] *Ibid.*, 134.

priations made under the fiction of "deficiency" or "urgent deficiency" were subject to little inflation; but the amounts to be expended on internal improvements and on pensions were capable of unlimited increase.[1] The principle that the government should compensate those who lost health or were disabled in the service of their country, and provide for dependent families of those who thus sacrificed their lives, was established by the law of 1792,[2] although the sum appropriated was insignificant until the Civil War. By thirty-seven acts passed between 1862 and 1882, the pension system was enlarged and extended until its payment formed one of the largest drains upon the federal government, and its disbursements became a dependable source of income for the northern section of the Union. The number of applicants for rewards of this kind reached 72,684 in 1865, and then slowly decreased until 1874, when the "pension-claim agent" found his vocation.

By various methods and by attractive advertising, these claim agents gradually increased the number of applicants and enlarged their influence in Washington until they were able to secure the passage in 1879 of the "arrears of pensions" act.[3] It provided that payment of all pensions allowed should commence from the date of the death or discharge of

---

[1] *North Am. Rev.*, CXXVIII., 572–586.
[2] *U. S. Statutes at Large*, I., 324.
[3] *Ibid.*, XX., 265; *Harper's Weekly*, XXV., 843.

the person on whose account the pension was issued. Under this alluring prospect of receiving accumulated back pay, the number of applicants increased from 44,587 in 1878 to 141,466 in 1880.[1] At the time this flood of applications reached the pension office, there were already pending not less than a hundred thousand claims, which were being investigated as rapidly as possible. One result of this legislation, which had been foreseen by Secretary Schurz but was not resisted by President Hayes, was to increase the pension expenditures from $27,000,000 in 1878 to $35,000,000 in 1879, and to $56,000,000 in 1880.

In 1880 the commissioner of pensions reported a total list of five hundred fraudulent pensioners, whose names had been dropped from the rolls.[2] Although the amount lost to the treasury from these pension frauds was not large, nevertheless, as President Arthur pointed out in his message of 1881,[3] temptation to make fictitious claims was strong, when the average sum obtained by each claimant was $1300. There were then pending 265,575 cases, of which about six-sevenths would be allowed. If no more claims were filed, it was estimated that the clerks in the pension office would be able to pass on those pending within six years. Arthur asked Con-

[1] Commissioner of Pensions, *Report*, 1880, in *House Exec. Docs.*, 46 Cong., 3 Sess., No. 1, p. 393.
[2] *House Reports*, 46 Cong., 3 Sess., No. 736, App.
[3] Richardson, *Messages and Papers*, VIII., 58.

gress to take steps to prevent fraud in filing claims and to increase the working force in the pension office.

Special statutes to provide rewards for deeds of heroism or humanity were not unknown from Revolutionary times; but not until the Civil War were private bills used to bring within the pale of federal bounty persons not included by the general pension laws, or to relieve individuals of charges of desertion and the like, which prevented their receiving pensions. During the latter part of the war special acts making payment to chaplains, surgeons, widows, and dependent relatives were mingled with acts for the settlement of claims, for losses by robbery, and for other "relief" measures, until they outnumbered the regular statutes passed at some sessions. Many of them were intended to set aside or overrule decisions of the pension office. In 1867 ninety-one of these special pensions were granted; in 1886 they aggregated two hundred and forty, occasioning many vetoes from President Cleveland.[1]

The temptation to extravagant expenditures, to which President Arthur referred, had been a subject of comment for fifty years past in connection with internal improvements. Madison, Monroe, Jackson, Polk, Pierce, and Buchanan had endeavored by pres-

[1] *House Reports*, 50 Cong., 1 Sess., No. 736; *U. S. Statutes at Large*, XIV., 615; XX., 493; XXIV., 130; Mason, *Veto Power*, 165-207; for later phases of the subject, see Dewey, *National Problems* (*Am. Nation*, XXIV.), chap. v.

idential vetoes[1] to repress the popular demand for these national benefits conferred on routes of internal commerce and transportation. Neither Congress nor presidents had been able to draw a satisfactory distinction between a waterway for external commerce upon which duties were collected, and an internal navigable waterway upon which no duties were collected and upon which, therefore, no national funds could legitimately be expended. The task of surveying and clearing the interior waterways produced the first "river and harbor" bill, in 1824.[2] Despite occasional vetoes, as mentioned above, sums were appropriated thereafter for this purpose, openly under lax presidents and cloaked in other appropriation bills under strict-constructionist presidents, until the Civil War. That conflict not only demonstrated on many occasions the need for better inland communication, but it also placed a quietus on the strict-construction theory which had been responsible for most of the presidential vetoes.

Naturally the industrial era, with its ruthless competition, demanded cheap methods of carrying raw materials and finished products. To bring coal and iron together required improved waterways and harbors. Logs could be rafted on navigable rivers cheaper than they could be carried by rail, and a supply of water-power was frequently obtained from the same beneficent agency. New industrial plants

---

[1] Mason, *Veto Power*, 95–105.
[2] Turner, *New West* (*Am. Nation*, XIV.), 236–243.

sought congressional aid in dredging a harbor or constructing a breakwater for individual benefit. It was argued that commerce and industrialism enriched the nation and should be encouraged and fostered by the federal government. A congressional appropriation brought a large sum of money into the state or the congressional district and enhanced the popularity of its representative. The money was now lying idle in the treasury; the surplus was a menace; why not distribute it among the people through the legitimate channel of public improvements?

These and kindred arguments produced a river and harbor bill in 1866,[1] which appropriated more than three million dollars to seventy-nine different places where work was already begun or to be inaugurated. That a new era of improvements was now being entered upon was evidenced by one item which set apart $255,000 for surveys on the Atlantic and Pacific coasts, the northwestern lakes, and the rivers of the West and Northwest. Federal bounty was carefully withheld from the states recently in rebellion.

Later sessions of Congress, through what President Buchanan had called "log-rolling," [2] increased the appropriations for rivers and harbors until in 1870 they aggregated nearly $4,000,000, in 1875 more than $6,000,000, in 1880 nearly $9,000,000, and in

[1] *U. S. Statutes at Large*, XIV., 70.
[2] Richardson, *Messages and Papers*, V., 605.

1881 over $11,000,000.¹ No equally potent method of "getting money into the district" existed, except appropriations for public buildings. The Cumberland national turnpike was long since turned over to the states through which it passed;² the canals no longer required treasury subscriptions to their stock; coast defences languished; and railroads received grants of land rather than cash to aid in their construction. The climax of these appropriations was reached in the session of 1882, when a river and harbor bill was passed applying $18,743,875 to nearly five hundred different localities for public works. While it carried gifts for the Mississippi, the Ohio, the Delaware, and other established highways of trade, it included also such doubtful avenues of commerce as the Potonowut, the Choptank, the Scuppernong, the Waccemaw, and the Yallabusha rivers, Goose Rapids, and Cheesequake Creek. Small wonder that a member in debate said that the only way to make some of these "rivers" navigable was to pave or macadamize them.

President Arthur in 1882 adopted the former Democratic expedient of placing a veto on this method of getting rid of the surplus.³ While some

[1] Statement of Appropriations, etc., *Senate Docs.*, 47 Cong., 1 Sess., No. 196, p. 286.
[2] Young, *Cumberland Road*, 85; Sparks, *Expansion of Am. People*, 259-264.
[3] Richardson, *Messages and Papers*, VIII., 120-122; Mason, *Veto Power*, 104; Hart, "Biography of a River and Harbor Bill," in *Practical Essays*, 206.

of the items before him were admittedly legitimate, and two of them—viz., reclaiming the Potomac flats in Washington city and constructing levees along the lower Mississippi, had been recommended by him, nevertheless many items were purely of local benefit, did not provide for the common defence, and did not promote commerce among the states. He regarded the extravagant expenditure of public money as an evil immeasurably greater than the loss of public money, because it also demoralized officials through all the ramifications of government. Notwithstanding the strong pleas of the veto message, the House yielded to the popular demand for a raid on the treasury and passed the measure over the veto by an affirmative vote of 66 Republicans, 56 Democrats, and 2 Independents, as against 31 Republicans, 28 Democrats, and 1 Independent. The vote in the Senate stood 41 to 16; and the accustomed "barrel of pork" was divided among the congressional districts notwithstanding the presidential objection.[1] Warned by the veto, the next session of Congress reduced the river and harbor appropriations to $8,000,000 before passing it; but the first session of the forty-eighth Congress in 1884 raised it to near $13,000,000.

Against the $15,000,000 assured of being returned to circulation by the river and harbor act of 1882, stood the $140,000,000 of the surplus. Opposed to

[1] McPherson, *Hand-Book of Politics*, 1882, p. 202; *Harper's Weekly*, XXVI., 498.

using this accumulation to redeem the outstanding legal-tenders stood the Greenbackers; equally opposed to calling in and redeeming the government bonds were the national banks. President Arthur continued to suggest a reduction of taxes as the proper remedy for over-prosperity of the treasury. Internal taxes had been abolished on one article after another, until, by 1881, they were retained only on spirits, liquors, tobaccos, bank checks and deposits, bank capital, friction matches, and proprietary medicines. In 1883[1] the tax was removed from all these articles except tobacco, spirits, and liquors. Public sentiment opposed the repeal of taxes on those manufactures, because they were wholly luxuries and caused a large part of the public burdens of charity and correction.

By a process of elimination, a reduction of tariff duties was the sole remaining method of preventing an undue accumulation of money in the national treasury. "Tariff reform" was demanded by the farmers, who saw themselves deprived of the benefits of the sharp rise of prices in 1881 and the years following, because some of our products were barred from European markets in retaliation for our tariff. Demand for tariff reform proceeded largely from the Democratic party, while the Republicans were daily becoming high protectionists as industrialism grew in the land. In 1876 the Republican platform de-

[1] *U. S. Statutes at Large*, XXII., 191; John Sherman, *Recollections*, 843.

manded an adjustment of the tariff to promote the interests of American labor and to advance the prosperity of the whole country; the Democratic platform denounced the tariff as "a masterpiece of injustice, inequality, and false pretence." Four years later the Republicans advocated levying duties discriminated to favor American labor, and the Democrats came out openly for a tariff for revenue only. During the campaign the Republicans assailed this position as an attack on American industrial interests.[1] In that way the Republican party became the protectors of American manufacturing interests, and by 1884 was ready to come out boldly for a tariff "not for revenue only, but . . . to afford security to our diversified industries and protection to the rights and wages of the laborer."[2] Manufacturing interests were beginning to make themselves felt, on the other hand, in the Democratic party; and its platform of 1884, instead of repeating the demand for a tariff for revenue only, advocated a reduction which "would not injure any domestic industry but rather promote their healthy growth . . . without depriving American labor of the ability to compete successfully with foreign labor."[3]

In order to ascertain the causes and the proper remedy for existing financial conditions, Congress in 1882 provided for a tariff commission. Its prime purpose was to lower taxation in order to relieve a

[1] Stanwood, *Am. Tariff Controversies*, II., 200.
[2] Stanwood, *Hist. of the Presidency*, 429.   [3] *Ibid.*, 436.

plethoric treasury,[1] and a horizontal cut on all dutiable articles would have been a legitimate suggestion and one that might have been expected; but the commission, true to its protective complexion, adopted discrimination as the proper principle. Taking up each class of dutiable goods, the report gave a history of its past and present condition, both at home and abroad, and recommended the steps necessary to maintain American precedence in its manufacture or production. In this manner the commission evolved a revised schedule,[2] which showed a reduction on most of the commodities averaging about 20 per cent., and ranging from no decrease on some articles to as much as 40 or 50 per cent. on others.

President Arthur, who spoke from experience gained in the New York custom-house, advocated in his message of 1882 the transfer of articles yielding small revenues to the free list, a reduction on cotton, iron, and steel, and a "substantial reduction" on sugar, woollens, and cotton goods.[3] The report of the tariff commission reached the Senate a few days after Arthur's message, and was considered systematically, section by section. The resulting bill, which the Senate took the liberty of drawing up,

[1] *U. S. Statutes at Large*, XXII., 64; Bolles, *Financial Hist.*, III., 475-481; McPherson, *Hand-Book of Politics*, 1883, pp. 109-113.
[2] Tariff Com. of 1882, *Report*, 49-82; John Sherman, *Recollections*, 851.
[3] Richardson, *Messages and Papers*, VIII., 136.

was fairly in accord with the recommendations of the report, although the Democrats tried to place a lower rate on at least forty different articles, while the Republicans attempted to place a higher rate on nearly as many, and by their party majority usually succeeded.[1] When the work was completed a bill revising the internal taxes, which had passed the House during the preceding session and been sent to the Senate, was taken up, and the Senate tariff-revision bill was attached to it and passed.

In this manner the Senate avoided the prohibition made by the Constitution against originating revenue bills. The protection leaders in the Senate were ex-Secretary Sherman, Senator Morrill, and a much younger man, Senator Aldrich, of Rhode Island. In the House the protectionists were led by William D. Kelley, whose devotion to the manufacturing interests of Pennsylvania had won for him the sobriquet of "Pig-iron" Kelley. He was well aided by Kasson, of Iowa, Haskell, of Kansas, and McKinley, of Ohio.

Meanwhile the House, after hearing the commission's report, was unable to agree on a tariff, and refused to concur in the Senate bill; and a conference committee was appointed on which several Democrats refused to serve. Finally the expurgated committee, headed by Sherman, "compromised" by raising the duties on many articles above the figure suggested by either house. Iron ore was taxed 50

[1] McPherson, *Hand-Book of Politics*, 1882, pp. 18-57.

cents a ton in both bills; the members of the committee raised it to 75 cents a ton. They shifted cheap painted crockery from the 50 per cent. to the 60 per cent. class, which put it on a par with china and porcelain. They imposed a tax on imported bottles containing mineral waters, and raised the rate on steel and on sugar.[1]

As finally reported to each branch for passage, the bill lowered the rate on the commoner kinds of cotton and woollen goods, but raised it on the higher grades. Reductions were made on certain goods by changing schedules or by abolishing duties on goods which could be made as cheaply in America as in Europe, thus bringing no relief to the consumer or to the treasury. Other decreases were made, but very slight, that they might satisfy the demand for reform and not affect the manufacturer. Although the pine forests of the Northwest were wellnigh exhausted, the tariff on lumber was continued, despite public opinion. The tax on manufactured tobacco was lowered about ten million dollars a year without a request from the manufacturers. Truly "a revision of the tariff by its friends" was realized. Mahone's iron ore was properly cared for; Kelley's pig-iron was put on the high list; and the interests of the Louisiana sugar-growers protected. Sherman alone of the Republicans was disappointed because the Ohio wool-growers were "sacrificed." A few

[1] Stanwood, *Am. Tariff Controversies*, II., 216, 217; John Sherman, *Recollections*, 851–855.

years later he said: "I have always regretted that I did not defeat the bill." [1]

These methods of "reform" were loudly denounced as "piddling trivialties" by the reform press. "Taking a shaving off the duty on iron wire and adding it to the duty on glue," was the characterization of one writer.[2] The Republican party was said to have fostered a child which had now become its master. An opposition speaker denounced "the swarms of lobbyists who are now here and have been for weeks, all begging for more bounty, more protection, or rather more taxation on the people to enrich themselves." [3]

Opposition to the proposed "reform" bill came also from the diminishing number of free-traders on principle, from the wealthy and active group of importers, especially in New York City, and from manufacturers whose interests chanced to be affected adversely by it. With the rise of industries demanding protection, the Democratic party was losing its early free-trade propensity as rapidly as the Republican party was assuming a high-tariff inclination. In the vote on the original bill in the Senate, 10 Democrats voted with the Republicans; but on the final passage, after the "compromise" by the conference committee, Senator McPherson, from the manufacturing state of New Jersey, stood alone with

[1] John Sherman, *Recollections*, 852; *N. Y. Tribune*, April 28, 1883. [2] *Nation*, XXVI., 204.
[3] *Cong. Record*, 47 Cong., 2 Sess., 3576.

the 32 Republicans. On the negative, 2 Republicans voted with 29 Democrats—viz., Cameron, of Pennsylvania, who was dissatisfied with the duty on iron, and Van Wyck, of Nebraska, who wanted a general reduction.[1]

Party lines were intensified in the House by an adroit parliamentary manœuvre whereby the protectionists secured the reference of the bill to the conference committee.[2] In the final vote 15 Democrats gave support to the bill, 12 of them being from the industrial states of Pennsylvania, New York, and New Jersey. Nine dissatisfied Republicans voted with the Democrats against the proposed measure, among them being William McKinley, a young member from Ohio.[3]

No party or even wing of a party was satisfied with the tariff act of 1883. Sherman confessed that the harmony of the bill was destroyed by Republican senators, "influenced by local interests."[4] Secretary of the Treasury Folger referred to it in slighting terms. Several attempts were made to amend it in the years immediately following,[5] the most important being the bill introduced in the House in 1884 by Morrison, of Illinois, chairman of the committee on ways and means. He proposed to place coal, lum-

[1] McPherson, *Hand-Book of Politics*, 1884, p. 65.
[2] Taussig, *Tariff Hist. of U. S.*, 232; McPherson, *Hand-Book of Politics*, 1882, pp. 51–56. [3] *Ibid.*, 1884, pp. 57, 58.
[4] John Sherman, *Recollections*, 851.
[5] McPherson, *Hand-Book of Politics*, 1884, p. 137; Perry, "Tariff Legislation, etc.," in *Quart. Journal of Econ.*, II., 69.

ber, and salt on the free list, and to make a "horizontal" reduction of 20 per cent. on all other dutiable goods. The changes would cause a decrease of at least thirty million dollars annually in the receipts of the custom-houses and tend to reduce the surplus. This method of framing a tariff schedule by a general reduction was denounced as unscientific and as likely to create more inequalities than existed at the time. It was killed by striking out the enacting clause, May 6, 1884. The Democrats retained possession of the House, and could have passed the bill had not 41 of them chosen to join the Republicans in throttling the measure.[1] These constituted a protectionist wing of the party, headed by Samuel J. Randall, who represented the industrial interests of Pennsylvania, and embraced Democrats from that state, from New York, New Jersey, Ohio, and California. Three Republicans from Minnesota and one from New York joined 151 Democrats in supporting the bill, the other Republicans voting *en masse* against it.

At the same session, Converse, an Ohio Democrat and warden of the wool-growing industry, made an unsuccessful attempt to restore the rates on foreign wool which had been reduced by the act of 1883.[2] Any effort to reduce the tariff showed the hold which protected interests had secured on both parties; and the act of 1883 remained unchanged

[1] Stanwood, *Am. Tariff Controversies*, II., 221.
[2] McPherson, *Hand-Book of Politics*, 1884, p. 137.

when the administration and the House passed to the Democrats in 1885. Fortune again favored the protectionists, because, by one of the vagaries of public finance, the tide turned in 1882 and the surplus declined to about sixty-five million dollars in 1885. The crusade for tariff reform which President Cleveland expected to lead thereby lost its chief argument.[1]

[1] Richardson, *Messages and Papers*, VIII., 341, 580; see for later phases, Dewey, *National Problems* (*Am. Nation*, XXIV.), chap. iv.

CHAPTER XVIII

INLAND COMMERCE
(1875-1885)

IN 1883 the United States was shipping to other countries raw cotton to the value of nearly $250,000,000, bread and bread-stuffs amounting to over $200,000,000, provisions worth $100,000,000, with mineral oil, woollen manufactures, iron and steel manufactures, tobacco, and cotton goods in decreasing order. In return for these she imported sugar to the value of $91,000,000, woollen goods worth $44,000,000, chemicals amounting to $43,-000,000, with coffee, iron, and steel products, cotton goods, and hides next in significance.[1] Because the people had spread from the seaboard over the interior of the continent, a large proportion of these exports came from the inland, and a corresponding share of the imports were carried thither for consumption. The development of a large inland commerce was a natural concomitant of the industrial era.

The balance of imports and exports is watched as the barometer of national prosperity, and its statis-

[1] *U. S. Statistical Abstract*, 1900, pp. 165-249.

tics are carefully collected; but domestic trade, more recently developed and more widely scattered, is accepted as matter of course. In 1875–1876 there was great rejoicing because the total value of the foreign trade was in excess of a billion dollars and because the exports surpassed the imports by nearly twenty million; yet the internal commerce of the United States was estimated at twenty-five times the total foreign trade.[1] The preponderance of foreign shipping in the American carrying trade was a constant matter of concern; but the capital employed in the railroads was twenty-three times that invested in all the shipping entering American ports. Water traffic on the inland rivers and the Great Lakes combined with the coastwise trade was thought to be ten times that carried to and from foreign lands.[2]

Internal commerce arose not only from the spread of the people, but also because new sources of raw material or of products were discovered, perhaps in remote regions. One or two cases will serve for illustration. Lying between the Mississippi and the Missouri rivers in the Dakotas was the broad valley of the Red River, stretching away hundreds of miles into the British provinces. In 1869 the British government purchased from the Hudson Bay Company the portion lying north of the international line, and formed it into the province of Manitoba. The

---

[1] *U. S. Statistical Abstract*, 1900, p. 92.
[2] U. S. Bureau of Statistics, *Report*, 1876; *House Exec. Docs.*, 44 Cong., 2 Sess., VI., No. 2.

soil of the entire valley was found to be specially adapted to the raising of a fine grade of hard wheat. A "rush" to the lands was instituted about 1876, immigrants coming not only from Europe, but also from the United States, averaging in 1879 as many as two thousand per week. Fort Gary speedily grew into the city of Winnipeg, with ten thousand inhabitants. By 1878 several lines of railways had pushed up through the valley from the American side, raising the local price of wheat from forty cents a bushel to the ruling Minneapolis price, less freight charges, and securing a hold on the wheat-carrying trade long before the Canadian Pacific reached Winnipeg in 1881. This enterprise was begun in 1872 under a guarantee from the Canadian government, was transferred in 1881 to a private company, was pushed rapidly through the wilderness and across the barren mountains to the Pacific, which it reached in 1883. A branch line was built *via* Sault Ste. Marie to St. Paul to compete with the American railway system.[1] The many trunk lines already constructed in the United States from the Northwest to the seaboard, when compared with the one in Canada, gave the former a decided advantage in wheat traffic which could not be overcome even by restrictive Canadian laws.[2]

Part of this surplus wheat went to the sea-shore in the shape of flour ground by the water-power of

[1] Roberts, *Hist. of Canada*, 373, 383, 402.
[2] *Appleton's Annual Cyclop.*, 1883, p. 511.

St. Anthony's Falls, at Minneapolis. By congressional appropriations, beginning in 1876, a concrete wall was constructed behind the falls to prevent erosion and to increase the volume of discharge. In 1881 the improved power operated twenty-eight flouring mills with a yearly capacity of over 20,000,000 bushels of wheat, representing the product of 1,250,000 acres. Nearly one-third the output of these mills found its way to England, Belgium, and Germany. The falls also supplied power to seventeen lumber mills, which produced 2,500,000 superficial feet during a single season. The logs for this purpose were floated down the Mississippi and its numerous upper tributaries.[1]

The long haul necessary to convey the products of the Northwest to the seaboard for export caused a steady effort to reduce the cost of carriage and to stimulate the business by reducing rates, so as to increase the railroad receipts. More than three-fourths the freight carried by the railroads in any year of the seventies was made up of agricultural products. The area of land under cultivation increased 5,000,000 acres annually; and the yearly crop of grain almost exactly doubled between 1874 and 1884. Food, fuel, and material for shelter constituted four-fifths of the inland commerce. The greatest amount of traffic was found in the central states, through which the food products and lumber were carried; the smallest amount was found in the

[1] *Appleton's Annual Cyclop.*, 1881, p. 588.

southern states, where cotton, hemp, and tobacco were light in weight and correspondingly high in value. The grain crop weighed 75,000,000 tons, and the cotton and wool crop combined only 2,000,000 tons.[1] For generations the cotton had found its way to New Orleans, Mobile, and other Gulf ports by water; but the railroads gradually turned it to the Atlantic ports. In 1883 it was estimated that a sixth of the crop was carried eastward by rail, causing the remarkable situation of a decrease of cotton receipts in the Gulf ports, although the crop had increased nearly one-half in the past seven years.[2]

Railroads also developed other sources of supply. They brought the fruits of Florida and of California to northern markets, developed the salt industry of the Gulf islands, and opened the phosphate beds of Florida, Tennessee, and South Carolina. They penetrated the coal and iron deposits of the lower Appalachian range, and caused the bogs of Louisiana to be drained and converted into rice-beds. The possibility of getting the product to market caused the drift-wood to be raised from the southern rivers and made into lumber, and the grazing industry to be introduced into the "pine barrens" of Georgia.

Chicago, situated at the head of the lakes, played a prominent part in the development of inland commerce. Into it poured the grain from the great

[1] *Appleton's Annual Cyclop.*, 1884, p. 682.
[2] *U. S. Statistical Abstract*, 1900, p. 371.

producing region of the Northwest, making it the largest grain market in the world. In 1874 fourteen great grain elevators or warehouses had been constructed, each capable of holding from 300,000 to 1,000,000 bushels of grain; railway tracks led to one side of the buildings, and the vessels to which the grain was to be transferred lay at the other. In 1880 nearly 250,000,000 bushels of grain were inspected passing to and from the Chicago elevators.[1] Some of the vessels loaded in Chicago were despatched direct to Europe through the St. Lawrence.

Another industry had grown from as small beginnings. In 1827, Archibald Clybourne erected a slaughter-house on the south branch of the Chicago River, in order to supply meat to the garrison in Fort Dearborn, located at the mouth of the river. Five years later he moved the plant out on the prairie near the river, and killed one hundred and fifty hogs the first year. In 1844 a drove of hogs was collected from the adjacent farms and driven on foot to New York, and sold for a profit averaging eight dollars a head. In 1854 this method was changed to that of killing the animals in Chicago, packing the meat, and shipping it by the newly built Michigan Central and the Michigan Southern railroads to New York. In 1865 a space of land near where Clybourne killed his animals on the prairie

---

[1] See the brief in Munn *vs.* Illinois, 94 U. S., 113; *Appleton's Annual Cyclop.*, 1880, p. 377; Nimmo, *Report on Internal Commerce* (*House Exec. Docs.*, 45 Cong., 3 Sess., No. 32, pt. iii.), 220.

became the Chicago stock-yards.[1] Refrigerator cars, in which the meat was shipped fresh and not salted, were put into use in 1879, and the export trade to Europe fully developed by refrigerating chambers on board vessels.[2] In 1880, 7,000,000 hogs were received at the yards, more than 1,000,000 cattle, and 30,000 sheep, making a total value of $62,000,000.

In transporting this large volume of trade, the railways easily supplanted the waterways for light goods and those demanding quick transportation. Before 1880 the Illinois Central, the Mobile & Ohio, and the Louisville & Nashville paralleled the lower Mississippi River; the Ohio & Mississippi, together with the Louisville & Nashville, took the Cincinnati-St. Louis trade from the Ohio River; and the New York Central on the one bank and the West Shore on the other absorbed a large part of the carrying trade of the Hudson River. Instances might be multiplied of railroads seeking the easy right of way afforded by the banks of a river and injuring the river trade. No traveller for business would go from Buffalo to Chicago by the Great Lakes, consuming almost a week, when he could traverse the distance by rail in less than twenty-four hours. While the number of miles of railroads in operation doubled between 1873 and 1883, the number of vessels constructed on the inland rivers and lakes declined after 1880 and had no revival until the

[1] *Harper's Weekly*, XXVI., 679.
[2] See above, chap. i.

full development of the iron-ore traffic about 1891.[1]

Notwithstanding the success of the railroads, Congress continued its internal improvement gifts to inland waterways, largely for the purpose of preventing extortionate railroad rates. In moving bulky freight, certain rivers could still compete with the railroads. A "fleet" of barges guided by one steam-tug frequently carried from the Pittsburg coal-field down the Ohio and Mississippi rivers over 25,000 tons of coal on a single trip. The Mississippi and its tributaries represented 15,000 miles of inland water carriage which must be maintained. Under precedent of the act of 1824 for improving the Ohio and Mississippi rivers, Congress passed more than sixty acts before 1882, appropriating a total of $105,796,403[2] for clearing the inland rivers, constructing lateral dikes, and otherwise improving the channel. Under direction of James B. Eads, a civil engineer of St. Louis, the deepening of the South Pass in the delta at the mouth of the Mississippi was begun in 1875 by the construction of "jetties," which constricted the waters into one comparatively narrow channel, the other outlets being closed. The current created by this volume of water carried the sediment brought down by the river out to greater depths in the Gulf, virtually making the stream clean its own channel. In 1877 a steamship drawing twenty-one feet eight

---

[1] *U. S. Statistical Abstract*, 1900, pp. 380, 440.
[2] *Senate Exec. Docs.*, 47 Cong., 1 Sess., No. 196, p. 286.

inches of water passed triumphantly between the jetties and thence up to New Orleans. In a few years the channel depth increased to thirty feet, and New Orleans was again a seaport, able to receive modern deep-draught steamers, thanks to the fostering hand of the general government.[1] This was felt to be a significant fact in view of the presumably speedy completion of an isthmian canal.[2]

Captain Eads unsuccessfully advocated similar walls along the upper river-banks to prevent washing and to form a deep waterway from the Gulf to the heart of the continent. These high levees would also prevent damage from the increasing number of freshets and floods caused by cutting off the forests. Levees constructed by individual planters were cheaply built and ineffective. In 1850[3] Congress gave the swamp-lands adjacent to the Mississippi in the various southern states to aid in building levees; the Civil War not only stopped the work, but destroyed much that had been accomplished.

President Johnson in 1866[4] recommended appropriations for the reconstruction of the Mississippi embankments; but little was done until a succession of overflows led Congress in 1879[5] to provide a commission consisting of three engineers from the army, three civilians, and a representative of the coast

[1] *House Exec. Docs.*, 45 Cong., 2 Sess., No. 1.
[2] See chap. xiii., above.
[3] *U. S. Statutes at Large*, IX., 519.
[4] Richardson, *Messages and Papers*, **VI., 454.**
[5] *U. S. Statutes at Large*, XXI., 37.

survey to form plans to "correct, permanently locate, and deepen the channel, and protect the banks of the Mississippi River; improve and give safety and ease to the navigation thereof; prevent destructive floods; and promote and facilitate commerce, trade, and the postal service." This "Mississippi River commission" was sustained for a number of years, and made careful surveys and many suggestions.[1] President Arthur, in a special message, April 17, 1882,[2] recommended the appropriation of a million dollars for closing existing gaps in levees. He called attention to the fact that the United States had imposed and collected some seventy million dollars by a "war tax" on cotton, and owed it to the planters to save their crops from devastating floods.

Beginning with a small sum spared by the commission from its appropriation in 1882, the levee system of the lower Mississippi River received many million dollars from the federal and state governments for improvements which maintained a channel for navigation and protected the adjacent lands from overflow. While inland commerce was thus fostered on the rivers, trade on the Great Lakes received a stimulus through the discovery of a new supply of iron ore. Prior to the Civil War the apparently inexhaustible timber supply caused a small demand

---

[1] Annual reports from 1880 to 1888 (except 1885) in *House Docs.*, beginning with the 46 Cong., 2 Sess., No. 58; *Appleton's Annual Cyclop.*, 1880, p. 530; *North Am. Rev.*, CXXXVI., 212.
[2] Richardson, *Messages and Papers*, VIII., 95.

for iron which was easily satisfied by the bog-ore deposits of the middle Atlantic states. Experience with iron-clad vessels during the war caused the building, gradually, of iron merchantmen. The railroads began to extend their lines, with heavy demands for rails, bridges, and cars, while the growing manufacture of agricultural implements, the invention of wire-fencing, and the replacing of wooden water-wheels by the turbine added to the increasing draughts on the iron supply.

Impelled by this demand, exploiters developed the mineral resources of the southern states, which had been neglected for agricultural pursuits. Seven distinct kinds of bituminous coal were found in Alabama, ranging from cannel to coke-producing and steam coal of a high order. Between 1870 and 1880 the output of coal increased in this state from 9000 tons to 400,000 tons. Markets were found in the Gulf cities and in Texas, while no small portion was used locally in the coke and iron industries. Ample deposits of hematite ore and of limestone were found adjacent to the coal, especially near Birmingham, destined to place the state in the first rank as an exporter of pig-iron and third in the production of coke. The iron and steel production of the state grew from 7060 tons in 1870 to 125,000 tons in 1884.[1] The demand for iron also disclosed large mining possibilities in Tennessee, extending the railroads and opening up inland commerce; but by far the

[1] *Appleton's Annual Cyclop.*, 1884, p. 7.

greatest revelations came from the upper peninsula of Michigan.

Deposits of copper on the south shore of Lake Superior were known to white men early in the seventeenth century; but it was not until 1844 that the variation in a surveyor's needle led to the discovery of ledges or outcrops of iron ore in the same region. In the following year a representative of a mining company organized at Jackson, Michigan, was conducted to the deposit by an Indian, and three hundred pounds of the ore were carried on the backs of men to the lake and thence to Jackson, where it was smelted in a blacksmith's forge.[1] In 1850 samples of the ore were shipped to the blast-furnaces in western Pennsylvania for reduction, resulting in the erection of several forges at Marquette, the nearest port to the iron mines. The Marquette iron belt, about twenty-five miles long and from three to ten miles in breadth, lies in an east and west direction, to the southwest of Marquette, and distant fifteen miles at the nearest point. Its limits are now marked by the cities of Negaunee and Michigamme. Pennsylvania iron manufacturers wished to bring this ore to their furnaces, but were barred by natural obstacles to transportation, especially the falls in St. Mary's River between Lake Superior and Lake Huron, about which a portage must be made. To relieve this difficulty, Congress gave to the state of Michigan a grant of public land

[1] *Geological Survey of Mich.*, I., 13-15.

in 1852 [1] to aid in the construction of a canal one mile long above the falls; and also gave large sums of money for clearing the channel of the river below the falls. To bring the ore to a shipping point, a railroad was built in 1857 between Marquette and the mines, and another line was constructed in 1864 to connect the mines with Escanaba, a city sixty-two miles to the southeast on Lake Michigan, where large ore docks were built, because shipments from this place would avoid the difficult and tedious passage through the St. Mary's River.

It chanced that the iron-mines of Michigan and the gold-fields of California were opened almost simultaneously; but where thousands rushed to search for gold scarce one fortune-hunter turned to the unattractive iron. The value of ore taken from the Superior fields has long since doubled in value that of the gold gathered with greater hardship from the valleys of California. It is true that the first iron companies at Marquette failed during the panic of 1857; but the demand for iron during and following the war soon made amends. In 1863 only three mines were developed; in 1866 there were nine; and in 1875 forty. Quarterly dividends of twenty-five per cent. were not uncommon.[2]

Iron deposits were known to exist a hundred miles to the west of the Marquette range for nearly forty years before being developed; but their remoteness

---

[1] Act of August 26, 1852, *U. S. Statutes at Large*, X., 35.
[2] Michigan Comr. of Mineral Statistics, *Report*, 1877–1878.

and inaccessibility prevented exploitation. In 1884 a railway under construction from Milwaukee to Ashland, Wisconsin, reached the deposits, and six car-loads of ore were taken to Milwaukee and the iron was found to be soft red hematite, with a high per cent. of iron and a low per cent. of phosphorus, and therefore well suited to the Bessemer steel process. When the railroad was completed to Ashland the following year, immense ore-docks were constructed and the Gogebic, the second of the great iron supplies of the Superior region, was sending its shipments along the Great Lakes. It lay partly in the state of Wisconsin and partly in Michigan, and is now marked by the cities of Bessemer, Ironwood, and Hurley.[1] In 1887 the Menominee range was discovered. It adjoined the Marquette on the south and strongly resembled that formation in the character of the ore.

Three iron-fields on the south of Lake Superior were now opened. On the northwest side were beds of large extent, noticed by geologists as early as 1850; but they lay a hundred miles to the north of Duluth, in a region accessible only to the foot-traveller or canoeist. They remained undeveloped until the high price of ore in 1875 seemed to warrant the construction of ore-docks at Two Rivers, the nearest harbor, on the shore northeast of Duluth, and the construction of a thoroughly equipped railroad to Vermilion

---

[1] Mussey, "Combinations in Mining Industry" (*Columbia Univ. Studies, Hist., Econ., etc.*, XXIII., No. 3), 84.

Lake, about which the ore-beds lay. The expenditure of three million dollars in these preparations was justified when the immense deposits were found to contain from three to four per cent. more iron and considerably less phosphorus than the Gogebic ore. Only eight feet of loose earth had to be removed to disclose beds of Bessemer ore so hard that it must be dynamited to be removed, and put through a crusher to be handled.[1]

Lavish nature was not yet done with her disclosures. A little more than half-way between Duluth and the Vermilion range, and about thirty miles from the latter, an explorer in 1890 found the famous Mount Iron, the pioneer mine of the Mesabec field.[2] In extent it more than doubled all the deposits previously found, and, unlike its neighbor, the Vermilion, was so soft that it could be scooped up with steam-shovels, effecting a saving in mining of perhaps five million dollars annually.[3] The five iron fields now disclosed made possible the forming of the United States Steel Company and the gigantic deals of a later time. The one million tons of ore taken out in 1873 grew to twenty-one million before the close of the century, although the number of companies engaged in the mining and shipping decreased from seventy-two in 1893 to forty-six before the century closed. The day of combinations was dawning.

[1] Mussey, in *Columbia Univ. Studies, Hist., Econ., etc.*, XXIII., 91.
[2] *Ibid.*,103.
[3] Winchell, *Geology of Minnesota*, IV., 581-616.

In smelting the first ores carried out by pack-horse from the mines to Marquette, charcoal was used as fuel. Wood for this purpose and limestone for flux were found near at hand; but when increased demand necessitated the use of coal, it was found to be cheaper to transport the ore to the coal-fields of Illinois and Pennsylvania than to carry the coal to the iron of Michigan and Minnesota. Further, the iron industry was already established in the vicinity of the coal-fields; expensive machinery was installed there; workmen could be obtained; and profitable markets were near at hand. For these and similar reasons the ore met the coal much more than halfway at South Chicago and Joliet, in Illinois; at Cleveland, Ohio; at Pittsburg, Pennsylvania; and at Youngstown and Sharon, in the valleys between the Ohio and Lake Erie.

Over the Great Lakes led the pathways of this enormous traffic, and to meet its demands Congress, in 1870 and again in 1890, was forced to enlarge the old canal about the Falls of St. Mary, to construct an additional one, and to improve the channel of the St. Mary's River and the St. Clair "flats" above Detroit.[1] A canal on the Canadian side of the St. Mary's Falls was opened in 1895. Thus were preparations made for the shipping through the St. Mary's, which grew eventually to be the largest in the world. The number of vessels passing through

[1] Chief of Engineers, in Sec. of War, *Annual Reports*, 1877–1896.

the St. Mary's canal increased eleven times between 1873 and 1900, while the number passing through the Welland Canal, between lakes Erie and Ontario, decreased nearly one-half.[1]

Lake traffic, carrying grain and ore from the source of supply at the head of the Great Lakes to the place of demand at the foot, was able to compete successfully with railroad carriage. About 1876 lake rates from Duluth to Buffalo were only one-twenty-sixth the all-rail rates. The character of the goods, being in bulk and not requiring speedy transportation, was favorable to water transit. Contract rates for carrying ore ranged in 1887 from $1.20 to $3.05 per ton, bringing large returns to vessel owners. In that year forty-seven vessels were added to the lake fleet at a cost of $6,000,000, reviving the inland ship-building industry. Vessels carrying ore averaged in 1872 about 650 tons; in 1889 ore-vessels of 2800 tons capacity were constructed, considered marvels at the time, but insignificant in comparison with later vessels of 10,000 tons capacity, loaded by machinery in an hour and a half. Under these conditions the price of pig-iron fell from $46 per ton in 1866 to $28 in 1880, and to $11 before the end of the century.[2]

The discovery of these apparently inexhaustible supplies of ore hastened the end of the "iron age"

---

[1] *House Exec. Docs.*, 42 Cong., 2 Sess., No. 134.
[2] Mussey, "Combinations in Mining Industry" (*Columbia Univ. Studies in Hist., Econ., etc.*, XXIII., No. 3), 95, 166.

and the advent of the "age of steel." In addition to the iron rails used by the railroad which carried ore to the docks, the cars in which it was carried were made of iron, and the bridges over which they passed were constructed of iron instead of wood. The vessels which carried the ore on the lakes were made largely of iron. In time these were all transformed into steel. Before the Civil War steel was produced in America in small quantities, by the "blister" or crucible process, and was worth $140 a ton. Then arose the Bessemer process, by which steel was made in large quantities direct from pig-iron by blowing out all the carbon and then reintroducing just enough carbon to create steel. The production of steel as a commercial article in this manner was introduced in 1866 at Steelton, near Harrisburg, Pennsylvania, and at Newburg, a suburb of Cleveland; and the following year steel rails for railways were rolled at Johnstown, Pennsylvania. The output of Bessemer steel in the United States grew from 3000 tons in 1867 to 1,000,000 tons in 1880, and passed the 2,000,000 mark in 1886, while steel made by all other processes in the latter year amounted to less than 300,000 tons.[1] At the time no one imagined that the Bessemer process could be improved upon; but in 1881 the improved "open-hearth" system was introduced, and the 95,000 tons of steel made in that manner opened the way for the later Jupiter steel and Harveyized armor-plate.

[1] *U. S. Statistical Abstract*, 1899, p. 361.

INLAND COMMERCE

The use of steel transformed the navy again and wrought great changes in railway construction. Before the Civil War iron rails cost at the mills in Pennsylvania about $50 a ton; during the war they trebled in price, but in 1867 declined to $80 a ton. In this year steel rails were put on the market at a cost double that of iron rails; but the development of the Superior iron region, and better means of transporting both iron ore and coal, reduced the price until American rails could compete successfully with those of European make. In 1882, 300,000 tons of steel rails were imported, and in 1891 only 134 tons; the amount exported grew from 3000 tons to 15,000 tons; while the total production rose from 864,353 tons to 1,871,425.[1] In 1880 only 30 per cent. of the trackage of the United States was laid with steel rails; ten years later the proportion had increased to 80 per cent.[2] Steel rails meant improved road-beds, locomotives of fifty tons weight, freight-trains scheduled at twenty miles an hour, and passenger-trains at fifty miles an hour. Ingenious devices lowered the time of through trains by supplying the locomotives with water, and by receiving and discharging the mails while the trains were moving at full speed.[3]

Inland passenger traffic developed rapidly under these conditions. Through trains were run on sev-

---

[1] *U. S. Statistical Abstract*, 1899, p. 362.
[2] Poor, *Railway Manual*, 1896, p. x.
[3] *North Am. Rev.*, CXXXV., 374.

eral lines from Boston, New York, and other Atlantic points to Chicago and St. Louis; and the extension of this service to the Pacific coast was confidently awaited. Sleeping-cars, first put into use about 1863 as an experiment, relieved prolonged journeys of their discomfort. By another Pullman patent in 1887, the platforms of cars were enclosed, forming a "vestibuled train." The extent of longitude traversed by the railway systems emphasized the difficulty of adjustment of time, because sun time at New York was four hours faster than sun time at San Francisco. Railway managers adopted the local time of prominent cities through which their lines passed, resulting in no less than seventy-five standards being employed on the various roads. Between Boston and Washington the traveller must set his watch five times if he conformed to the time on which his train was run. Frequently trains would leave the same city on three or four different times to conform with the standards employed by different roads. England overcame this difficulty in 1848 by making all clocks conform to Greenwich time; but with the geographical extent of the United States this was not possible.

In 1883, after long consideration of the problem, the United States was divided into four vertical zones—viz., the eastern, to cover all the United States east of a line drawn irregularly from Buffalo through Pittsburg to Charleston, South Carolina; the central, from Buffalo to a line drawn north and south through Kansas; the mountain, from that point to the Salt Lake City line; and the Pacific, to include the remainder of the country. The 75th, 90th, 105th, and 120th meridians, each of which passed through the middle of one of these zones, were selected as governing lines, the fifteen degrees between each being equal to an hour of time.[1] It was now possible for a traveller passing from any zone to turn his watch back one hour if going westward, or to set it forward one hour if travelling eastward, and so maintain exact railroad time. Canada also adopted the plan. Gradually the people of both countries overcame their prejudices and for the most part accepted the railroad or "standard" time of their respective zones.[2]

The industrial age was now fully developed, its lines indicated, and its inevitable results apparent. "Combination" was henceforth to be the watchword of capitalist and of laborer. Strife between the two would transform the remarkable age of prosperity, which should have brought untold peace and happiness to its participants, into an unfortunate period of intermittent strife and bloodshed, involving national parties, invoking national agencies, and often humiliating national pride. Fortunately, coeval with the growth of industrialism grew the spirit of reform to quicken national life, to cor-

---

[1] *North Am. Rev.*, CXXXI., 528; *Appleton's Annual Cyclop.*, 1883, p. 761; *Science*, II., 499; *De Bow's Review*, new ser., VIII., 464.   [2] *Railway Gazette*, November 16, 1883.

rect aberration of party vision, and to lend a new value to the civic conscience. "Reform" was largely responsible for the political revolution which marked the presidential election of 1884, and "reform" of capitalistic combinations was to play an important part in future campaigns.

Corporate combinations were rare as yet, and simply indicative of future tendencies. In 1880 the railway mileage of the United States was being operated by 1514 different companies, and their patronage came from a large number of small shippers.[1] Modern aggregations of capital were unknown. Of 183 manufacturing companies or combinations listed in the report of the industrial commission of 1901, only three were chartered before 1885. These were the New Jersey Zinc Company, organized in 1880; the Standard Oil Company, chartered finally in 1882; and the Brunswick-Balke-Collender Company, for the manufacture of billiard-tables and accessories, whose charter was granted in 1884.[2] The history of such enterprises belongs properly with the problems they were destined to present.[3]

[1] Poor, *Manual of Railways*, 1880, pp. 1–1001.
[2] Industrial Commission, *Report*, XIX., 1120–1127 (1901).
[3] Dewey, *National Problems* (*Am. Nation*, XXIV.), chap. xii.

CHAPTER XIX

THE ELECTION OF 1884
(1882–1884)

THE administration of President Arthur was an exception to the saying, caused by Tyler and Johnson, that a president coming into office through the death of his predecessor breaks with his party. Nominated to the vice-presidency as a sop to Conkling, and as a vindication for his removal from the New York custom-house, bearing the repute of a New York spoilsman and "good fellow," Arthur was expected to discharge his New York obligations through federal patronage, and to select his advisers from the worst element of the party. But he surrounded himself with excellent counsellors, broke with his former associates, and exhibited in many instances evidences of a high degree of statesmanship.[1] His foreign policy, if not as aggressive as Blaine would have made it, was at least dignified and safe. If he did not administer the civil service act of 1883 in the militant spirit of the reformer, he accepted it in good faith, made excellent appoint-

[1] McCulloch, *Men and Measures*, 484; *Harper's Weekly*, XXIX., 246, 257.

ments to its commission, and withstood all pressure to misconstrue its provisions.[1] During the first fourteen months of his administration his appointments necessitated one removal in thirteen; while those of Garfield in four months included removals in nearly a fourth of the cases.[2]

Improvements in the coast defences were begun under his administration, and the building of a steel navy inaugurated.[3] Letter postage was reduced, special delivery of letters commenced, and the star-route frauds were stamped out. These popular acts, due largely to the suggestion of the president, would seem to warrant him and his party a continuance in power. Unfortunately, the financial depression continued. The crops of 1883, although surpassing the unfortunate yield of 1881, were scarcely up to the average, and the corn crop fell nearly four hundred million bushels behind. Large quantities of stocks and bonds had been watered by extensions and consolidations which could not be expected to yield immediate dividends, and they declined steadily during the year. Northern Pacific threw on the market in October, 1883, an issue of twenty million dollars and created a mild panic. More than ten thousand firms became bankrupt during 1882, a larger number than marked any year since 1873. Causes for the depression were found in over-production, financial

[1] Andrew D. White, *Autobiography*, I., 193-195.
[2] Richardson, *Messages and Papers*, VIII., 147.
[3] McPherson, *Hand-Book of Politics*, 1884, pp. 165-169.

troubles abroad, over-railroad building, and capital lying idle because rates of interest were unattractive.

For no one of these misfortunes was President Arthur accountable; yet with proverbial shortsight the people placed the responsibility on the shoulders of the party in power. Conviction was growing that the tariff enriched the few at the expense of the many; and disappointment over the failure of the Republican party to revise the tariff in 1880–1882, when it was in full command of the government, rapidly changed to a desire for revenge. Discontent in the party ranged from the habitually disgruntled, who felt that the party had been in power long enough, to thoughtful reformers, who accused the party leaders of being professional politicians, guilty of corrupt practices, and negligent of needed reforms. In truth, the germ of reform was in the air. Antimonopolists held meetings in various states demanding restriction of corporations by the federal government, post-office savings-banks, government ownership of telegraphs, abolition of convict labor, woman suffrage, and legal restraint of combinations intended to advance prices.

Some of this animosity was engendered by a combination effected in 1881, whereby the Western Union Telegraph Company absorbed its great rival, the American Union Company. The two companies came into litigation over the extension of telegraph lines along new railways in Kansas in the preceding year, fought through the courts, and made a compromise which combined the two, after the dissolution of an injunction to prevent their union. Stock in the Western Union was increased to eighty million dollars, about one-fourth being assigned to the stockholders in the American Union Company and fifteen million dollars being distributed as a dividend among the Western Union stockholders.[1] As if to add to the public indignation at thus being deprived of the benefits of competition, a syndicate was formed for the purpose of acquiring control of the Northern Pacific Railroad and preventing it entering Washington and Oregon as a competitor of the Oregon Railway and Navigation Company, which connected at Ogden with the Union Pacific Company.[2] Still another evidence was given of the approaching days of consolidation when the three New York elevated roads were merged. "Monopoly" soon became a word for political parties to conjure with.

In some states the two reform wings known as "Greenback" and as "Labor" united on resolutions demanding state ownership of railways and telegraph lines, and that all land owned by individuals or corporations in excess of what was required for personal use should be taxed so as to render its ownership valueless. Prohibitionists made nominations in the gubernatorial elections of 1882 and 1883. Temperance agitation was responsible for local-option bills being passed in many states, and Maine and Kansas

---

[1] *North Am. Rev.*, CXXXIII., 369; *Appleton's Annual Cyclop.*, 1881, p. 130.　　[2] Henry Villard, *Memoirs*, II., chap. xli.

set up prohibitory regulations against the selling of liquors. Women's rights reformers held conventions in many cities and passed resolutions. In Massachusetts and New York, which had adopted civil service reform, its advocates kept constant watch over its interests, questioning candidates and exacting pledges.[1]

That the popular spirit of reform was not to be ignored was manifest in Pennsylvania in 1882, when Robert Pattison, a young Democratic reformer, who had made a record as comptroller of the city of Philadelphia, was chosen governor of that "solid Republican" state on a pledge of retrenchment, anti-spoils, and no party favoritism.[2] During the same year Benjamin F. Butler, former Republican, was elected governor of Massachusetts on a Democratic platform of protest against extravagant expenditures, class legislation, and the existing tariff, and was with difficulty defeated, after one year, in a campaign for re-election.[3]

Even more significant was the situation in New York, the president's state. Governor Cornell, Republican, sought re-election in 1882, but was opposed by ex-Senator Conkling, presumably because of vetoes hostile to certain corporations in which Conkling was now interested as legal adviser.[4] The

[1] Stanwood, *Hist. of the Presidency*, 420.
[2] *Appleton's Annual Cyclop.*, 1882, p. 679; *Harper's Weekly*, XXVI., 724. [3] *Independent*, November 9, 1882.
[4] *Harper's Weekly*, XXVI., 546.

ex-senator was supposed to possess powerful influence with President Arthur, and turned the support of the administration from Governor Cornell to Charles J. Folger, secretary of the treasury. Backed by the administration and by the Stalwarts, or "machine Republicans," Folger easily secured the nomination over Cornell. The Democrats took advantage of the reform movement to nominate Grover Cleveland, who had been chosen mayor of Buffalo in 1881 in a reform campaign and had made a reputation for independence, conscientiousness, and ability. Dissatisfaction with the Republican nomination was manifest from the beginning of the campaign; charges of political trickery were made; and the ancient feud between Stalwart and Half-Breed was revived. The Democrats made use of a letter written by Secretary Folger suggesting that the shrinkage of forty million dollars in the value of the great properties of the country, following the election of several Democratic congressmen in Ohio in the October elections, showed an evident dread on the part of the business interests of the country lest the Democratic party should be returned to power. The vote for governor of New York, cast in November, 1882, gave Cleveland five votes to every three cast for Folger, making 192,000 plurality.[1] It was a crushing defeat for the Republicans, a severe blow to President Arthur and the Stalwarts, and

[1] Stanwood, *Hist. of the Presidency*, 420; *Appleton's Annual Cyclop.*, 1882, p. 611.

significant in its bearing upon the approaching presidential election. Governor Cleveland was thenceforth a factor which could not be overlooked.[1]

The political "reforms" were part of the general ethical movement which purified the civil service in nation and in state, reduced the rates of postage, attempted to eradicate polygamy, rehabilitated the temperance cause in the "crusade" of 1874, prosecuted the star-route frauds, and made war on the Louisiana lottery. Neither the Republican party nor its ancestor, the Whig party, made use of the word "reform," as did the Democratic party. Two of the greatest Democratic victories, that of Jefferson in 1800 and that of Jackson in 1828, were won almost entirely on "reform" issues.

Another reason why the Republican party could not turn reformer was the tenacity with which its leaders clung to the old war issues, to the waving of the "bloody shirt," and to charges of treason hurled at its opponents. Its reluctance to adopt tariff reform in 1882, and its tardiness in hearkening to the demand for civil service reform, caused the loss of the House in the "land-slide" of that year. These and other causes operated in cutting down the Republican lead at every presidential election. In the presidential canvass of 1872 the Republican majority of the popular vote was 763,007; in 1876 it was 252,224; and in 1880 it fell to 9464.[2]

[1] *Harper's Weekly*, XXVI., 690, XXVIII., 342.
[2] Stanwood, *Hist. of the Presidency*, 352, 383, 417.

However, New York, Massachusetts, and other wandering states returned to the Republican fold in 1883, and each party approached the presidential year with good grounds for hope. The Democratic party escaped the evils that befell the party in power both during and after the war. Its relegation to inactivity through misguided secession was not without certain advantages, as now became apparent. Restoration to control in the South gave assurance of a majority in the electoral colleges, provided a few populous northern states could be added to the Democratic list by pointing out Republican extravagance and improbity. The Democratic was still the party of "reform." [1]

The Republican party was not without warning of the coming of this era of reform. In April, 1876, upon call of prominent Republicans, including William Cullen Bryant and Theodore D. Woolsey, a conference was held in New York City at which resolutions were passed not to support a Republican candidate for the presidency who in public position ever countenanced corrupt practices or combinations, who impeded their exposure and punishment, or opposed necessary measures of reform.[2] In 1880 a strong reform or independent movement was inaugurated for Senator Edmunds, but was turned into an anti-third term for Grant, and as such held

[1] *Independent*, October 2, 1884.
[2] *Appleton's Annual Cyclop.*, 1876, p. 779; *Harper's Weekly*, XX., 342, 362.

a conference in St. Louis in April of that year.[1] The reform contest of 1876 was largely responsible for the choice of Hayes over Blaine, and in 1880 for the nomination of Garfield instead of Blaine. "The man from Maine" had a record which made him unacceptable to the reformers. In December, 1883, the former Independent movement was revived in Boston, and in February following in New York, by conferences which resolved that the Republican candidates must be men of good character, record, and associations.

Nevertheless, Blaine was the most prominent man in the party. Six years speaker of the House, leader of the Republican minority, senator from Maine, and secretary of state under Garfield, there was no further reward for his service to the party except the presidency. He had the highest number of votes on the first ballot in the Republican convention of 1876, and the second highest in the convention of 1880. His failure to be nominated on these occasions was thought to establish a claim. "It is now Blaine's turn," naïvely declared Platt, ex-senator and Stalwart leader of New York. Blaine was no more acceptable to the reform element of the party in 1884 than he had been in preceding years. The reformers included Senator Hoar and Governor Long, of Massachusetts, George William Curtis, Andrew D. White, and two younger men, Henry Cabot Lodge and Theodore Roosevelt. They had the support of

[1] *Appleton's Annual Cyclop.*, 1880, p. 693; cf. chap. xii., above.

many newspapers, the most prominent being the *New York Times*. They favored Senator Edmunds, leader of the reform movement against polygamy,[1] and the man who once said of Blaine that he was always bobbing up from behind any evil that they tried to attack. Arthur was the favorite of the office-holding element, who argued that he would have a chance of defeating Grover Cleveland if the latter should be nominated by the Democrats; but Arthur had offended Massachusetts by his veto of the river and harbor appropriation bill in 1882. Logan was the choice of the "old soldier" element, and Sherman had part of the Ohio delegation.[2]

The Republicans met at Chicago, June 3, under these rather discouraging conditions, with a "Hurrah for Blaine" which overthrew every combination effected by the reformers in the convention to compass his defeat. A helmet and plume, reminders of Ingersoll's allusion to the "plumed knight" in the convention of 1876, were passed about the convention hall; roosters were brought in; placards and banners displayed; every mention of Blaine's name greeted by prolonged cheering; and no device omitted which might stampede the convention to him.[3] It was claimed that he would "sweep the country like prairie wild-fire." On the fourth ballot he re-

[1] *Harper's Weekly*, XXVIII., 134.
[2] Wise, *Recollections of Thirteen Presidents*, 165; Andrew D. White, *Autobiography*, I., 209; John Sherman, *Recollections*, 886.
[3] *Harper's Weekly*, XXVIII., 379.

ceived the nomination over Arthur, Edmunds, Logan, Sherman, and a few scattering names.[1]

The reformers immediately divided. Lodge, White, and Roosevelt, being held by party ties and hoping to persuade Blaine to come out for civil service and other reforms, supported him;[2] William Walter Phelps, Senator Edmunds, Senator Hoar, and others, unwillingly accepted the candidate.[3] On the other hand, radical reformers, who were immediately dubbed "Mugwumps," from an Algonquin word meaning "chief," united with a few Democrats who despaired of reform in their party and launched the Independent movement, which had long been impending. Within ten days, George William Curtis, who said in the convention, "I was at the birth of the Republican party and I fear I am to witness its death," presided over a meeting of protest in New York City.[4] A Boston meeting was addressed by James Freeman Clarke, Thomas Wentworth Higginson, President Eliot, of Harvard, and others equally prominent. Wendell Phillips Garrison turned the editorial columns of the *Nation* against Blaine; and *Puck* joined the movement by cartooning him as a man tattooed with his questionable record. *Harper's Weekly* and scores of daily and weekly newspapers joined the Independents.[5] Blaine was denounced by

[1] Stanwood, *Hist. of the Presidency*, 432; McPherson, *Hand-Book of Politics*, 1884, pp. 197–210.
[2] Andrew D. White, *Autobiography*, I., 209; *Harper's Weekly*, XXVIII., 544. [3] *Ibid.*, 592. [4] *Ibid.*, 451.
[5] *Nation*, XXXVIII., 496.

them as a corrupt man, a professional politician, a spoilsman, a theatrical poser, and the candidate of a "packed" convention. His henchman, Powell Clayton, an Arkansas carpet-bagger of the worst type,[1] had been slated for temporary chairman of the convention, but was repudiated by the delegates, who placed a negro in the position. The manager chosen for his campaign was a star-route contractor. These were said by the Independents to be fair specimens of the men with whom he would surround himself in the White House.

So hot grew the indignation of the Independents that they were ready to support the candidate of the opposite party if a man to their liking should be nominated. Senator Bayard, of Delaware, would have been acceptable to them; but his attitude of "let them go" when the southern states were attempting to secede, and certain unfortunate allusions to the "unjust war being waged by Mr. Lincoln," made him a presidential impossibility.[2] Tilden, even had he been physically equal to the canvass, was not acceptable to the "reformers" because of the methods ascribed to him in the campaign of 1876. Congressman Flower, of New York, said to be Tilden's heir to the nomination, was declared by the Independents to lack qualifications for the high office, and likely to be influenced by Tammany and other elements which were banded together to defeat

[1] *Nation*, XXXVIII., 475.
[2] *Ibid.*, 520; *Independent*, June 26, 1884.

the aspirations of the leading Democratic reformer, Grover Cleveland.

Cleveland's career was that of an unknown lawyer rising on the crest of the reform movement with no political record to damn him. His national reputation was as limited as that of Blaine was extensive, and, personally, he was almost antipodal to the magnetic "plumed knight." He lacked the glamour attending a soldier candidate, because he had sent a substitute to the front in the Civil War. He was a party man, but no partisan; a forceful thinker, but no astute logician; a ponderous speaker, but no orator. He depended for his success upon candor, pertinacity, and a will power which often verged upon stubbornness. His frankness and radical views concerning public honesty and the conduct of the party estranged him from "Boss" Kelly and Tammany Hall, but attracted the Independents to his support. As governor of New York during the session of the state legislature of 1883–1884, he maintained his reputation for courage by vetoing the "five-cent-fare" bill for elevated roads in New York City,[1] the most popular measure of the session, and by placing a pocket veto on an unprecedented number of bills at the end of the session, although both branches of the legislature were Democratic. "We love him for the enemies he has made," became the slogan of his supporters.

The Democratic national convention met at Chi-

[1] *Nation*, XXXVIII., 244.

cago, June 8, with the New York delegation uninstructed, but the majority favoring the nomination of Cleveland, though Tammany was opposed to him as a dangerous reformer. The platform arraigned the Republican party for having failed to relieve the people of unjust war taxes, pledged the Democratic party to tariff reform, to "honest" civil service reform, and to the revival of an American merchant marine through an American policy. On the first ballot votes were cast for Cleveland, Bayard, Hendricks, Thurman, Randall, McDonald, Carlisle, Flower, Hoadley, and Tilden, with Grover Cleveland leading and lacking only nineteen votes of a majority. On the second ballot he was nominated, and his closest competitor, Hendricks, of Indiana, was given second place on the ticket.[1]

Encouraged by the manifest dissatisfaction in the Republican ranks and by their success in the preceding campaign, the Prohibitionists gathered at Pittsburg, July 23, and named ex-Governor St. John, of Kansas, as their candidate.[2] Two conventions of ultra-reformers, "antis" of various sorts—a kind of political junk but indicative of the unrest of the times—nominated ex-Governor Butler, of Massachusetts, who had withdrawn from the Democratic convention because it would not adopt a protective

---

[1] Stanwood, *Hist. of the Presidency*, 433–440; *Harper's Weekly*, XXVIII., 458.
[2] Stanwood, *Hist. of the Presidency*, 442; *Harper's Weekly*, XXVIII., 458, 512.

tariff plank. To add to the diversified nature of
the campaign, Belva A. B. Lockwood, a woman
lawyer of Washington, D. C., was put in nomination
by a National Equal Rights party in California. An
American, or anti-secret society convention, named
S. C. Pomeroy as its candidate.[1]

The Republicans at first made light of the Independent or "Mugwump" movement, comparing it
with that of the Liberal Republicans who supported
Greeley in 1872 and ended in a fiasco.[2] Recruited
largely from the ranks of scholars, the Independents
were ridiculed as "dudes" and as "Pharisees" and
their claims for purity as the "Holier than thou"
pose. In turn, they insisted that they did not reject
Blaine because he was a Republican, but because he
was Blaine and an unfit candidate. They called
attention to his persistence in keeping himself before
the public by means of professional "boomers" and
"wire-pullers." They criticised the taste shown by
him in publishing chapter by chapter his *Twenty
Years in Congress*, immediately preceding the Republican convention, and insinuated that the writer
was endeavoring in his book to soothe old enmities
rather than to tell the truth of history. They revived
the charge that Blaine, as secretary of state in 1881,
pushed the bogus claims of Landreau to the guano
beds of Peru; that he injudiciously recognized Calderon as president of Peru; and that he came near

[1] Stanwood, *Hist. of the Presidency*, 441.
[2] Dunning, *Reconstruction* (*Am. Nation*, XXII.), chap. xii.

involving the United States in war with Chile by his rashness in making political capital out of his responsible position.[1] They wanted no more of Blaine's "brisk foreign policy."

A conference of Independents assembled in New York a short time after Cleveland's nomination, indorsed his candidacy as a rebuke to "increasing public corruption and the want of official integrity in the highest trusts of the government," and appointed committees to compass the defeat of the Republican candidate. Carl Schurz, who had been a member of Hayes's cabinet, stumped the country for Cleveland; George William Curtis gave his potent pen to the same purpose; Henry Ward Beecher added his eloquence; William Everett contributed his lively individuality; and prominent Republicans, headed by ex-President Woolsey, of Yale College, endeavored to persuade the Prohibitionist candidate to retire in favor of Cleveland. Butler was charged with being in league with the Republicans to draw votes from the Democratic ranks in return for the payment of his campaign expenses. From its beginning the campaign was abusive. Blaine's supporters were embittered against the Independents and the Prohibitionists, who drew votes from the Republican ranks, and the Democrats were exasperated with Tammany for its apathy.

Having introduced the slinging of mud, all parties indulged to the full. Blaine's long public record

---

[1] See page 224, above.

was examined anew, and the "Mulligan letters" brought afresh to the public view, reminders of his unfortunate connection with certain railroad bonds as speaker of the House at the time when railway corporations were especially active in soliciting favors in rights of way through public lands and in adjustment of land grants.[1] Although he produced some of the letters with dramatic effect in the House in 1876,[2] the charge defeated him for the nomination in that year and in 1880, and now bade fair to defeat him before the people in 1884. Finding it impossible to retaliate on the scanty public record of Cleveland, the Republicans brought charges of sexual immorality against him; but his reply of "Tell the truth" broke the force of the blow.[3] The Democrats countered with alleged scandals concerning Blaine's marriage, and accused Logan of being in a plot to steal the lands of the Zuñi Indians.[4]

In the course of the "mud slinging," the Democrats attempted to prove Blaine part owner of a mine in Ohio where a strike of miners was in progress. Republicans, in turn, revived the campaign cry of 1880, that the Cobden Club, a free-trade organization of England, was sending over large sums of money to be used by the Democrats in the dissemination of free-trade doctrine. Blaine was next accused of

[1] Dunning, *Reconstruction* (*Am. Nation*, XXII.), chap. xix.; Follett, *Speaker of the House*, 108, 109.
[2] *Cong. Record*, 44 Cong., 1 Sess., 3604.
[3] *Independent*, October 30, 1884.
[4] *Harper's Weekly*, XXVIII., 480.

being a drunkard, but his managers produced a certificate from Neal Dow, the Prohibitionist of Maine, to prove that he was a total abstainer. Aside from Blaine's transactions with the railroads, he was charged with having defeated the House appropriation for the civil service commission in 1873. The Democrats also republished a speech by Logan in 1869 adverse to the Jenckes civil service reform bill.

The use of personalities in the campaign was due largely to the absence of a prominent issue between the parties; there was no line of demarcation; each declared for "good money," pure citizenship, and a tariff which would not destroy American industries or injure American workingmen. These generalities furnished no ground and formulated no plan for a definite line of action to be pursued, whichever party should win. Reformers and the reform press, whose ambitions were to set a high standard in American politics, were disgusted with the low moral standard set for the campaign. The Mugwumps were partly responsible for having opened their guns on Blaine's record; but they did not foresee the direction the missiles would take. Said one editorial, "The campaign is one worthy of the stairways of a tenement-house, which reflects shame and disgrace on the whole country." The same paper again asserted that "party contests have never before reached so low a depth of national humiliation."[1]

[1] *Nation*, XXXVIII., 378; XXXIX., 150.

If the campaign was a disgrace from the standpoint of courtesy and decency, it showed improvement in the matter of levying political assessments. In February of the campaign year the civil service commission presented its first annual report, eliciting a congratulatory message from President Arthur to Congress upon the good results already accomplished and expressing his conviction that it would in the future be of still more signal benefit to the public service. Although the Republican national committee could not abandon readily the old plan of levying a "voluntary contribution," and the Democratic state committees assessed officials in states and in municipalities which they controlled and where civil service laws did not protect incumbents, nevertheless both the great parties depended upon contributions made by private individuals and by corporations rather than those made by officeholders. The reformers were indignant when the Republican committee announced that it would make a list of officials who responded to its appeal and of those who failed to heed — a veiled threat likely to be coercive. The Independent and reform press also criticised the action of Commissioner of Pensions Dudley, who tendered his resignation to take effect after election day, and then took the stump in Indiana and Ohio for Blaine, thus apparently avoiding a lesion of the principle that federal officials should take no part in a political campaign.

One other attempt was made to employ old

methods of campaigning, when Lot Wright, United States marshal for the southern district of Ohio, swore in and armed a number of deputy marshals, many of them negroes, to preserve peace at the polls. His defence, when brought before a committee of the House of Representatives the following session in an attempt to impeach him, was that large numbers of voters, both colored and white, had been imported from Kentucky and Indiana into Cincinnati during the October state elections, with the purpose of fraudulently increasing the Democratic vote. He further claimed that the city officials were imprisoning colored men during the days preceding the November election to prevent them voting the Republican ticket. The committee presented a report March 3, 1885, that Wright was guilty of the acts as charged, but that the near approach of the close of the session would not permit proceedings to be brought against him. One of his henchmen was sentenced to imprisonment by the local courts, and public opinion clearly warned future campaign managers that old methods were passing away with old ideals.[1]

The Republicans based large hopes on the Irish vote because Tammany, although ostensibly indorsing Cleveland, made its own nominations for state offices and would supposedly throw away its vote

---

[1] *Cong. Record*, 48 Cong., 2 Sess., 17-25; *House Reports*, 48 Cong., 2 Sess., No. 2681; *Appleton's Annual Cyclop.*, 1885, pp 204-206.

for presidential electors. When the Republican managers pointed with pride to the Irish maternal grandmother of Blaine, the opposition raised the anti-Catholic alarm, and Blaine's church affiliation became a prominent issue of the campaign. Cleveland's maternal Irish ancestry was offered to counterbalance that of Blaine. As the campaign drew to a close, these issues became paramount in and about the city of New York. Blaine partly conciliated the reformers by indorsing civil service reform in a Brooklyn speech after his return from his western campaign; but the following afternoon, October 30, he gave an audience in New York City to more than five hundred Protestant clergymen, who wished to assure him that they as well as the Roman Catholic clergy were his supporters. The spokesman, Rev. Samuel D. Burchard, in the course of his address referred to the Democratic party as one whose antecedents were "rum, Romanism, and rebellion." [1] The unfortunate alliteration probably escaped the notice of Blaine, or its potency was unforeseen, for he failed to correct it in his response and it was immediately taken up by the enemy as an expression of the opinion of the Republican party and its candidate, and was used to hold the doubtful Tammany vote. On the evening of that day Blaine was the guest of the representative business men of New York; immediately the country was placarded with Burchard's alliterative phrase, and with pictures of

[1] Andrews, *Last Quarter-Century*, II., 87.

Blaine's millionaire dinner. Hendricks made a personal appeal to "Boss Kelly," and secured a promise that Tammany would support the Democratic ticket for the sake of the vice-presidential candidate.[1]

The vote of New York was essential to Democratic success, because while the "solid South" and New Jersey could be counted on for 163 electoral votes, the number would be 39 short of the 201 required for a choice. If the 36 could be secured from New York, the addition of any state, even Nevada, would mean a Democratic victory. On the other hand, the Republicans could not depend on the 228 electoral votes they had received in 1880, because New York, Indiana, and Connecticut had gone Democratic in the mean time. Omitting Indiana and Connecticut, the Republicans were sure of success if they could carry New York.

The electors were chosen November 4, and early returns showed that Cleveland had carried all the southern states, together with Connecticut, New Jersey, and Indiana, giving him 183 electoral votes. Blaine had 182 electoral votes, and New York was to be the umpire. So close was the vote in that state that a recount was necessary.[2] For ten days the result of the election was uncertain, and intense excitement prevailed. A rumor spread that Jay Gould was withholding the returns for stock speculative purposes. Remembering the disputed elec-

---
[1] *Appleton's Annual Cyclop.*, 1884, p. 774.
[2] Stanwood, *Hist. of the Presidency*, 449.

tion of eight years before, the Democrats were determined to maintain their rights. Two days after the election a small riot occurred in Indianapolis, caused by the Democrats attempting to carry a banner into the post-office building and being resisted by Republicans, who tore the banner to bits. Crowds of angry partisans surrounded newspaper bulletins, and a large window in a newspaper office was broken by a missile. The mayor of Chicago made a public request that newspapers refrain from issuing bulletins.[1] Fortunately the electoral commission of 1876 had established the principle that no higher authority than that of the states could "go behind the returns" to question the count of votes. A careful recanvass of the popular vote in New York gave Cleveland 563,154, and Blaine 562,005; by this margin of 1149 votes the Democracy was triumphant in a national election for the first time in twenty-five years; and delirious rejoicing followed throughout the country.

The usual attempts were made to explain the result of the election. Stress was laid on the Burchard incident, on the conciliation of Tammany, and on the fact that Cleveland remained for the most part at Albany while Blaine made a campaign tour of the central states. Although he received a magnificent ovation, it was predicted that no future candidate would commit the error of taking the stump in his own behalf. Others attributed the

[1] Andrews, *Last Quarter-Century*, II., 88–90.

Republican defeat to Conkling, who had twice prevented the nomination of Blaine in the convention, and who now refused to give his still powerful influence in New York to his ancient enemy. The Independents claimed the credit for the victory, and, having administered a rebuke to the party for adopting an unacceptable candidate, were ready, for the most part, to return to their allegiance. Advocates of tariff reform claimed to have chastised the party for refusing to listen to their plea. Lovers of universal freedom thought the defeat a punishment administered to the Republicans for allowing the Chinese to be excluded.

In a larger view, the Democratic victory of 1884 may be taken as the natural end of a cycle—the unavoidable result of forces working for the previous twenty years. The end of the national Republican régime, inaugurated by the radicals in 1866, was at hand; and a change was taking place as marked as that which characterized the original transition of 1866. No longer could the people be persuaded that secession was in danger of being revived; that the "rebel brigadiers" were planning to seize Congress; or that any one party was essential to the preservation of the Union. It was not so much an acknowledgment that Reconstruction was a failure, as that Reconstruction methods were no longer possible, and that Reconstruction issues were no longer potent. Expediency in matters of finance and currency was to determine political issues in the immediate future.

Former political issues were to be relegated to oblivion with former methods of manufacture, of transportation, of business, in the new industrial era. Thousands of young men who voted independently of party in 1884 were too young to remember the war, and too cosmopolitan in their business relations and travel to feel the influence of sectionalism. Added to them were thousands of foreigners, naturalized since 1865, to whom the war issues meant nothing. Blaine was the sole surviving statesman of the old Reconstruction group still in active life; when he withdrew, after a valedictory in which he placed all the blame for his defeat on the suppression of the colored vote in the South, the last word of the old language was spoken; the past was decently interred; and hope turned expectantly towards the new order of things, towards new types of statesmen, new ideals of government, and new activities for conscientious citizenship.

CHAPTER XX

CRITICAL ESSAY ON AUTHORITIES

BIBLIOGRAPHIES

BIBLIOGRAPHICAL aids in the shape of reference lists and guides, so valuable for earlier periods of American history, are wanting for the decade assigned to this volume. J. N. Larned, *Literature of American History* (1902), contains under the title, "American Development" (Nos. 2687–2821), notes on occasional volumes bearing on this period; and the Library of Congress has issued lists on the Isthmian Canal, the Monroe Doctrine, Trades-Unions, and other subjects. Brookings and Ringwalt, *Briefs for Debate* (1897), contains topics and references of value; as does Ringwalt, *Briefs on Public Questions* (1905). See also the "Critical Essay" at the end of J. H. Latané, *America the World Power* (*Am. Nation*, XXV.).

GENERAL SECONDARY WORKS

None of the standard historians covers the field of this volume. James Ford Rhodes closes his admirable *History of the United States* with the contested election of 1876. E. Benjamin Andrews, *History of the Last Quarter-Century of the United States, 1870–1895* (2 vols., 1896), enlarged by added chapters to *The United States in Our Own Time* (1903), covers in a popular way the entire period, although it is hastily written amid other duties, and omits industrial features. Among the popular histories covering this period may be mentioned Woodrow Wilson, *History of the American*

People (5 vols., 1902), and Edwin Erle Sparks, *The United States of America* (2 vols., 1904). Of the single volumes, the *Cambridge Modern History*, Vol. VII., *The United States* (1903), gives in chaps. xx.–xxii. a scholarly treatment of modern industrial and economic questions. Henry William Elson, *History of the United States* (1904), (somewhat enlarged edition, 5 vols., 1905), mentions the principal events of this period, although necessarily condensed.

DOCUMENTARY SOURCES

The debates in Congress will be found in the *Congressional Record*, as the official report is called after 1874. Many important House and Senate documents are cited in the foot-notes on preceding pages of this volume. Others may be found from Ben. Perley Poore, *Descriptive Catalogue of Government Publications to 1881;* and for later years in the less voluminous but more accurate *Tables of and Annotated Index to the Congressional Series of United States Public Documents* (1902). Presidential messages are most easily found in Richardson, *Messages and Papers of the Presidents* (10 vols., 1896–1899). Acts of Congress for this decade are in *Statutes at Large*, Vols. XX. to XXV. Akin to documents is Edward McPherson, *Hand-Book of Politics*, published biennially after 1872, in which are printed the votes of Congress on important measures, being arranged according to political parties, together with valuable statistical information. The more important acts of Congress may be found in William MacDonald, *Select Statutes of the United States, 1861–1898* (1903); and many illustrative sources are reprinted in Albert Bushnell Hart, *American History told by Contemporaries, 1845–1897* (4 vols., 1897–1901). On the presidential elections, Edward Stanwood, *History of the Presidency* (1898), stands supreme. Election statistics and statistics bearing on finance and industries are collected in the various almanacs, of which the *American Almanac* and the *World Almanac* enjoy the largest popularity. A large part of this valuable material also appears annually in the *United States Statistical Abstract.*

CYCLOPÆDIAS

Appleton's Annual Cyclopædia (new series), 1876, is not to be classed with the usual bureau of general information, but contains year by year well-written articles on prominent events of the year, with occasional historical surveys. James A. Woodburn, *American Political History, 1763–1876* (1906), reprints Alexander Johnston's useful articles from John J. Lalor, *Cyclopædia of Political Science, Political Economy, and United States History* (3 vols., 1881).

BIOGRAPHIES AND COLLECTED WORKS

Materials of this kind for this period are scanty. John Sherman was connected with most of the events, and his *Recollections of Forty Years* (1897) gives valuable personal views, although unevenly written. John Bigelow, *Life of Samuel J. Tilden* (1896), presents the Democratic view of the controversy of 1876. The lives of Hayes by Howells and by Howard are campaign documents. The correspondence and papers of Hayes are in Indianapolis and not accessible. The campaign of Garfield and his death brought out a number of "lives," those of Bundy, Conwell, Ridpath, Stoddart, McCabe, and Mason being of like unimportance. That by James A. Gilmore (1880) is more complete. Fuller, *Reminiscences of Garfield* (1881), bears little on his public life. The sketches by Stoddart, *Lives of Hayes, Garfield, and Arthur* (1888), have more merit than the others named above. B. A. Hinsdale, *Works of James A. Garfield* (1882), is taken largely from his speeches made in Congress. George S. Boutwell, *Reminiscences of Sixty Years* (1902), covers the political aspects of this period, especially the presidential election of 1880. Edward Stanwood, *James G. Blaine* (American Statesmen Series, 1905), includes very briefly Blaine's candidacy for the presidency and still more briefly his work in Garfield's cabinet. Gail Hamilton [Abigail Dodge], *Life of James G. Blaine* (1895), gives a personal view of the Maine statesman. George F. Hoar, *Autobiography of Seventy Years* (1903), and W. D. Foulke, *Life of Oliver P. Morton* (1899), may be consulted on a few points.

PERIODICAL LITERATURE

The periodicals, especially the *North American Review*, the *Fortnightly Review*, the *Nation*, and the *Forum*, contain articles of merit on events of this period, in addition to those mentioned elsewhere. These may be reached through William F. Poole, *Index to Periodical Publications*. Of the departmental monographs, the following from the American Statistical Association, *Publications*, have a bearing on this volume: No. 6, *American Railroad Statistics;* No. 23, *Growth of Cities in the United States between 1880 and 1890;* No. 24, *Geographical Distribution of the Population of the United States;* No. 42, *Concentration of Pig-Iron and Coal Production;* No. 46, *Comparative Study of Statistics of the Tenth and Eleventh Census;* and No. 53, *Industrial Associations in the United States.* In Columbia University, *Studies in History, Economics, and Public Law*, see I., No. 2, *History of the Tariff Administrations;* XI., *Growth of Cities;* XII., No. 3, *History of Military Pension Legislation in the United States.* In Johns Hopkins University, *Studies in Historical and Political Science*, see XX., Nos. 5, 6, *Trust Companies in the United States;* XXIV., Nos. 3, 4, *Finances of American Trade-Unions.*

CIVIL SERVICE REFORM

The literature on this subject is rather meagre for the early stage discussed in this volume. Dorman B. Eaton has valuable articles on the Spoils System, Patronage, etc., in Lalor, *Cyclopædia of Political Science, etc.* (1881), I., 153, 472, 478, II., 640, III., 19, 139, 565, 782, 895. Fish, *Civil Service and the Patronage, Harvard Historical Studies*, No. XI. (1905), is the most comprehensive study of the subject. For the evils of the spoils system, see Lyon G. Tyler, *Parties and Patronage* (1888), George William Curtis, *Orations and Addresses* (1893), II., 477; Henry Cabot Lodge, *Historical and Political Essays* (1892), 114 (reprinted from the *Century*, October, 1890); Theodore Roosevelt, *American Ideals* (1904), No. 7; and Dorman B. Eaton, *Government of Municipalities* (1899). For the working of the merit system, consult the annual reports of the federal civil service commission, especially that for 1886-1887; and of the commissions of New York and Massachusetts. James Bryce, *American Commonwealth* (ed. of 1893), II., chap. lxv., describes the evils and attempted cures of the American civil service. The *Congressional Record*, 47 Cong., 2 Sess., contains the speeches on the passage of the first reform bill. The various reports presented in the House and Senate are noted in the foot-notes to chapter xiv., above. In the periodicals, see especially *Political Science Quarterly*, III., 247, and *Atlantic Monthly*, LXV., 433.

DIPLOMACY

Treaties made during this period may be found in *Treaties and Conventions between the United States and Other Powers* (1889), or in more convenient form, with comments, in Freeman Snow, *Treaties and Topics in American Diplomacy* (1894). The diplomatic correspondence of the United States is printed annually in *Papers Relating to the Foreign Relations of the United States*. James Bassett Moore, *American Diplomacy* (1905), takes deservedly high rank as a secondary work. It is rivalled by John B. Foster, *Century of American Diplomacy* (1901). A topical treatment of certain questions is followed in John B. Henderson, Jr., *American Diplomatic Questions* (1901), and in Theodore S. Woolsey, *America's Foreign Policy* (1898). A more ephemeral sketch is William Eleroy Curtis, *The United States and Foreign Powers* (1899). On the few instances of arbitration during this period, one may consult John Bassett Moore, *International Arbitrations* (1898).

THE INTEROCEANIC CANAL

Senate Document, 56 Cong., 1 Sess., 59, is a reprint of a Library of Congress pamphlet by Hugh Morrison, *List of Books and Articles Relating to an Interoceanic Canal and Railway Routes* (1900). On the Monroe Doctrine, see the Critical Essay on Authorities by Fredrick J. Turner, in *Rise of the New West* (*American Nation*, XV.). The Doctrine as applicable to De Lesseps and his isthmian canal scheme is considered by John B. Henderson, Jr., *American Diplomatic Questions* (1901), 137–158; by T. B. Edgington, *The Monroe Doctrine* (1905), 145–147; and by John W. Foster, *A Century of American Diplomacy* (1901), 461–467. The periodical literature on the subject is extensive between 1878 and 1888, including many articles by De Lesseps himself. It may be traced in Poole, *Index to Periodical Literature* (1884). The most authentic account of the French enterprise and its accomplishments is in the nine parts of the report of the *Commission d'étude institué par le liquidateur de la Compagnie Universelle*, Paris, 1890. The diplomatic debates between Blaine and Frelinghuysen on the one side, and Lord Granville on the other, concerning the abrogation of the Clayton-Bulwer agreement, are to be found in the first volume of *Foreign Relations* for 1881, 1882, 1883, and 1884. That for 1883 contains also valuable historical information on early canal companies. *House Documents*, 47 Cong., 2 Sess., 107, makes comparisons of the various routes proposed for an isthmian canal, with résumés of different surveys. The Rogers report of 1884, *Senate Executive Documents*, 48 Cong., 1 Sess., No. 123, contains illustrations of the progress made by the De Lesseps company on the Isthmus. A monograph by Ira D. Travis, *The History of the Clayton-Bulwer Treaty* (1899), contains a few pages on the De Lesseps era. W. E. Hall, *International Law* (1904), discusses the relations of the United States to the De Lesseps scheme. The relation of the United States towards the canal in general is also given in L. M. Keasby, *The Nicaraguan Canal and the Monroe Doctrine* (1896).

Later phases of the canal may be studied in D. R. Dewey, *National Problems*, chap. xii., and in J. H. Latané, *America the World Power*, chap. xii. (*Am. Nation*, XXIV., XXV.).

THE DEVELOPMENT OF THE WEST

The transition period occupied in the construction of the Pacific railroads, and the influence of their completion on the West, may be studied in Robert P. Porter, *The West from the Census of 1880* (1882). Of the experiences of travellers, that of Robert Louis Stevenson, *Across the Plains* (1892), and *The Amateur Emigrant; the Silverado Squatters* (1893), are best written, although far from optimistic. Of contemporary descriptions, one may read with interest William F. Rae, *Westward by Rail* (1874), and L. P. Bracket, *Our Western Empire* (1882). An earlier view may be found in Samuel Bowles, *Our New West* (1869). On individual occupations and industries, one of the best works is Joseph G. McCoy, *Historic Sketches of the Cattle Trade of the West and Southwest* (1874). William Shepard, *Prairie Experiences in Handling Cattle and Sheep* (1885), is of some merit, although not written by a trained hand. The Indian campaigns of the West find a place in Nelson A. Miles, *Personal Recollections and Observations* (1896); in Philip Sheridan, *Personal Memoirs* (1888); in George A. Custer, *My Life on the Plains* (1874); and in Elizabeth B. Custer, *Tenting on the Plains* (1888). The series entitled "Story of the West" is graphically written, but gives few facts for the student. Among the best numbers is Cy Warman, *Story of the Railroad* (1903), and Charles Howard Shinn, *Story of the Mine* (1896), especially the Comstock lode of Nevada.

THE CHINESE QUESTION

The Library of Congress has published by A. P. C. Griffin, *References on Chinese Immigration* (1904), an indispensable guide to literature on the subject. Conditions in California are set forth in the *Report of the Senate Committee* [of the California legislature] (Sacramento, 1877, 49 pp.). Conditions in Canada may be studied in the *Report of the Royal Commission on Chinese and Japanese Immigration* (Ottawa, 1902). The situation in Wyoming is described in Secretary of the Interior, *Report*, 49 Cong., 1 Sess., II., 1223, 1284 (*House Executive Documents*, pt. v.). The report of the Senate investigating committee of 1876 is printed as *Senate Reports*, 44 Cong., 2 Sess., Nos. 689-1281. Relations of the Chinese to American labor may be examined in *House Reports*, 46 Cong., 2 Sess., No. 572, 39 pp. The negotiations for the extension of the act of 1882 are printed in *Senate Executive Documents*, 48 Cong., 1 Sess., No. 62, 76 pp.; and the regulations of the treasury department for the admission of excepted classes are given in *House Executive Documents*, 48 Cong., 2 Sess., No. 214. Among the general writings that of George F. Seward, sometime minister to China, *Chinese Immigration in its Social and Economical Aspects* (1881), is among the best. Richard Mayo-Smith, *Emigration and Immigration* (1890), gives valuable statistics and comments. James A. Whitney, *Chinese and the Chinese Question* (1888), is authoritative. The California presses produced a large number of pamphlets both pro- and anti-Chinese. The periodical literature of the period is voluminous, the editorials of E. L. Godkin in the *Nation* forming the best defence of the Chinese. The *Overland Monthly* presents chiefly the opposite view. Articles by Chinese will be found in the *Cosmopolitan*, V., 297-311 (August, 1888); in the *North American Review*, CXLVIII., 476-483 (April, 1889); and the *Overland Monthly*, new series, XXIII., 518-526 (May, 1894). Among the best public documents on the Chinese question are *Senate Reports*, 44 Cong., 2 Sess., No. 689; 57 Cong., 1 Sess., No. 776. *Senate Executive Documents*, 48 Cong., 1 Sess., No. 62; 52 Cong., 2 Sess., No. 54; *Senate Documents*, 55 Cong., 1 Sess., Nos. 120 and 167; *House Reports*, 46 Cong., 2 Sess., No. 57; 51 Cong., 2 Sess., No. 4048; *House Executive Documents*, 49 Cong., 1 Sess., No. 102; *House Miscellaneous Documents*, 45 Cong., 1 Sess., No. 9.

FINANCIAL AND COMMERCIAL

The Tenth Census (1880) contains statistics on the industrial progress of the preceding decade, although of limited character compared with similar reports of later dates. Davis R. Dewey, *Financial History of the United States* (American Citizen Series, 1903), is the best outline on American finance; A. D. Noyes, *Thirty Years of American Finance* (1898), is valuable for the connection of national finance with Wall Street; and A. S. Bolles, *Financial History of the United States* (3 vols., 1883–1886), is of service for resumption, the silver question, and the tariff. Frank W. Taussig, *Tariff History of the United States* (1905), may be consulted on the tariff act of 1883, and on the Mills bill, although not with pleasure by advocates of high protection. D. A. Wells, *Practical Economics* (1885), includes essays on the tariff, on silver coinage, etc. The silver question, in its earlier stages, is considered by J. Laurence Laughlin, *Bimetallism in the United States* (1897); by D. K. Watson, *History of American Coinage* (1899); and by F. W. Taussig, "Silver Situation in the United States" (American Economic Association, *Publications*, VII., No. 1, 1892). Of periodical literature on the tariff of 1883, two readable articles are in *North American Review*, CXXXVI., 270, and *Fortnightly Review*, XXXVII., 369. The further consideration of these questions is continued in D. R. Dewey, *National Problems* (*American Nation*, XXIV.), passim.

MODERN INDUSTRIALISM

An excellent sketch of the rise of industrialism is presented by Katharine Coman, *Industrial History of the United States* (1905), and a less up-to-date view by Carroll D. Wright, *Industrial Evolution of the United States* (1895). Other aspects of the industrial age are to be seen in J. M. Swank, *History of the Manufacture of Iron* (1897); T. M. Young, *American Cotton Industry* (1903); and W. J. Mitchell, *Story of American Coals* (1897). The agricultural aspects are presented in Edward W. Martin, *History of the Grange Movement* (1874), and the mechanical achievements in Edward W. Bryce, *Progress of Invention in the Nineteenth Century* (1900). For the influence of the Pacific railways in the development of interior commerce, see J. P. Davis, *The Union Pacific Railway* (1894), and E. V. Smalley, *The Northern Pacific Railroad* (1883). The successive issues of the United States Census contain a vast amount of valuable material on the different industries, on agriculture, on transportation, and on labor. On the earlier phases of the industrial combination problem, see William Z. Ripley, *Trusts, Pools, and Combinations* (1905), a compilation.

THE RAILWAY PROBLEM

In its early stages, the question of federal and state control of railways may be examined in A. T. Hadley, *Railroad Transportation* (1890), William Larrabee, *The Railway Question* (1893); W. D. Dabney, *Public Regulation of Railways* (1889); Charles F. Adams, *Railroads, their Origin and Problems* (1888); F. H. Dixon, *State Railroad Control* (1896); B. H. Myers, *Railway Legislation in the United States* (1903). For an early view, also see Edmund J. James, *Agitation for Federal Regulation of Railways* (American Economic Association, *Publications*, II., No. 3). James F. Hudson, *Railways and the Republic* (3d ed., 1889), is answered by Appleton Morgan, *The People and the Railways* (1888). The railway argument is presented by A. B. Stickney, *The Railway Problem* (1895). For later aspects of the railway problem, one may profitably read Henry R. Hatfield, editor, *Lectures on Commerce* (1904).

TRADES-UNIONS

For this subject a valuable bibliography is A. P. C. Griffin, *Select List of Books on Labor, Particularly Relating to Strikes*. For the English labor organizations, see William Trant, *Trade-Unions* (1899); Sidney and Beatrice Webb,

History of Trade-Unionism (1902); and George Howell, *Conflicts of Labor and Capital* (1889). American labor organizations may be studied in R. T. Ely, *The Labor Movement in America* (1890); in John Mitchell, *Organized Labor* (1903) in George McNeill, *The Labor Movement in America* (1888); and in Terence V. Powderly, *Thirty Years of Labor* (1889). James Brownson Reynolds, *Benefits of Labor Unions* (1898), and F. J. Stimson, *Labor in its Relation to Law* (1895), treat of phases indicated in the titles. The strike of 1877 brought out a popular illustrated history, J. A. Dacus, *Annals of the Great Strikes in the United States* (1878). For this strike see also United States Department of Labor, *Annual Report*, 1888, *Strikes and Lockouts*.

INDEX

AGRICULTURE, Centennial exhibit, 15; export trade, 16–18, 305; development in West, 25, 257; Red River wheat lands, 306; internal commerce, 308.
Alabama, coal and iron mines, 315.
Aldrich, N. W., and campaign assessments, 196; protectionist, 299.
Allison, W. B., silver bill, 142; and campaign assessments, 196.
American Steamship Company organized, 56.
American Union Telegraph Company absorbed by Western Union, 329.
Ammen, Daniel, at international canal congress, 205, 208.
Anderson, T. C., prosecuted, 111.
Angell, J. B., Chinese treaty, 243.
Apache Indians, war (1879), 273.
Arctic exploration, 51.
Arizona, growth of population (1870–1880), 23; "cow-boys," 253. *See also* Far West.
Army, use in suppressing rioting (1877), 74; use at polls forbidden, 125–127, 131.
Art, influence of Centennial, 11–13.
Arthur, C. A., removed from collectorship, 158; defence, 159;
nominated for vice-president, 171; elected, 177; Stalwart, 182; takes oath as president, 191; and civil service reform act, 198–200; Chinese exclusion veto, 246; and Arizona "cow-boys," 253; on Indian policy, 278; on surplus, 288, 296; river and harbor bill veto (1882), 294; on tariff, 298; character of administration, 327, 328; and financial depression, 328, 329; candidacy for renomination, 336; bibliography of administration, 352–362.
Atchison, Topeka & Santa Fé, construction, 255.
Atrato-Napipi canal route, 207, 212.

BALTIMORE & OHIO RAILROAD, development of trunk line, 54; and rate agreement, 58; reduction of wages (1877), 71; strike, 72.
Bannock Indians, war (1878), 272.
Bayard, T. F., and silver, 141; candidacy for presidential nomination (1880), 173; (1884), 338; on French Panama company, 210.
Beaver Falls, Pa., Chinese laborers, 239.
Beecher, H. W., supports Cleveland, 342.

Bell, A. G., telephone, 43.
Bibliographies, of period 1877–1884, 352; of Isthmian canal, 357; of Chinese question, 358.
Bicycle, introduction, 44.
Biographies of period 1877–1884, 354.
Birmingham, iron industry, 315.
Blaine, J. G., denunciation of Hayes's southern policy, 100, 107, 109, 113; on federal election laws, 122, 126; candidacy for presidential nomination (1880), 168–171; secretary of state, 183; and Conkling, 183, 184; conceit, 184; Isthmian canal diplomacy, 220; attempt to abrogate Clayton-Bulwer treaty, 221–223; and rights of naturalized citizens, 223; South American diplomacy, 224; opposition of reformers, 335, 337, 338; as candidate for presidential nomination (1884), 335; nominated, 336; campaign charges against, 342–344; and Burchard's alliteration, 347; defeated, 348; reasons for defeat, 349–351; bibliography, 354.
Bland, R. P., monetary commission, 140; silver bill, 142.
Bogy, L. V., monetary commission, 140.
Bonds, movement to pay in silver, 137–140; refunding, 152, 288; variety (1880), 287.
Boston, absorption of suburbs, 30.
Boutwell, G. S., monetary commission, 140; bibliography, 354.
Bowen, Francis, monetary commission, 140.
Bradley, J. P., and prosecution of Louisiana returning board, 111.

Brady, T. W., star-route frauds, 188–190.
Brown, J. C., Louisiana commission, 91.
Brown, J. Y., and charge against Hayes of bargaining, 95.
Brush, C. F., electric light, 41.
Bryant, W. C., and political reform (1876), 334.
Burchard, S. D., political alliteration (1884), 347.
Burke, E. A., and charge against Hayes of bargaining, 96.
Burlingame, Anson, Chinese-American treaty (1868), 233.
Burnside, A. E., resolution on Isthmian canal, 212.
Butler, B. F., elected governor, 331; nominated for president (1884), 340; campaign charge against, 342.
Buzzi incident, 223.

CABINET, Hayes's, 104–107; Garfield's, 183.
California, agricultural development, 28. *See also* Chinese.
Cameron, J. D., senator, 107; and tariff bill of 1883, 302.
Cameron, Simon, and Hayes's cabinet appointments, 106; and Grant's candidacy (1880), 167.
Canadian Pacific Railway, construction, 307.
Canadians as immigrants, 33, 249.
Canals, railroad competition, 54; abandonment, 55; St. Mary's, 317, 320. *See also* Isthmian.
Cannon, A. M., sentenced for polygamy, 264.
Centennial Exhibition, plan, 4; difficulties, 5; federal aid, 6–9; opening, 9; stimulates travel, 9–11; educational and artistic results, 11–14; influ-

INDEX

ence on technical education, 13-15; agricultural exhibits, 15; admissions, 15; financial success, 16; effect on exports, 16.
Chamberlain, D. H., rival governor of South Carolina, 90; retires, 94, 99; denounces Hayes, 108.
Chambers, B. J., nominated for vice-president, 172.
Chandler, W. E., denounces Hayes, 113.
Chandler, Zachariah, denounces Hayes, 108.
Cheyenne Indians, war (1878), 273.
Chicago, and development of inland commerce, 309; development of meat packing, 310.
Chili, Blaine's diplomacy, 224.
Chinese, and organized labor, 230; beginning of immigration, 231; qualities as laborers, 231, 234, 239; work on Pacific railroads, 232; treaty guaranteeing right of residence (1868), 233; competition with white laborers, 233, 234; development of anti-Chinese sentiment, 235; Los Angeles riot, 235; habits preclude amalgamation, 235; not admissible to citizenship, 236; congressional investigation, 237; political "sand lots" agitation against, 238; menace eastern labor, 239; discriminating state and municipal enactments against, declared unconstitutional, 239 - 241; and California's electoral vote (1880), 241, 244; exclusion bill vetoed (1879), 241-243; treaty permitting suspension of immigration (1880), 243; Morey letter, 244, 245; Denver riot (1880), 245; second exclusion bill vetoed (1882), 245-247; party platforms on (1880), 245; first exclusion act (1882), 247; its inefficiency, 248; second exclusion act (1884), 249; later acts, 249; bibliography, 358.
Chittenden, S. B., on evils of greenbacks, 145.
"Cipher despatches," 115-117.
Cities, growth (1860-1880), 29-31; development of street railways, 37-39.
Civil service, Hayes's attitude on reform, 154; he forbids political participation and assessments, 155, 156; reform in New York post-office, 157; Hayes and New York custom-house, 155-161; reform movement, 161; state and national reform associations, 167; campaign assessments, 162-164, 185, 189, 196-198, 344; Garfield and office-seekers, 187; star-route frauds, 188-190; spoils system and assassination of Garfield, 191, 192, 194; reform bill, 194, 195, 198; prosecution for political assessments, 197; Arthur and reform, 198; provisions of reform act, 199; commission, 200; execution of act under Arthur, 200; purpose of reform, 200; bibliography of reform, 355.
Clarke, J. F., Mugwump, 337.
Clawson, Rudger, sentenced for polygamy, 263.
Clayton, Powell, Blaine's henchman, 338.
Clayton-Bulwer treaty, attempt to abrogate, 213, 221-223, 225; bibliography, 357.
Clearing-House, federal government as member of New York, 146.

Cleveland, Grover, elected governor, 332; character, 339; nominated for president, 340; Mugwump support, 342; campaign charges against, 343; elected, 348.
Cleveland, strike of iron-workers (1882), 81.
Clybourne, Archibald, meat-packing industry, 310.
Coal-mining in South, 34, 315.
Collins, Frederick, survey of Isthmian canal route, 212.
Colorado, admission, 22; silver and lead mining, 22; development of railroads, 23; growth in population (1870-1880), 23. *See also* Far West.
Commerce, development of export food trade, 16-18; favorable balance of trade, 19; regulation of interstate, 28; engineering feats in aid of, 49; foreign (1883), 305; size of inland, 306; inland, of raw material, 306, 308; Chicago and inland, 309; river transportation, 311-314; of Great Lakes, 314, 320, 321; bibliography, 360. *See also* Internal improvements, Isthmian canal, Railroads, Shipping, Travel.
Congress, *Forty-fifth:* and Hayes's appointments, 107; extra session, 110; debate on Hayes's southern policy, 111-114; election investigation, 114-117; complexion, 111 *n*, 119, 120; federal election laws, 120, 125-127; monetary commission, 140; Bland-Allison silver law, 142, 145; attempts to delay resumption, 143-145; and Halifax award, 149; Chinese exclusion, 241-243; pension arrears, 289.
Forty-sixth: complexion, 119, 120, 128-130; extra session, 127; federal election laws, 130-132.
Forty-seventh: complexion, 120, 184; Conkling feud, 184-187; civil service reform, 194, 195, 198-200; Chinese exclusion, 245-247; restrictions on immigration, 250; anti-polygamy laws, 262; tariff, 297-302.
Forty-eighth: bureau of labor statistics, 83; complexion, 120; Chinese exclusion, 248; restrictions on immigration, 250; tariff, 302, 303; election investigation, 346.
Conkling, Roscoe, and Hayes, 113; and removal of Arthur, 158, 159; and Grant's candidacy (1880), 167, 169, 170; stumps for Garfield, 176; heads Stalwarts, 182; and Garfield's cabinet appointments, 182, 183; and Blaine, 183, 184; and nomination of Robertson, 184, 185; resigns senatorship, 185; fails of reelection, 186; and Cornell, 331.
Converse, G. L., wool tariff bill, 303.
Cornell, A. B., removed from custom-house office, 158; elected governor, 160; defeated for renomination, 331.
Corporations, combinations before 1880, 326; telegraph combination, 329; agitation against monopolies, 329.
Corruption, star-route frauds, 188-190.
Cotton, size of crop (1876, 1881), 17; southern mills, 35, 50; International Exposition (1881), 50; utilization of "storm" cotton, 50; of seed, 50; tariff bill of 1883 on manufactures, 300; export

INDEX

(1883), 305; inland transportation, 309.
"Cow-boys" in Arizona, 253.
Cremation, introduction, 47.
Crook, George, and removal of Poncas, 271.
Cumberland, Md., miners' strike (1882), 80.
Curtis, N. M., prosecuted for political assessments, 197.
Curtis, G. W., and civil service reform, 159, 161, 197; political reformer (1884), 335; Mugwump, 337; supports Cleveland, 342.

DAVENPORT, J. I., enforcement of federal election laws, 123.
Davis, J. J., on greenbacks, 145.
De Long, G. W., Arctic exploration, 51.
Delfosse, Maurice, Halifax commission, 147.
Democratic party, denunciation of Hayes, 109; gains control of Congress, 119, 120, 128–130; solid South, 129; and silver, 140, 143; and civil service reform, 195; and tariff, 296; and reform, 334. *See also* Elections.
Denver, anti-Chinese riot (1880), 245.
Devens, Charles, attorney-general, 106.
Dorsey, S. W., star-route frauds, 189, 190.
Dow, Neal, nominated for president, 173.
Dudley, W. W., in campaign of 1884, 345.
Dundy, E. S., decision on personal status of Indians, 271.

EADS, J. B., Tehuantepec ship-railroad scheme, 211; Mississippi jetties, 312.
Eaton, D. B., and civil service reform, 161; civil service commission, 200.
Economic conditions, period of reconstruction of industries, 3; revival after resumption, 152; beginning of combinations, 325, 326, 329; depression (1883), 328; anti-monopoly agitations, 329; bibliography, 360–362. *See also* Agriculture, Commerce, Finances, Fisheries, Inventions, Labor, Live-stock, Manufactures, Mining.
Edison, Thomas, electric light, 41; phonograph, 45; other inventions, 45.
Edmunds, G. F., candidacy for presidential nomination (1880), 168; (1884), 336; anti-polygamy bill, 262; supports Blaine (1884), 337.
Education, influence of Centennial, 11; growth of technical, 14; Indian, 276, 277.
Election laws, federal, provisions, 120, 121; motive, 122; operation, arrests under, cost, 123–125, 346; use of troops at polls forbidden, 125–127, 131; vetoes of attempted repeal, 130–132; judicial decision on, 133–135; dead letter, 135; repeal, 136.
Elections (*1876*): Hayes takes oath, 84; his inauguration, 86; validity of Hayes's title, 101; prosecution of Louisiana returning board, 111; congressional investigation, 114; attempt to invalidate Hayes's election, 115; cipher despatches, 115; Greenback platform, 144; popular majority, 333; Republican reform movement, 334.
1880: campaign assessments, 162–164; corporation contributions, 163, 164;

Grant's third-term candidacy, 167–170; Republican convention, 169–172; Greenback convention, 172; Prohibitionist convention, 173; Democratic convention, 173; Hancock as candidate, 174, 175; Republican slogans, 175; attacks on Garfield's record, 176, 244, 245; results, 177, 178; platforms on Chinese, 245; popular majority, 333.
1884: party prospects, 331–334; Blaine's candidacy for nomination, 335; attitude of Republican reformers, 335; other Republican aspirants, 336; Republican convention, 336; Mugwump bolt from Blaine, 337, 338, 341, 342; Democratic aspirants, 338, 339; Democratic convention, 339; other conventions, 340; campaign of abuse, 342–344; campaign funds, 345; use of federal election laws, 346; Irish vote, 346; Burchard's alliteration, 347; importance of New York, 348; result, 348; significance of Republican defeat, 349–351.
Electric light, introduction, 39–42.
Eliot, C. W., Mugwump, 337.
Elk *vs.* Wilkins, 281.
Ellis, John, and charge against Hayes of bargaining, 96.
Enforcement acts. *See* Election laws.
Engineering, Sutro tunnel, 48; bridge building, 49; elevated railroad, 49; destruction of Hell Gate, 49; Ohio River dam, 50; Mississippi jetties, 312.
English, W. H., nominated for vice-president, 174; defeated, 177.
Erie Canal, railroad competition, 54; widening, 55.

Erie Railroad, development of trunk line, 54.
Evarts, W. M., secretary of state, 106; international monetary conference, 153; and civil service reform, 159; on Isthmian canal, 217; and Peruvian-Chilian war, 224.
Everett, William, supports Cleveland, 342.
Expenditures, (1866–1882), 283; fixity of usual appropriations, 288; temptation of surplus, 288, 289, 291.
Exploration, Arctic, 51.

FAR WEST, development (1870–1880), 22–24; cattle thieves, 251–253; troops withdrawn, 254; transcontinental railroads, 254, 255; land grants to railroads, 255, 256; homestead applications, 256; military reservations, 256; lawlessness, 257; agricultural development, 257; bibliography, 358. *See also* Indians, Pacific Coast, and states and territories by name.
Field, S. J., candidacy for presidential nomination (1880), 173.
Fifteenth Amendment, judicial interpretation, 133–135.
Finances, federal deficit and surplus (1873–1882), 282, 283, 287; temptation of surplus, 288, 289, 291; bibliography, 360. *See also* Bonds, Paper money, Resumption, Silver, Tariff.
Fink, Albert, and railroad pools, 59.
Fisheries, treaty of Washington, 147; award of Halifax commission, 147–149; agreement under treaty terminated, 149; payment of award, 149; Fortune Bay affair, 150.

INDEX 369

Flower, R. P., candidacy for presidential nomination (1884), 338.
Folger, C. J., on tariff bill of 1883, 302; defeated for governor, 332.
Food. *See* Agriculture, Fruit, Meat.
Foreign affairs, bibliography, 356. *See also* Chinese, Isthmian, and nations by name.
Fortune Bay incident, 150.
Foster, Charles, and charge against Hayes of bargaining, 95-97.
Fourteenth Amendment, judicial interpretation, 132; not applicable to Chinese, 237; or to Indians, 281.
France. *See* Isthmian canal.
Frelinghuysen, F. T., Isthmian canal diplomacy, 225.
Fruit, development of export trade, 17; inland commerce, 309.

GALT, Sir A. T., Halifax commission, 147.
Garfield, J. A., and charge against Hayes of bargaining, 96; Republican leader of House, 129; and campaign assessments (1880), 164, 185, 189; nominated for president, 170, 171; campaign attacks on record, 176; Morey letter, 176, 244, 245; elected, 177; inauguration, 180, 181; and Conkling's cabinet demand, 182, 183; cabinet, 183; Conkling feud, 184-187; and office-seekers, 187; removals by, 188; and Brady and star-route frauds, 188-190; assassinated, 191; effect of assassination on civil service reform, 192, 194; bibliography, 354.
Garrison, W. P., Mugwump, 337.

Germans as immigrants, 258.
Germany and military service of German-Americans, 224.
Gibson, R. L., monetary commission, 140.
Gogebic iron-field, 318.
Gordon, J. B., and charge against Hayes of bargaining, 95.
Grand Trunk Railroad, completion, 54; and rate agreement, 58.
Granger laws, 61, 62; judicial decisions on, 62, 65; repeal of laws, 64.
Grant, U. S., candidacy for presidential nomination (1880), 167-170; stumps for Garfield, 175; heads an Isthmian canal company, 211; on Chinese immigrants, 235; Indian policy, 266.
Gray, Elisha, telephone, 43.
Great Britain, attempt to abrogate Clayton-Bulwer treaty, 213, 221-223, 225; control of Suez Canal, 222.
Great Lakes, commerce, 310, 314, 320, 321; St. Mary's canal, 317, 320; ship-building, 321.
Greely, A. W., Arctic exploration, 52.
Greenback party, platform, 144; vote (1876-1884), 144; convention (1880), 172; (1884), 340.
Gregory, J. M., civil service commission, 200.
Grenville, Lord, on Clayton-Bulwer treaty, 222.
Groesbeck, W. S., monetary commission, 140.
Guiteau, C. J., assassinates Garfield, 191; purpose, 192; hanged, 192.

HALE, EUGENE, and campaign assessments, 196, 197.

Half-Breeds, 182.
Halifax commission, 147-150.
Hampton, Wade, rival governor of South Carolina, 90; secures control, 93; re-elected, 117; senator, 130.
Hancock, W. S., nominated for president, 173; as candidate, 174, 175; defeated, 177.
Harlan, J. M., Louisiana commission, 91.
Harper's Weekly denounces Hayes, 113.
Haskell, D. C., protectionist, 299.
Hawley, J. R., Louisiana commission, 91.
Hayes, Lucy W., as lady of White House, 179.
Hayes, R. B., and railroad strike riots, 75; takes oath as president, 84; inauguration, 86; personality as president, 87; auspicious party beginnings checked, 88; proclaimed attitude towards South, 89, 97; withdraws troops from Louisiana, 91-93; from South Carolina, 93; accused of bargaining with southerners, 94-98; rewards southern returning boards, 98; southern trip, 99; radical denunciation, 99, 100; validity of title, 100-102; justification of withdrawal of troops, 101, 110; effect of southern policy on Republican party, 103; party and cabinet appointments, 104-107; nominations rejected, 107; Republican denunciation, 107-109, 113, 114, 160; Democratic denunciation, 109; debate on policy, 111, 112; attempts to invalidate title to presidency, 114-117; southern ingratitude, 117; decline of Republican denunciation, 117; vetoes of repeal of federal election laws, 125, 130-132; signs bills forbidding use of troops at polls, 127, 131; and silver, 141, 151; on resumption and business, 152; and civil service reform, 154; forbids political participation and assessments, 155, 156; and New York custom-house, 157-161; character of administration, 178; and Isthmian canal, 216; vetoes Chinese exclusion, 242; negotiation on Chinese immigration, 243; proclamation against New Mexican partisan war, 253; and removal of Poncas, 271; on Indian wars, 274; bibliography of administration, 352-362; papers, 354.
Hell Gate, destruction, 49.
Hendricks, T. A., candidacy for presidential nomination (1880), 173; nominated for vice-president (1884), 340; elected, 348.
Hewitt, A. S., and repeal of federal election laws, 126.
Higginson, T. W., Mugwump, 337.
Hoar, G. F., and Hayes, 113; political reformer (1884), 335; supports Blaine, 337; bibliography, 355.
Howe, T. O., on Hayes's southern policy, 114; international monetary conference, 153.
Hubbell, J. A., Garfield's campaign assessment letter to, 189; assessment circular (1882), 196.
Hunt, W. H., secretary of navy, 183.

IMMIGRATION, as barometer of prosperity, 32; nativity, 32; ignores the South, 34; early

INDEX 371

lack of restrictions on, 229; encouragement, 230; and organization of labor, 230, 249; restrictive legislation, 249. See also Chinese.

Indians, problem, 229; development of reservation system, 265; Grant's peace policy, 266; encroachment on reservations, 267; Nez Percé Wallowa campaign, 267, 268; removal of Poncas, 268–272; judicial decision on personal status, 271; wars, causes, cost (1865–1882), 272–274; Hayes on wars, 274; damage claims against, 274; cost of reservation system, 275; education, 276, 277; allotment in severalty of reservation land, 277; labor on reservation, 278; Arthur on policy, 278; number (1870 – 1880), 279, 280; not citizens under Fourteenth Amendment, 280; bibliography, 358.

Industry. See Economic conditions.

Injunctions against labor strikes, 76.

Internal improvements, river and harbor legislation, 55, 292–295; of Mississippi River, 312–314; St. Mary's canal, 317, 320.

Internal revenue, decrease (1866–1874), 282; increase, 283; removal from various articles (1883), 296.

Inventions, for street railways, 37–39; electric light, 39–42; telephone, 42; bicycle, 44; phonograph, 45; other inventions by Edison, 45; improvements in telegraph, 46; photography, 46; cremation, 47.

Iron, southern mines and manufacture, 34, 315; tariff bill of 1883 on, 299; Michigan and Minnesota deposits, 316–319; transportation of ore, 320, 321; fall in prices, 321; development of uses, 322. See also Steel.

Isthmian canal, development of demand for American control, 202, 203, 213, 216–218, 227; De Lesseps' survey, 203; Wyse's concession, 204, 205; international congress on, 205; possible routes, 205–207; De Lesseps' French company, 207; alarm in America, 207–209; De Lesseps' explanation of scheme, 209, 215; suspicious of corruption, 210; fear of war with France, 210; movements to anticipate French company, 211; Nicaragua company, 211; Eads's ship-railroad scheme, 211; report of American surveys, 211; action of Congress, 212, 213; and Monroe Doctrine, 212, 225; attempt to abrogate Clayton-Bulwer treaty, 213, 221 – 223, 225; question of neutrality, 214, 215; Hayes on demand for American control, 216; French assurances of private character of De Lesseps' company, 218; De Lesseps begins work on tide-level canal, 218–220; estimates of cost, 219; Garfield's attitude, 220; Blaine's diplomatic note on American control, 220; draught treaty with Nicaragua, 226; failure of French company, 226, 227; bibliography, 357.

JACKSON, ANDREW, and no-third-term principle, 166.

James, T. L., and civil service reform, 157; Stalwart, 182;

postmaster-general, 183; and star-route frauds, 188.
Jay, John, report on New York custom-house, 158; and civil service reform, 161.
Jefferson, Thomas, and no-third-term principle, 166.
Johnston, J. E., and Hayes's cabinet, 105.
Jones, J. P, monetary commission, 140.
Joseph, Chief, and Wallowa campaign, 267, 268.

KASSON, J. A., protectionist, 299.
Kearney, Dennis, anti-Chinese agitation, 238.
Kelley, W. D., protectionist, 299.
Kellogg, E. H., Halifax commission, 147.
Kellogg, W. P., admitted to Senate, 110.
Kelly, John, opposes Tilden, 173; and election of 1884, 348.
Key, D. M., postmaster-general, 105; urges southern support of Hayes, 117.
Kirkwood, S. J., secretary of interior, 183.
Knights of Labor, rise, 80.
Ku-Klux act pronounced unconstitutional, 135.

LABOR, ten-hour day for federal employés, 68; eight-hour day, 68; state bureaus, 69; early unions, 69; beginning of hostility to capital, 69; reduction of wages of railway employés (1877), 70-72; railway strike and rioting, 72-76; federal injunctions, 76; coal-miners' strikes (1877, 1882), 78, 80; strike at Leadville (1880), 79; rise of Knights of Labor, 79, 242; strike of Cleveland iron-workers (1882), 81; of New York freight-handlers, 81; lessons of these troubles, 82; federal bureau of labor statistics, 83; organization and immigration, 230; tariff and wages, 285; bibliography, 361. *See also* Chinese.
Lapham, E. G., elected senator, 186.
Lawrence, C. B., Louisiana commission, 91.
Lead-mining in Colorado, 22.
Leadville, rise, 22; miners' strike (1880), 79.
Lesseps, Ferdinand de, survey of Panama canal route, 203; canal company, 207; opposition in United States, 207-209; his explanation of character of scheme, 209, 215; suspected of purchasing influence, 210-212; French assurances of private character of company, 218; begins construction, 218-220; failure of company, 226, 227.
Lincoln, R. T., secretary of war, 183.
Live-stock, improvement in breed, 18; development in Wyoming, 25; in Texas, 26-28; drives, 27, Texas fever, 27; cattle thieves, 251-253; cattle and sheep wars, 252; and farmers, 252. *See also* Meat.
Lockwood, Belva A. B., nominated for president, 341.
Lodge, H. C., political reformer (1884), 335; supports Blaine, 337.
Logan, J. A., and Grant's candidacy (1880), 167; candidacy for presidential nomination (1884), 336; campaign charges against, 343, 344.
Long, J. D., political reformer (1884), 335.

INDEX

Los Angeles, anti-Chinese riot (1871), 235.
Louisiana, rival governments (1877), 89; Hayes's commission, 91, 92; federal troops withdrawn, 92; overthrow of carpet-bag government, 92; Democratic reforms, 93; debt, 93; proceedings against returning board, 93, 111; Hayes rewards returning board, 98.
Lull, E. P., survey of Isthmian canal route, 212.

McCRARY, G. W. secretary of war, 106.
McKinley, William, protectionist, 299; and tariff bill of 1883, 302.
McLin, S. B., accuses Hayes of bargaining, 95.
McPherson, J. R., and tariff bill of 1883, 301.
MacVeagh, Wayne, Louisiana commission, 91; attorney-general, 183.
Manufactures, Centennial exhibit, 13; southern, 34, 35, 50.
Marquette iron-field, 316.
Massachusetts, board of railroad commissioners, 60; labor bureau, 69; civil service law, 201; goes Democratic (1882), 331.
Matthews, Stanley, and charge against Hayes of bargaining, 95, 96; and silver, 141.
Meat, development of export trade (1876-1884), 17; development of Chicago industry, 310. See also Livestock.
Menocal, E. G., at international canal Congress, 205.
Menominee iron-field, 318.
Merritt, E. A., appointed collector, 159.
Mesabee iron-field, 319.

Michigan, iron deposits, 316-318.
Militia, feebleness in suppressing riots, 74.
Miller, Warner, leads Republican faction in New York, 182; elected senator, 186.
Mining, lead, in Colorado, 22; coal, in South, 34, 315; Sutro tunnel, 48; iron, in South, 315; iron, in Michigan and Minnesota, 316-319.
Minneapolis mills, 308.
Minnesota iron deposits, 318, 319.
Mississippi River, jetties, 312; levees, 313, 314.
Money. See Paper money, Silver.
Monroe Doctrine, and Isthmian canal, 212, 225; bibliography, 357.
Morey letter, 244, 245.
Mormons. See Utah.
Morrill, J. S., and silver, 141; protectionist, 299.
Morrison, W. R., candidacy for presidential nomination (1880), 173; tariff bill, 302.
Morton, L. P., minister to France, 183.
Morton, O. P., and Hayes, 113; bibliography, 355.
Mugwumps in campaign of 1884, 337, 338, 342.
Munn vs. Illinois, 63.

NATURALIZATION and duties to native country, 224.
Negro suffrage. See Election laws.
Negroes, southern exodus, 35; effect on, of Hayes's southern policy, 101; race problem, 229.
Nevada, decline, 28; Sutro tunnel, 48. See also Far West.
New Mexico, Chisholm partisan war, 252. See also Far West.

New Orleans, debt (1877), 93; seaport, 313.
New York, Republican factions, 182; Conkling-Platt resignations, 185–187; civil service law, 201; goes Democratic (1882), 331–333; importance in election of 1884, 346–349.
New York City, absorption of suburbs, 30; elevated roads, 37, 49, 330; Brooklyn bridge, 49; strike of freight-handlers (1882), 81; Hayes, and custom-house, 157–161.
New York Times, denounces Hayes, 113; and political reform (1884), 336.
Nez Percé Indians, Chief Joseph and Wallowa campaign, 267, 268.
Nicaragua. *See* Isthmian canal.
Nicholls, F. T., rival governor of Louisiana, 89; secures control, 92; reform administration, 93.
Nominating conventions, unit rule, 170. *See also* Elections.
North Adams, Mass., Chinese laborers, 239.
Northern Pacific Railroad, construction, 254; bond issue (1883), 328; syndicate to control, 330.
Noyes, E. F., and charge against Hayes of bargaining, 96.

OREGON, development, 28.

PACIFIC coast, economic development (1860–1880), 28. *See also* Chinese, Far West.
Pacific railroads, four lines completed, 48, 254, 307; land grants, 255, 256; bibliography, 358, 361.
Packard, S. B., rival governor of Louisiana, 89; federal support of, withdrawn, 92; retires, 92; denounces Hayes, 99.
Panama. *See* Isthmian canal.
Paper money, contraction of greenbacks stopped (1878), 144; Greenback party, 144. *See also* Resumption.
Pattison, Robert, elected governor, 331.
Pendleton, G. H., civil service reform bill, 195.
Pennsylvania goes Democratic (1882), 331.
Pennsylvania Railroad, development of trunk line, 54.
Pensions, development of system (1862–1882), 289; arrears act (1879), 289; resulting increase, 290; frauds, 290; private bills, 291.
Periodicals of period 1877–1884, 355.
Peru, Blaine's diplomacy, 224.
Phelps, W. W., supports Blaine (1884), 337.
Phonograph, invention, 45.
Photography, improvements, 46; composite, 46; motion pictures, 47.
Pittsburg, railroad strike and rioting (1877), 73.
Platt, T. C., and campaign assessments, 163; Stalwart, 182; resigns senatorship, 185; fails of re-election, 186.
Political assessments of civil service employés, 155, 156, 162–164, 185, 189, 196–198, 345.
Politics. *See* Elections and parties by name.
Pomeroy, S. C., nominated for president, 341.
Ponca Indians, removal, 268–272.
Population, increase (1860–1880), 20; shifting of "frontier," 21, 22; expansion in West, 22–28; growth of cities,

INDEX

29-31; interstate migration and sectionalism, 31; Indian (1870-1880), 279, 280. *See also* Immigration.
Post-office, star-route frauds, 188-190.
Potter committee investigation, 114-117.
Potts, William, and civil service reform, 197.
Presidency, no-third-term principle, 165-167; succession questions raised by Garfield's illness, 192; succession laws, 193. *See also* Elections.
Prohibitionists, convention (1880), 173; (1884), 340. *See also* Temperance.
Public lands, grants to railroads, 255, 256; homestead applications, 256; military reservations, 256; desert land, 256; Indian reservations, 265, 267.

RACES, problems of non-amalgamating, 229. *See also* Chinese, Immigration, Indians.
Railroads, development in Colorado, 23; transcontinental lines (1884), 48, 257, 307; transcontinental service, 48, 323; miles (1850-1880), 53; development of trunk lines, 53; competition with waterways, 54, 311, 321; rate war, 56, 57; rate agreement, 57; pools, 58-60; federal and state aid, 60, 255, 256; state commissions, 60; federal act favoring consolidations, 61; hostile Granger legislation, 61, 62; Supreme Court on state regulation, 62, 65; depression, 63; decline of hostile legislation, 64; federal reports and bills for regulating, 64, 66; inconsistent rating, 65; popular demand for federal regulation, 65; recovery from depression, 66; reduction of wages (1877), 70-72; strike and riots, 72-76; federal injunctions against strikers, 76; demand for federal protection, 77; strike of New York freight-handlers (1882), 81; judicial decision on duties during strike, 82; development of commerce by, 307-309; steel rails and their effect, 323; sleeping-cars, 324; vestibules, 324; railroad time, 324; demand for state ownership, 330; bibliography, 361. *See also* Street railways.
Randall, S. J., speaker, 129; protectionist, 303.
Reconstruction, Hayes promises self-government, 89; rival governments in Louisiana and South Carolina, 89; Hayes withdraws federal troops from these states, 90-94; final overthrow of carpet-bag government, 92-94; Hayes accused of bargaining, 94-98; effect of Hayes's policy, 98-101; effect of policy on Republican party, 103; Republican denunciation of policy, 107-109, 113, 114; Hayes's justification, 110; debate in Congress on policy, 111, 112; southern ingratitude to Hayes, 117; "solid South," 118, 129; federal supervision of elections, 120-125; attempts to repeal election laws (1877-1880), 125-127, 130-132; judicial interpretation of legislation, 132-135; final repeal of election laws, 136; dead issue, 350, 351.
Red River of North, wheat belt, 306.

Red Star Line, formation, 56.
Reform, spirit (1882), 325, 329–333; party attitude, 333–335; Republican conference (1876), 334; Mugwumps, 337, 338, 341, 342. *See also* Civil service.
Religion. *See* Utah.
Republican party, effect on, of withdrawal of troops from South, 101, 103; and Hayes's cabinet appointments, 104–107; denunciations of Hayes, 107–109, 117, 160; decline and loss of control of Congress, 119, 120, 128; and silver, 140, 143; and unit rule, 170; nominations of 1880 heal dissensions, 172, 175; dissensions in New York, 182; and protection, 296; and reform, 333–336. *See also* Elections.
Resumption, attempts to postpone, 143–145; preparation for, 145; success, 146, 151.
Revenue, deficit and surplus (1874–1882), 282, 287.
Riots, railroad strike (1877), 73; inadequacy of militia, 74; use of federal troops, 74.
River and harbor bills, purpose, 55, 292; various (1866–1882), 293; Arthur's veto (1882), 294; passage over veto, 295.
Robertson, W. H., supports Blaine (1880), 171; nominated for collectorship, 184–186.
Roebling, J. A., Brooklyn bridge, 49.
Roosevelt, James, nominated for customs collectorship, 158.
Roosevelt, Theodore, political reformer (1884), 335; supports Blaine, 337.
Russian Jews as immigrants, 249.

St. Anthony Falls, water-power, 308.
St. John, J. P., nominated for president, 340.
St. Mary's River, canal, 317, 320.
San Francisco, cable roads, 37; Chinatown, 235; sand-lot agitation, 238.
Scandinavians as immigrants, 32, 258.
Schley, W. S., Arctic exploration, 52.
Schurz, Carl, secretary of interior, 106; and civil service reform, 161; and removal of Poncas, 270; supports Cleveland (1884), 342.
Schwatka, Frederick, Arctic exploration, 51
Sectionalism and interstate migration, 31.
Sherman, John, and charge against Hayes of bargaining, 96; approves of Hayes's southern policy, 113; on federal election laws, 122; and silver, 141; preparation for resumption, 145; and removal of Arthur, 158, 160; candidacy for presidential nomination (1880), 168–171; (1884), 336; protectionist, 299; and tariff bill of 1883, 299, 302; bibliography, 354.
Shipping, decline of American ocean, 55; American transoceanic lines, 56; inland, 311, 321.
Siebold, *ex parte*, 134.
Silver, decline in value, 137; trade dollar, 137; limited legal tender, 137; movement for free coinage and payment of bonds in, 137–139; argument against it, 139; monetary commission (1875), 140; party attitude towards, 140; attitude of Hayes, 141, 151; Bland-Allison law, 142, 143;

INDEX

operation of the law, 151, 153; international conference, 153; bibliography, 360.
Sitting Bull pardoned, 273.
Slaughter Houses cases, 133.
Social conditions, influence of Centennial, 9–13; Mormon polygamy, 259–264; spirit of reform, 325, 329–333. *See also* Chinese, Education, Immigration, Indians, Negroes, Population.
Sources on period 1877–1884, documentary, 353; annual publications, 354; periodicals, 355.
South, industrial development (1870–1880), 33–35; immigrants ignore, 34; exodus of negroes, 35; in election of 1880, 177, 178; coal and iron mines, 315. *See also* Reconstruction.
South Carolina, rival governments (1877), 90; Hayes's conference with governors, 93; federal troops withdrawn, 94; Democratic control and reforms, 94.
Southern Pacific Railroad, construction, 254.
Southern Railway and Steamship Association, 59.
Spofford, H. M., rejected by Senate, 111.
Stalwarts, 182.
Standing Bear and removal of Poncas, 270, 271.
Star-route frauds and trials, 188–190.
Steel, "age," 322; effect of Bessemer process, 322; open-hearth process, 322; development of uses, 323.
Strander *vs.* West Virginia, 133.
Street railways, elevated, 37; cable, 37; electric, 38, 39.
Strikes. *See* Labor.
Suez Canal, British control, 222.

Suffrage. *See* Election laws.
Supreme Court, on state regulation of interstate trade, 28, 62, 65; on reconstruction legislation, 132–135; on antipolygamy law, 261, 263, 264; on Indian citizenship, 281.
Sutro tunnel, 48.
Swift, J. F., Chinese treaty, 243.

Tariff, receipts (1873–1882), 282, 283; war tariff, 283; internal revenue taxes and protection, 284; protection and new industries, 284, 287; and wages, 285; post-war increase, 286; free list, 286; chief sources of collections, 287; demand for reform, 296; and surplus, 296, 304; party attitude (1876–1884), 296; commission (1882), 297; Arthur's attitude, 298; bill (1883), 298–302; Morrison bill, 302; Converse wool bill, 303; bibliography, 360.
Taxation. *See* Internal revenue, Tariff.
Tehuantepec route for canal, 205; Eads's ship-railroad scheme, 211.
Telegraph, improvement, 46; Western Union's monopoly, 329; demand for state ownership, 330.
Telephone, introduction, 42.
Temperance agitation, 330. *See also* Prohibitionists.
Tennessee iron-mines, 315.
Texas, development of cattle industry, 26–28.
Thoman, L. D., civil service commission, 200.
Thompson, A. M., nominated for vice-president, 173.
Thompson, R. W., secretary of navy, 106; resigns to serve French Panama company, 210.

Thurman, A. G., international monetary conference, 153.
Tilden, S. J., accepts defeat, 102; and cipher despatches, 116; and nomination in 1880, 173; in 1884, 338; bibliography, 354.
Time, railroad, 324.
Transportation. *See* Commerce, Railroads.
Travel, influence of Centennial, 9–11; transcontinental service, 48, 323.
Trescot, W. H., envoy to South America, 224; to China, 243.
Tyner, J. N., as assistant postmaster-general, 105.

UNITED STATES *vs.* Harris, 135.
United States *vs.* Reese, 133.
Utah, growth, 24; rise of Mormonism, 258; polygamy, 259; federal act against polygamy (1862), 259 – 261; attempt to discourage Mormon immigration, 260; Mormon foreign propaganda, 261; Protestant missions, 262; Edmunds anti-polygamy law (1882), 262; prosecutions under it, 263, 264.
Ute Indians, wars (1879), 273; surrender reservation, 278.

VAN WYCK, C. H., and tariff bill of 1883, 302.
Vance, Z. B., senator, 130.
Vanderbilt, Cornelius, development of trunk line, 53, 54; and rate agreements, 58.
Vermilion Lake iron-field, 318.
Vetoes, Hayes's, of repeal of federal election laws, 125, 130, 132; of Chinese exclusion, 242; Arthur's, of Chinese exclusion, 246; of river and harbor bill, 294.

WALLACE, LEW, and charge against Hayes of bargaining, 95.
Washington, George, and no-third-term principle, 165.
Washington, development, 28.
Watterson, Henry, and charge against Hayes of bargaining, 96.
Weaver, J. B., nominated for president, 172.
West, shifting of frontier (1860–1880), 21, 22; Granger laws, 61–63. *See also* Far West, Pacific coast, and states by name.
Western Union Telegraph Company absorbs its rival, 329.
Wheat, Red River region, 306.
Wheeler, E. P., and civil service reform, 197.
White, A. D., and civil service reform, 161; political reformer (1884), 335; supports Blaine, 337.
Willard, George, monetary commission, 140.
Williams, J. S., senator, 130.
Windom, William, secretary of treasury, 183.
Winnipeg, rise, 307.
Women's rights agitation, 331; nomination for president, 341.
Wool, crop (1876), 17; tariff bill of 1883 on, 300; Converse bill, 303.
Woolsey, T. D., and political reform (1876), 334; in campaign of 1884, 342.
Wright, Lot, use of federal election laws (1884), 346.
Wyoming, cattle-grazing, 25; cattle wars, 26. *See also* Far West.
Wyse, L. B., canal concession, 204, 205.

YOUNG, BRIGHAM, and polygamy, 259.

END OF VOL. XXIII